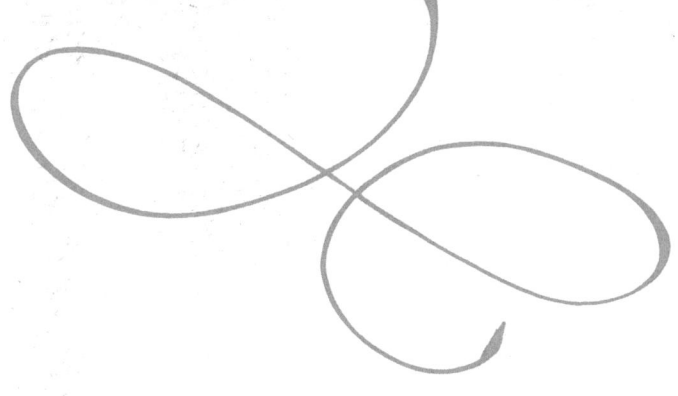

P9-DHH-997

To my beloved

husband-shepherd-friend
earthly head and king
my bridegroom

And to my Beloved

Savior-Shepherd-Friend
eternal Head and King
my Bridegroom

My beloved is mine, and I am his.

With great delight I sat in his shadow,
and his fruit was sweet to my taste.
He brought me to the banqueting house,
and his banner over me was love.

THE SONG OF SONGS

She's done it again! In *Adorned*, Nancy gives us another rich resource to help us become Titus 2 women. As I read this book I felt that I was sitting in Nancy's kitchen enjoying a cup of tea and a Titus 2 conversation. She invites us into her heart. She encourages and equips us to share the gospel and our lives with other women. This is a lovely book.

SUSAN HUNT
Author of *Spiritual Mothering—The Titus 2 Mandate for Women Mentoring Women*

I have seen firsthand and have benefitted personally from Nancy living out this message. I am so grateful for her as a sister in Christ, a mentor from afar, and a spiritual mother to many through True Woman/Revive Our Hearts!

LAUREN CHANDLER
Pastor's wife, worship leader, author

This is a beautiful book, written by someone who beautifully lives out its truths. Each chapter is chock-full of wisdom and faithful instruction to help you grow—woman to woman—into someone whose life adorns the beauty of the gospel. What a tremendous treasure for this generation!

MARY A. KASSIAN
Speaker, author of *Girls Gone Wise*

Adorned is a beautiful call to Titus 2 living—life on life, woman to woman, one generation to another. We need this book. Nancy shares with wisdom and insight the importance of female discipleship in the local church. Her words will inspire you to faithfully pick up the baton of truth and pass it on to others.

MELISSA KRUGER
Author of *Walking with God in the Season of Motherhood* and *The Envy of Eve*

I am so, so thrilled for you to experience this book! *Adorned* is beautifully written from beginning to end, and Nancy so thoughtfully reminds us how very much we women need each other. It blessed my heart and I know it will yours too.

JENNIFER ROTHSCHILD
Author of *Lessons I Learned in the Dark* and founder of Fresh Grounded Faith events

Nancy's practical insight, ageless wisdom, and warm fervor rang like bells through my spirit as I read this book. Both like an alarm waking me and a recurring melody inspiring me to understand again how my womanhood is beautified and can blossom in a multigenerational community of women following the Lord day by day together.

KRISTYN GETTY
Hymn writer/singer and mother of four daughters

Nancy is one of the women God has used to shape me into a better reflection of Himself. Her book *Adorned* crams a thousand coffee shop conversations about life, love, and godliness into a single, riveting book. Women in every season of life need to read it, reread it, and pass it along to the other women in their circle.

ERIN DAVIS
Women's ministry leader, wife, and momma who would be adrift without the encouragement and support of her sisters in Christ

This is truly Nancy's legacy work. Through what feels like a personal conversation, she takes women back to the Greek and Roman culture to grasp Titus 2, and urges us to rise up today to adorn the Bride of Christ. This book will influence the church and the personal lives of women in a way that few books ever have.

DANNAH GRESH
Bestselling author of *And the Bride Wore White*

Adorned is a Christ-exalting, mind-renewing, life-altering presentation of Titus 2 that will help women, young and old, embrace their call to learn from one another, to the glory of Christ our Savior.

JACKIE HILL PERRY
Writer, speaker, artist

Nancy's instruction, wisdom, and grace will challenge you to not only pray for a woman who you might call a spiritual mother, but you'll also desire to be the type of woman others might call on—for the good of the church and to the glory of God.

TRILLIA NEWBELL
Author of *Enjoy*, *Fear and Faith*, and *United*

Adorned is more than a book that articulates the virtues of the Titus 2 woman. You will be inspired to be biblically beautiful, adorned in the sound doctrine of God, and prepared for the kingdom work of God no matter your season of life.

KAREN LORITTS
Speaker and teacher

Nancy's new book is a call for all Christian women—young and old—to live out the Titus 2 command of life-on-life discipleship. More than ever, we need women to show us how to live out the gospel in our daily life. Older women, we need you!

CHRISTINA FOX
Licensed counselor, speaker, author of *A Heart Set Free: A Journey to Hope through the Psalms of Lament*

Nancy has penned her most significant work yet in *Adorned*! This delightful, fresh look at the biblical mandate in Titus 2 is profound, yet practical. You will sense the Holy Spirit calling you to live the life God has made you for and called you to.

REBECCA LUTZER
Retired RN and wife of Dr. Erwin Lutzer, pastor emeritus of The Moody Church

Adorned calls the women of the church to the vital and joyful work of cultivating real-life relationships centered on the gospel of Jesus. I am thankful for Nancy's work to develop a resource on Titus 2 that is substantive, faithful, and practical.

AMANDA BIBLE WILLIAMS
Chief Content Officer of She Reads Truth, author of *Open Your Bible*

. . . so that in everything they may adorn the doctrine of God our Savior.

TITUS 2:10

Living Out the Beauty
of the Gospel Together

NANCY DEMOSS
WOLGEMUTH

MOODY PUBLISHERS | CHICAGO

Contents

Teach what accords with sound doctrine.

Older men are to be sober-minded, dignified, self-controlled,
sound in faith, in love, and in steadfastness.

Older women likewise are to be reverent in behavior,
not slanderers or slaves to much wine.

They are to teach what is good,
and so train the young women
to love their husbands and children,
to be self-controlled,
pure,
working at home,
kind,
and submissive to their own husbands,
that the word of God may not be reviled.

. . . so that in everything they may adorn
the doctrine of God our Savior.

TITUS 2:1–5, 10

CHAPTER 1

A Woman Adorned and Adorning

Beauty Secrets of Titus 2

Let us rejoice and exult,
and give him the glory,
for the marriage of the Lamb has come,
and his Bride has made herself ready;
it was granted her to clothe herself
with fine linen, bright and pure.

REVELATION 19:7–8

IT HAD BEEN A SHORT NIGHT OF SLEEP. But that didn't matter to me. I knew this day—Saturday, November 14, 2015—would be one I'd never forget. At the age of fifty-seven, I was about to be a bride for the first time. Today I would say "I do" before God and several hundred witnesses and become Mrs. Robert Wolgemuth. It was a day I had eagerly anticipated and for which I had been earnestly preparing for months.

My phone alarm woke me at 5:15 a.m. An hour later, a sweet young friend and her husband knocked on the door of my hotel room. Emerging into the predawn stillness, we drove twenty minutes through the western Chicago suburbs and finally pulled into a vacant church parking lot in Wheaton, Illinois.

Inside the church, we were directed to a small, sparsely furnished room, where over the next few hours a transformation would take place. I slipped on a robe and took a seat as first a hair stylist, then a makeup artist, quietly got busy. We had been through trial runs, so they knew just what to do.

My wedding gown, purchased months earlier, painstakingly altered and carefully steamed by a friend the night before, hung off to the side, ready for me to slip into. An elegant bracelet and "diamond" earrings sat out on a table along with sparkly silver shoes—which yet another friend would take to a shoe store as soon as it opened so they could be stretched. (They were brand-new and killing my feet!) Everything was ready to complete the ensemble.

Why was I going to all this trouble? Why was I getting more dressed up than I had ever been in my life? Why had I endured the seemingly endless attention to details that commandeered my life over so many months? Why did I enlist and gratefully accept the help of so many friends who had plenty of other important things to do?

I'll tell you why. All the time, thought, money, and effort expended for that one day were for a single purpose. I wanted to be *adorned*— beautiful, ready for my bridegroom. And I wanted to *adorn* my husband-to-be with my affection and attention. I wanted him to be honored and admired by others. I wanted our guests to see how much I loved this man and what a gift he was to me.

We had decided to take our photos prior to the wedding ceremony. So promptly at nine-thirty, arrayed in my dress, train, and white faux-fur wrap, I was carefully loaded into a car that would take me to an outdoor location nearby for our photo shoot.

Robert was already at the site, his back toward me. On cue, he turned around to get his first glimpse of the adorned bride he had only been able to picture in his mind till that moment. His response—the look in his eyes, his involuntary gasp—was priceless to me. It made all the effort worthwhile.

We walked the fifty feet or so toward each other, bracing against the brisk, late fall chill, our hearts warmed with each other's presence. Robert reached out to embrace me, and I fell into his arms.

Never had I felt more beautiful.

Woman to Woman

Back in the bride's room, just moments before the ceremony was to begin, as Robert and I and several others were tending to last-minute details, someone came in to let me know that one of our guests had asked to pray with me before the wedding.

Vonette Bright, a dear, lifelong friend, was like a second mother to me. Eighty-nine years old and widowed for a dozen years, she had been battling leukemia and had just been told she had only months to live. But she had been eager to be at my wedding if it was the last thing she did—and she'd made it. (As it turned out, she would be with the Lord just six weeks later.)

I was eager to see this beloved friend, so we invited her to join us for a few moments. Vonette's caregiver gently pushed her wheelchair into the room. Beautifully dressed in bright red, Vonette turned a radiant countenance toward us. We circled around her wheelchair as cameras flashed and video rolled and this venerable woman of God led us in prayer, blessing our marriage.

When she finished, Vonette turned to me and whispered, "I had hoped to be able to speak to you alone." In response, I quickly asked everyone to clear the room. Then she turned to me and spoke gently but forthrightly: "Honey, I'm a mama . . . and I'd like to know . . . Is there anything you'd like to ask a mama before you get married?"

No cameras or recorders were privy to the sweet exchange that took place in those next few moments, but that scene and our conversation will forever be etched on my heart.

A woman in the winter of her life imparting encouragement and exhortation to a woman in an earlier season who was eager to glean everything she possibly could.

A seasoned wife—having enjoyed a vibrant, loving marriage for fifty-four years— mentoring a novice in how to make much of Christ in her own marriage.

Two women, one older and the other younger, living out the beauty of the gospel—together.

Woman to woman.

The picture brings to mind another pair of women. I envision the elderly Elizabeth, after decades of infertility and unfulfilled longings, now supernaturally expecting a son . . . taking Mary of Nazareth into her heart and home . . . imparting faith and wisdom to the teenage virgin in whose womb was miraculously growing an infant who would one day be our Savior.

Precious little is recorded of their conversation, but what was preserved for us speaks to the beauty of the gospel being lived out by women walking in company with each other. Women whose lives are adorned by the presence of Christ and who adorn His gospel and make it believable for the next generation by their humble, joyful obedience.

After Vonette had shared with me what was on her heart, she took my hands in hers and once again prayed, praising our Father for the wedding about to take place and pleading for His blessing and favor on the marriage to follow. One could almost hear heaven whisper *Amen*.

That small, plain room, littered with hair and makeup gear, assorted clothing items, jewelry, and more, was transformed, through the Spirit of God knitting our hearts together, into a place of beauty, a temple adorned by and for the living Christ.

The Loveliness of Christ

As this modern-day Elizabeth and I exited that holy place, we could hear strains of the prelude flowing from the nearby sanctuary. Magnificent.

Not wanting to miss a moment of the celebration, Robert and I made our way to a secluded room just off the balcony, where we could see and hear the prelude and the first part of the worship service until it was time for the processional to begin.

The sanctuary with its colonial design was a visual feast. Tall, gleaming organ pipes lining the chancel wall. Gold banners proclaiming "Worthy is the Lamb" and "Unto Him be the glory." Massive arrangements of red roses and white calla lilies adorning the platform, with sprays of roses and ribbons at the end of the pews. Candles in elegant gold and silver stands. Exquisite.

And in the center of it all, prominently displayed on the platform, a twelve-foot, rough-hewn cross that made the whole setting even more striking.

For was it not at Calvary that our Savior took upon Himself the rags of our sin and shame, adorning us in exchange with the robes of His righteousness? Is not the cross the only source of any eternal beauty we may ever hope to experience or to offer other souls starved for love and loveliness?

> Jesus, Thy blood and righteousness
> My beauty are, my glorious dress.[1]

At the beginning of the ceremony, ten young girls whose families I have known and loved for years processed down the aisle ringing tiny bells. They were attired in darling dresses—some red, others white—with tights and fancy shoes, their hair curled and styled so sweetly.

A photo of the ten children surrounding the bride, all of us seated on steps at the front of the church, brought tears to my eyes the first time I saw it. For in these precious, beautifully dressed girls, I saw ten young women of God in the making.

I love the thought of inspiring those girls with a vision of what it means to be a bride who has experienced the love and grace of Christ and who radiates His beauty to others. I pray they will grow to have hearts that are adorned with grace and that their lives will adorn the gospel of Christ for their generation.

Children adorned. Guests adorned. A sanctuary adorned. A bride adorned.

All of it intended to fulfill the vision Robert and I had for our wedding from the time we announced our engagement—namely, *to showcase the loveliness of Christ.*

Or, as the apostle Paul put it in the second chapter of the book of Titus, to "adorn the doctrine of God our Savior" (v. 10).

Love and Beauty

Women love beauty. We enjoy the process of adorning ourselves and our environment.

Shopping for the clothes, makeup, or jewelry that will help us look our best.

Picking paint and accessories to make our homes more welcoming or comfortable or fashionable.

Carefully garnishing the food we put on the table.

Dressing our little ones in cute outfits.

Adding those special touches that make our surroundings, our relationships, and our activities a little more beautiful and personal and fun.

There's just something about assembling and creating beauty that's deeply satisfying.

And *feeling* beautiful—that's a longing deep in many women's hearts that has spawned and fueled countless industries.

I've never considered myself to be particularly beautiful in a physical sense. It's not that I think I'm unattractive or that I think there's something wrong with physical beauty. It's just not something I've focused on a whole lot. Mindful of the fleeting, deceptive nature of external beauty, I've tried to focus on cultivating the kind of beauty that can't be photographed (or photoshopped)—beauty of character and the heart.

Yet I can still remember how my heart skipped a beat the first time Robert told me I was beautiful.

I grew up in a loving home with a dad who adored me. I've been blessed to have many good, kind men in my life. It's possible my memory has failed me. But prior to that point, I cannot recall ever hearing a man say to me, "You're beautiful."

Robert kept telling me I was beautiful. He really seemed to mean it. And gradually I began to believe that he truly saw me that way—even when I had just finished working out at the gym, even on days when I hadn't taken time to apply makeup or fix my hair. As our courtship progressed, I told a friend, "I don't think there is anything I could do that would make him love me less or think I'm less beautiful."

But I also noticed that something even more significant was happening. As the persistent, gentle love of this man took root in my heart, it had a tenderizing, beautifying effect. In fact, to my amazement, people began to

> *Our calling is to make His love and His truth visible, believable, and beautiful to skeptical observers.*

comment on my new "glow." Over and over again on my wedding day, friends said to me, "You're so beautiful!"

I say this not to shine a spotlight on myself, but to make the observation that to be adorned with another's love is to develop a greater capacity to reflect love and beauty to others.

You see, God has placed us here on earth as ambassadors of the gospel of Christ. And our calling as His followers is to make His love and His truth visible and believable—and beautiful—to skeptical observers.

Because they see it in *us*. Because they see it *changing* us.

His love making us beautiful. Adorning us.

And, through us, adorning His gospel.

Why We Need Each Other

It's a wonderful picture, isn't it?

But sadly—as you and I well know—it doesn't always work that way.

We may claim to love Jesus, but for some reason people don't always see His beauty reflected in our attitudes and actions. They don't always see in us the transforming power of His love.

Instead, too often, they see women who are just as overwhelmed, preoccupied, petty, or unloving as everyone else around us. If we're honest, that's the way we sometimes see ourselves.

But we long to do better. We really do want our lives to show the gospel in its very best light—even when we're

- up to our elbows in work and family life, with little time for personal prayer and Bible reading
- doubled over in worry and frustration because of a child who's running hard from God
- suffering through a lonely, loveless stretch of marriage with a husband who's pulled away
- retired to a shallow routine of crawling out of bed, making the coffee, watching television, and working the morning crossword puzzle
- or perhaps trapped in one of those tedious, one-foot-in-front-of-the-other seasons of life when the motivation to press on is almost more than we can muster.

But *how* do we do better? That's the question, isn't it?

How in the world do we manage to adorn the gospel and let it adorn us in the midst of our mundane or agonizing realities?

With help.

Lots of help!

The good news is that this task of being adorned by the gospel and enhancing the way it's perceived by others isn't something we're called to do alone. To help us accomplish what He has given us to do, God has graciously given us His Spirit and His church. And for us women, God has given us a community of other believing women for inspiration and support.

On my wedding weekend, a cadre of women friends, younger and older, banded together to provide personal and practical support in every way imaginable. The dear friend who took me to get my nails done (and secretly paid the bill). The young woman who accompanied me to the church for my makeup routine. Loving friends who baked and decorated cupcakes and others who managed guest lists and cared for administrative details for four different events. The sweet women who slipped away early from the reception to adorn Robert's and my hotel suite with an abundance of flowers, candles, and tasty snacks.

The love and combined efforts of these special women (along with many kind, helpful men) resulted in an indescribably lovely weekend. I couldn't have done it without the encouragement and help they provided. And in much the same way, I can't make it through life without walking in community with women who band together to support and beautify each other in Christ.

I need older women like my friend Vonette, who prayed for me from the time I was a child, watched me grow into a woman, often spoke into my life with wisdom, vision, and faith, and then, near the end of her life, endured the rigors of travel to be there for me and to share her love and wisdom when I got married.

I also need younger women in my life, even girls as young as those sweet little women-to-be who participated in my wedding. They help keep me from becoming narrow and brittle, and they bring me such joy and hope.

And I need women in my own season of life—like a small group of "sisters" I am a part of who gather periodically, on the phone or in person, for mutual encouragement, accountability, and prayer. I treasure the companionship and influence of these women in my life.

The biblical model of older women living out the gospel and training younger women to do the same is vital for all of us to thrive.

Older women, younger women, women who are peers—we all need each other if we are to adorn the gospel and show its beauty in our lives. And that reality brings us back to Titus 2 and the heart of this book. Because this important passage offers a primer for how and why this all works. It paints for us a picture of generational wisdom flowing downhill into inexperienced hearts, where it can cycle around and back up again in a continual process of godly care and counsel.

Woman to woman.

Older to younger.

Day to day.

Life to life.

This is God's good and beautiful plan. The biblical model of older women living out the gospel and training younger women to do the same, of younger women recognizing the value of older women in their lives—of women adorning the gospel together—is vital for all of us to thrive. Living our lives as Titus 2 women enables us to fulfill the purpose for which we were created. It helps our families and churches to flourish and the beauty of the gospel to shine forth in our world.

Together in the Race

We sometimes hear life compared to a marathon, the defining mark of which is *endurance*. And for sure, the race of life calls for endurance over the long haul.

But life is so much more than just staying the long course, gritting our teeth and enduring. We're also meant to grow, thrive, and celebrate. We're meant to enjoy beauty—awe-inspiring, life-enriching, God-exalting beauty.

And we're meant to experience the strength and encouragement that flow out of doing life together, helping each other live gospel-adorned lives that in turn adorn the gospel in the eyes of the world.

So I like to envision us Christian women participating in another kind of race. We're not just solo competitors slogging it out toward a distant finish line. Instead, we're a team. We run *together*.

Think of it as a *relay*—passing the baton from one person to another, each of us involved in the process, both giving and receiving as we press on toward our destination. It's teamwork, not just individual performance, that counts.

Or think of it as one of those charity runs where we all move forward in a group, helping one another, pooling our energies for the sake of a beloved cause. Knowing that our individual efforts count but that it's not entirely up to us to make it happen—and that the race itself has meaning, not just crossing the finish line.

Picture a vast field of runners—some older, some younger, some more mature, some less seasoned—and you and me, right there with them. We each need our own, personal relationship with God and His Word, of course, but we are not running by ourselves. God intends for our lives to intersect with one another, to carry each other forward under the strong, victorious, beautiful banner of Christ.

Now if all of this seems a bit too philosophical and esoteric, I assure you the practical implications will soon be clear. And they are huge, because this marathon, this relay, this race for a cause runs right through your living room. The baton passes directly over your kitchen table and through seemingly insignificant conversations and encounters.

When older women and younger women support each other in living out God's transforming love, the entire body of Christ grows more beautiful.

This is for you and me . . . real women living real, everyday lives.

And when it's working, believe me, it *works*. When older women choose to invest themselves in the lives of younger women, whole families and churches feel the blessing. When young moms and singles widen their close-knit groups to include women who have already run a few laps and lived to tell about it, both sides of the relationship are strengthened and grow. When older women and younger women support each other in living out God's transforming love, the entire body of Christ—the bride of Christ—grows more beautiful.

So if you're an *older woman* (and willing to admit it—as I am), the message of this book is for you.

And if you're a *younger woman* (as I still am to some), the message of this book is for you too. It's for all of us—because each of us is an older woman to somebody and each of us is a younger woman to someone else. And each of us, in different ways, in different seasons, can be on both the giving and receiving end of this life-to-life process.

Where We Begin

The heart of this powerful pattern can be seen in a single paragraph of Titus 2. And yet the rich, practical, gospel-drenched insight found in Titus 2:3–5 is sufficient to keep us nourished and growing for a lifetime.

These words were originally written by the apostle Paul to a young pastor named Titus, who was struggling to lead a church on the island of Crete. The Roman Empire, which ruled Crete, was just coming under the tyrannical reign of the ruthless emperor, Nero. Just imagine what Nero's maniacal threats felt like to the fledgling churches of his day, especially when his government officially outlawed Christianity throughout the empire.

Do you think it's hard being a Christian today? Try knowing you're a hunted species. Try thinking that if this young, revolutionary movement is to survive, plans must be put in place both to spread and to deepen its impact. It can't just be a religious order or a theological system; the gospel must soak through people's hearts and lives and families so pervasively that no emperor, no persecution, no reviling would be able to rock the church of Christ from its foundations. No amount of pressure, fear, or fatigue could dilute the church to the point that it would lose its light—its distinctiveness, vibrancy, and impact in the world.

Those were some of the concerns behind Paul's letter to Titus. Christians were wondering:

- How are believers supposed to think and act in such times?
- How can we keep from being deceived by false doctrine and teachers?
- How can we pass our faith on to the next generation, rather than seeing it become extinct?
- How can the church not just survive, but thrive, in a world that is hostile to our faith?
- How can we effectively fulfill our mission to reach a corrupt world with the beauty of Christ's gospel?

Sound familiar? Those questions are still with us.

Which is why we still need the book of Titus today.

We may not live in Nero's Rome, but we do live in a decadent, deceptive culture that threatens the church of Christ with its allure as well as its accusations and attacks. We need help to see how our lives can portray the gospel so beautifully that others see in us the transforming power of Christ and are drawn to know and follow Him. And (dare we say it?) we need help keeping His gospel attractive enough to *ourselves* that we—who claim to believe it—will actually trust Him, obey Him, and experience the power, peace, and joy He promises, even while living as exiles on this earth.

We all need to understand how to adorn the teaching of the gospel of Christ with the way we live—and to help each other do the same. And that's exactly what Titus 2 provides for us. With its succinct summary of the character qualities that delight God's heart and attract the hearts of those around us, this passage provides a timeless curriculum meant to be handed down from generation to generation. It lets older women know what is most important to share and younger women know what they're called to aspire to become.

Years ago, when I first began preparing to teach on this theme, I read this short book of the Bible scores of times—meditating on it, memorizing it, pondering individual words, letting my spirit soak in it.

I hope you'll do the same. Read it over and over again—all three chapters at first, to give you the overall setting, then narrowing down to chapter 2, with special emphasis on verses three through five. Immerse yourself in the text and its meaning because this is a passage you and I need to *get*. The more we let it define our lives and relationships, the more lovely Christ will be to us, and the more clearly the beauty of His gospel will shine through us to others.

Life, the Way It's Supposed to Be

Several years ago, I received an unforgettable email from a young woman in her early thirties, a single mom I had known since she was a little girl. The subject line said simply, "Happy Mother's Day."

Intrigued, I opened it and read on.

Her note brought back some memories that, while fuzzy in my mind, were still fresh in hers. She referenced a handful of activities I'd planned for her and several of her middle-school friends and a brief conversation here and there as she grew up—nothing particularly significant in my mind. But God had used these periodic connecting points as an enduring means of grace and encouragement in her life.

Her closing paragraph touched me deeply:

> Although you may not have biological children here
> on earth, your spiritual motherhood and its impact
> have been among the greatest blessings in my life.
> Thank you for being a shining example of Christ's
> likeness. Happy Mother's Day!

The note was signed, "From one of your many spiritual children." It doesn't get much better than that.

I assure you that I fall far short of being the "shining example of Christ's likeness" I long to be. But how I thank God for the way He uses our lives and efforts—imperfect as they are—to accomplish His purposes here on earth.

My response to my young friend captures the essence of this book, as well as my heart for you—whatever your season of life—as we begin this journey together:

> I was pretty close to the age you are now when some
> of what you describe took place. I had no idea then
> how those simple things would impact the lives of
> you girls. I just wanted to love and encourage you.
> And God in His grace caused those seeds to take
> root and produce sweet fruit.
>
> Now God has given you a precious daughter to
> disciple, and undoubtedly has put others in your

sphere of influence. I pray your life will be a fragrance of Christ to them and that one day you will have the joy of receiving a note that will bless you as much as your note has blessed me.

Love,
Nancy

And so the race goes on. Each of us supporting others and encouraging them to press on. One generation passing the baton to the next, preserving and inspiring godliness and gospel witness. And, in the process, the beauty of Jesus shines forth and His kingdom is advanced in our world.

This is a joy you can experience. It's not about having a big platform or an official teaching role (though God may entrust one or both to you). More than that, it's about living the life He has made you for and called you to, right where you are.

Older women modeling holiness, obedience, and love, and investing intentionally in the lives of younger women.

Younger women seeking and receiving, with humility and gratitude, the blessings given to them from seasoned women, only to pass the treasure on to others down the line.

Women of all ages—growing ever more beautiful as the gospel of Christ adorns our lives.

Adorning that gospel by the way we live.

And doing it all, step by step, together—the Titus 2 way.

Making It Personal

Older women

1. Can you think of two or three younger women with whom you could share your life and experience—as Vonette Bright did for me? Who are they? How might you go about approaching them?

2. Older women are called to pass the baton to younger women. What have you learned or experienced that you would like to pass to the next generation?

Younger women

1. Does the note I received from my young friend inspire you to send a similar one to a spiritual mother in your life? If so, what specific things can you express gratitude for?

2. Name an older woman who speaks wisdom, vision, and faith into your life—as Vonette Bright did for me. If you don't have anyone like that currently, ask the Lord to direct you to a woman you could approach about investing in your life.

To get the most out of this book, invite a group of women—younger and older—to read through it together. You'll find a group discussion guide and lots of helpful companion resources at adornedbook.com. Connect there with other women about how to apply the Titus 2 calling in your life and relationships.

PART ONE

A Woman under God

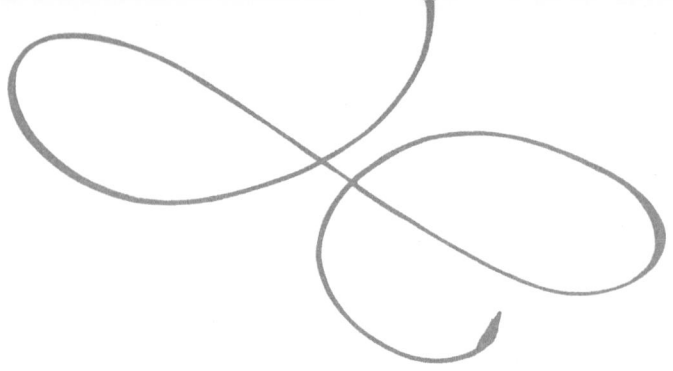

Teach what accords with sound doctrine.

Older men are to be sober-minded, dignified, self-controlled,
sound in faith, in love, and in steadfastness.

Older women likewise are to be reverent in behavior,
not slanderers or slaves to much wine.

They are to teach what is good,
and so train the young women
to love their husbands and children,
to be self-controlled,
pure,
working at home,
kind,
and submissive to their own husbands,
that the word of God may not be reviled.

**. . . so that in everything they may adorn
the doctrine of God our Savior.**

TITUS 2:1–5, 10

CHAPTER 2

Doctrine, You, and Titus 2

The "What" and the "Now What"

Do not settle for a wimpy theology. It is beneath you.
God is too great. Christ is too glorious.
JOHN PIPER

MY HUSBAND IS A SELF-ADMITTED ACROPHOBIC. He has a fear of heights. Put him at the top of a ladder or peering over the balcony of a tall building, and he confesses that his heart pounds and his knees turn to Jell-O.

Robert is also a gifted handyman and amateur builder. Over the years, he has taken on some impressive building projects. I've seen the pictures. And some of these projects—building a thirty-foot chimney, painting a two-story house—have required him to do his work high in the air.

So how does he deal with his fear while perched twenty-five feet above the ground? "That's easy," he says. "I never climb a ladder or step onto scaffolding until I'm certain I have taken the time to level the legs of the ladder or plant the feet of the scaffolding on a perfectly solid place."

What Robert describes is a perfect metaphor for this chapter.

My heart's desire is to be a Titus 2 woman. Consistently. Contentedly. Beautifully. To be adorned with the gospel and to adorn the gospel in the eyes of others.

I hope that's your desire too.

But the starting point on the journey to get us there might not be what you expect.

Maybe you turned the page to this chapter ready to jump right into the heart of the noble calling and qualities Paul outlines for women. Like Robert scampering up the ladder or scaffolding to get started with his work, you're eager to get *on* with it. You're hoping for something useful, something you can put into practice in your day-to-day life.

Instead, you're about to run smack dab into one of those "church words" that doesn't seem to have much to do with how you live.

Doctrine.

That's right. This chapter is about doctrine.

It's a word that reminds me of my husband taking time to make sure his ladder is secure, that his scaffolding is built on solid, level ground before he climbs up.

I understand you may be tempted to skip ahead to the "good stuff," looking for "news you can use"—practical insights and tools to help you become a more godly, fruitful woman. And you'll find lots of that in Titus 2 and in this book. But Paul addresses doctrine before laying out specifics of our practice, and he does so for a good reason. Doctrine—what we believe—is foundational to how we live. And if you miss it, you'll never get to where you want to be.

Belief and Behavior

So what's your first reaction to the word *doctrine*? Sound dull? Dry? Divisive or disagreeable? Maybe you share the sentiment of a man who once told a friend of mine, "At our church we don't preach doctrine. We just love Jesus."

But the fact is, every one of us and every situation we encounter in life is fueled by some kind of doctrine. It is the ground we stand on as we build our lives.

Your kids may go to public schools—supposedly religion-free zones. But don't think for a minute that doctrine is not being taught in secular grade schools, high schools, and colleges. Every course taught in every school is informed by some sort of doctrinal framework.

The afternoon talk shows have a doctrine. The evening dramas and sitcoms have a doctrine. Books on the *New York Times* bestsellers list, just like the ones on the feature display at your local Christian bookstore, all contain doctrine. Even atheists have a doctrine. Not *good* doctrine, but a doctrine that leads them to certain conclusions and values and that determines the way they think and live.

Doctrine, you see, simply means teaching. It's the *content* of what we believe, the understanding of reality that shapes our faith. Like soil in a garden, doctrine provides the context for growing character.

The soil of doctrine in which we're planted can make us beautiful and help us point others to the beauty of Christ and His gospel.

But only if it's the *right* doctrine.

Even those of us who are longtime Christians can be misled by false or skewed beliefs we've picked up somewhere. If we aren't intentional about where our hearts and minds are planted and watered, we can't expect to end up with a healthy crop. Bad doctrine, bad fruit. Good doctrine, good fruit.

Let me give you an example: my longtime friend Holly Elliff is a pastor's wife, the mother of eight children. She has a vibrant ministry to her family and to other women. But there was a time in her late twenties when her experience of the abundant Christian life was hindered by a bad case of bad doctrine.

Early on, Holly, like many, had somehow picked up the belief that if she did her best to be a good Christian woman, if she prayed and read her Bible faithfully, if she loved her husband and children and checked off all the right religious boxes, then God could be counted on to return the favor by placing her in a no-trouble zone. Given this assumption—this incorrect doctrine of God—you can imagine how Holly's world was shaken when trouble started showing up.

After giving birth to her first two children, she had a miscarriage. Her next child had a birth injury that required months of therapy. In the midst of all this, her father-in-law, who had been a godly role model for many years, was unfaithful to his wife, resulting in her in-laws divorcing after forty-three years of marriage. Then her mother-in-law developed Alzheimer's disease, and Holly—now with four young children still at home—became the primary caregiver.

As if that wasn't enough, a loud, vocal faction began stirring up dissent in their church and targeting her husband, Bill, with their criticism. Something like that is hard enough to take when you're the object, but even harder when it's someone you love.

On Sunday mornings, one of Holly's jobs was to serve at the welcome table. This task, which she had always enjoyed, became uncomfortable during this season, when contentious conversations were taking place in the church hallways and meeting rooms, around dinner tables, and on phone calls. Nor did it help that the saccharine-sweet woman who sometimes shared Holly's hospitality duties was married to one of Bill's most outspoken critics.

Now, put yourself in Holly's place. If you were faced with this set of circumstances and were coming from the doctrinal standpoint Holly had embraced as a young woman—the one that says God shields obedient believers from overwhelming challenges or difficulties—what would your response be? Would you be "reverent" in your behavior, "self-controlled" in your demeanor, "kind" in your remarks, as Titus 2 urges you to be?

You see, belief affects behavior. Doctrine matters.

This whole experience forced Holly to examine what she really believed; it challenged her to build a solid foundation for her life by getting into the Word more seriously and getting to really know God. The fruit of that resolve, coming out of a difficult season in her life, has been extraordinary and beautiful.

So the starting place—the foundation—for becoming Titus 2 women is exactly where Paul begins—by calling us to a life that "accords with sound doctrine."

Desperate for Doctrine

The culture in first-century Crete, where Titus served as a pastor, was the furthest thing from good or godly. Quoting a contemporary philosopher of the day who had said, "Cretans are always liars, evil beasts, lazy gluttons," Paul added simply, "This testimony is true" (Titus 1:12–13). He described unbelievers there as being "detestable, disobedient, unfit for any good work" (v. 16).

As is invariably the case, rampant false teaching went hand in hand with the irreverent lifestyle that was so prevalent in Crete:

> There are many who are insubordinate, empty talkers
> and deceivers. . . . they are upsetting whole families
> by teaching for shameful gain what they ought not to
> teach. (Titus 1:10–11)

This false teaching was no small matter. That word translated "upsetting" means to "overthrow, overturn, destroy."[1] That's the kind of upheaval that unsound doctrine was causing for entire Christian families.

So what were those first-century believers to do in light of such pervasive unsound teaching and godless living? And what are we to do in similar circumstances today? Wring our hands in despair? Curse the darkness? Give up and just hold on for Jesus to come back?

"But as for you," Paul said to Pastor Titus, *"teach what accords with sound doctrine"* (2:1).

That's it? Teach God's people how to live according to truth?

That's it. That is God's plan—truth and light overcoming deception and darkness.

The Cretan culture was in desperate need of believers and churches that valued right doctrine. Our culture has the same need. Because where such doctrine is taught, believed, and put into practice, the gospel of Christ is put on display; it is proclaimed with power and becomes believable. That's why Paul urged Titus to appoint elders and overseers in each church who could "give instruction in sound doctrine" (v. 9) and whose example would back up their teaching.

The Greek word translated "sound" (as in "sound doctrine") is *hugiaino*. It's the term from which we get our English word *hygiene*.[2] Sound doctrine is a means of keeping us healthy. It's wholesome. It's life-giving. It helps make spiritually sick people well in every way that matters for eternity.

We hear a lot these days about clean energy sources and healthy lifestyle choices. Our activist culture is quick to fight the overuse of pesticides in the farming industry or in mosquito-infested neighborhoods. And we all know people who like to keep their friends close but their hand sanitizer closer.

But many who are fastidious about washing their fruits and vegetables are not nearly as careful about what they ingest in the form of doctrine. Contaminants don't seem to bother them when it comes to what they believe.

Sound, healthy doctrine is pure. It's hygienic. It's safe. It's free from poisonous error. As a result, it produces sound, healthy believers. Their lives show the difference good doctrine makes.

But too often, little if any such difference is evident in the lives of those who call themselves Christians.

Not long ago, I was struck by the results of a survey I read. Nonbelieving older teens and young adults were asked if they had a personal friend or acquaintance who was a Christian. Of the roughly 85 percent who said they did, only *15 percent* indicated they saw any lifestyle differences between their Christian and non-Christian friends.

> *Sound doctrine is radically transformational. Lived out it changes everything about us.*

And it's not only students and young adults who see it that way. This problem applies to both older and younger generations.

It should not be this way. Believers should be noticeably different. True believers *will* be noticeably—beautifully—different.

And sound doctrine is what makes it so.

How Sound Doctrine Changes Us

Sound doctrine is radically transformational. Lived out, it changes everything about us. It counsels us. It corrects us. It's like an onboard guidance system, directing and determining our course. And ultimately it transforms the culture through us and around us.

The teaching of sound doctrine was so foundational to Paul's thinking that he actually included this phrase nine times in the three New Testament letters known as his "pastoral epistles" (1 and 2 Timothy and Titus). Five of those instances are in Titus alone.

Sound doctrine.

It mattered then. It matters now. It's the complete body of truth, revealed in Scripture, that explains and defines our faith. Among other things, it tells us:

- who we are
- who God is

- what it means to be a Christian
- what the gospel is
- who Jesus is
- why He came
- why He died
- why He lives again

Sound doctrine tells us that God is sovereign over all—over time, over nature, over us, over every minute detail in the universe. That means when everything in our world seems to be giving way, spinning out of control, we can trust that "He's got the whole world in His hands."

Sound doctrine tells us that we exist to bring glory to God and that every circumstance that comes into our lives can contribute to that end. If we could get just that one truth fixed in our hearts, we would never look at our circumstances the same way again.

That belief—that doctrine—would certainly change us.

Sound doctrine tells us that sin entered our world and infected it all the way down to the dust specks and the groundwater. It tells us that our natural tendency (going all the way back to Adam and Eve) is to try to remedy the situation on our own, apart from God, to hide from Him behind our hand-sewn fig leaves in hopes of avoiding notice and accountability. It also tells us that conflicts at home, at work, in our families, and in our world are evidence of what sin has done to us and to others.

Knowing this, our only hope is found in turning to the One who, while certainly within His rights to write us off, has chosen instead to introduce redemption and reconciliation into our world. In light of His truth, we see our sin and the sin of the world for what it is, and we recognize our utter dependence upon Him who is our righteousness and our life.

That, too, changes us.

Sound doctrine tells us that our personal opinions are inconsequential compared to God's, that individual rights do not trump eternal absolutes, that truth is not subjective and relative but consistent across all times and all places to all people—including us.

It tells us that the way things are is not the way they will always be, that the goal of the Christian life is not mere survival nor peaceful coexistence with a lost culture, but rather the ultimate triumph of Christ *over* culture.

Sound doctrine tells us that even as believers we can expect to struggle with indwelling sin, fleshly appetites, and self-centeredness. It reminds us that if we are not abiding in Christ and allowing His Spirit to do His sanctifying work in us, we may be capable of producing religious work but not of bearing spiritual fruit.

Yet sound doctrine also goes on to tell us that every time we say *yes* to Jesus and *no* to our flesh, allowing His love and power to flow through us, we become more and more like the King whose heavenly kingdom we represent here on earth.

It tells us that the cross is God's message of hope to the world and that the primary evidences of its present reality are lives in which His mercy and grace are actively at work.

And all that, my sister, should totally transform us.

The Gift of Sound Doctrine

Yes, sound doctrine changes us.

It is the *what* that leads to our *now what*.

"Give instruction in sound doctrine," Paul says to Titus (1:9). Lay a solid biblical and theological foundation in the hearts of your people. That's the *what*. It's the starting place.

Then "teach what accords with sound doctrine" (2:1)—that is, make personal and practical application of the truth. That's the *now what*. It's the practical application that follows. Sound doctrine is not just a collection of abstract theological concepts. It is always connected to duty. It requires, motivates, and enables us to live lives that are pleasing to the Lord.

Sadly, many believers and churches today seem to lack an appetite for sound doctrine. We live in a consumer culture. We want to be entertained. We want to be comfortable. We don't want to have to think. And we don't want outsiders to think we're narrow, exclusive, or boring. We've learned that "doctrine lite" often attracts bigger crowds than strong doctrinal teaching and preaching.

But the impact of the gospel in our world is inevitably weakened when our focus on programs, productions, marketing, and relevance outranks our emphasis on sound doctrine. When that happens, people are deprived of the very thing that gives the Christian message its greatest persuasiveness—the winsome witness of changed lives that reflect the beauty of Christ and His truth. To crave anything less than sound teaching is a dangerous place to be.

But this tendency is not unique to our era. Nor should it surprise us. Paul warned his young pastor friend Timothy of this very thing:

> The time is coming when people will not endure
> sound teaching, but having itching ears they will
> accumulate for themselves teachers to suit their own
> passions, and will turn away from listening to the
> truth and wander off into myths. (2 Tim. 4:3–4)

Paul was quick to point Timothy toward the timeless solution:

> I charge you in the presence of God and of Christ Jesus
> . . . preach the word; . . . reprove, rebuke, and exhort,
> with complete patience and teaching. (2 Tim. 4:1–2)

This is essentially the same message Paul gave Titus at the beginning of his letter, when he spelled out the qualifications for church leaders. Pastors and elders are responsible for providing spiritual *direction* and *protection* for the flock of God. An unswerving commitment to sound doctrine is central to that calling:

> He must hold firm to the trustworthy word as taught, so that he may be able to give instruction in sound doctrine [*direction*] and also to rebuke those who contradict it [*protection*]. (Titus 1:9)

If the pastors and leaders of your church love and live and teach sound doctrine, you have been given a huge gift. Be sure to let them know how blessed and grateful you are. If you're looking for a church home, make sure to choose one where you and your family will find a steady diet of solid, biblical teaching that encourages you to live out the implications of sound doctrine. And if your church is searching for a new pastor, pray that God will bring a man who will "teach what accords with sound doctrine" (Titus 2:1). He doesn't have to be a spellbinding orator or a superb administrator. He doesn't have to possess great charisma or the ability to build a megachurch. But he does need to be able to "preach the Word"—to "exhort and rebuke with all authority" (v. 15).

Dual Dangers

Without sound doctrine, we have no moorings, no firm footing for our lives. If we are not grounded in sound doctrine, we will be easily deceived and led astray—susceptible to false doctrine. We won't know how to discern truth from error when we hear a popular preacher or read a bestselling book that is not fully aligned with Scripture. Without sound doctrine, we can't know how to live in a way that pleases God.

That's why we so often see professing Christians falling prey to off-base teaching and justifying unbiblical and immoral choices—because they have fallen away from sound doctrine and its life implications.

Having said all of this, we need to acknowledge that it is possible to hold tenaciously to sound doctrine in a way that is cold, lifeless, and devoid of the Spirit. (Can you say Pharisee?) In fact, there are two dangers equally to be avoided when it comes to doctrine.

So far in this chapter we have emphasized the first danger—that of *life without sound doctrine*. On the other hand, those who value and promote sound Bible teaching can be in danger of having *doctrine without life*.

> *Doctrine that produces self-righteous, critical, contentious, dry-eyed defenders of truth is not truly sound—because sound doctrine is not only true and right; it is also beautiful and good.*

This was Nicodemus' problem when he first came to Jesus. This Jewish spiritual leader was well versed in the Old Testament Scriptures. He observed their precepts meticulously. He had his doctrine down. But he didn't have the Spirit. He didn't have life. And when he came to talk with Jesus under cover of night, it quickly became clear that Nicodemus was missing the basics of life in the Spirit. This caused Jesus to marvel: "Are you the teacher of Israel and yet you do not understand these things?" (John 3:10).

Nicodemus was a prime example of the fact that it is possible to *know* right and *do* right and yet not *be* right.

Further, doctrine that produces self-righteous, critical, contentious, dry-eyed defenders of truth is not in accord with the heart and character of God. It is not truly sound—because sound doctrine is not only true and right; it is also beautiful and good.

Would people see that as they look at our lives? We may have the right answers to hard questions, but do we exhibit tenderness as we share those answers? We may be able to quote "chapter and verse" for our favorite doctrinal distinctives, but are genuine love and kindness—

the fruit of the Spirit—manifest in our theological correctness? We may have mastered the Word of God, but is it evident to others that our hearts are moved by the wonder of what we know?

As Paul told Titus, the goal is that "in everything," we would "adorn the doctrine of God our Savior" (Titus 2:10). As we live out His truth in the power of the Holy Spirit, our lives are made more beautiful. And that truth becomes more compelling and irresistible in the eyes of those around us.

The Only Difference

When Paul urges Titus to teach what accords with sound doctrine, that implies that some ways of life are *not* in accordance with sound doctrine. Throughout the book of Titus, Paul identifies ways that Christians' lives should differ radically from those of unbelievers.[3] Let's look at some of these distinctions:

- *Consistency of belief and behavior.* Unbelievers may "profess to know God, but they deny him by their works" (1:16)—whereas true believers' lives are expected to be consistent with what they claim to believe.
- *Purity.* Paul describes unbelievers as being "defiled" and lawless (1:15; 2:14), acting like "evil beasts" (1:12). By contrast, the doctrine of God's holiness calls us to be "above reproach" (1:6–7) in every area of our lives.
- *Self-Control.* Unbelievers are slaves to "various passions and pleasures" (3:3) such as drunkenness and laziness (1:7, 12). But believers in Christ are empowered by Him to be self-controlled.
- *Composure.* Unbelievers are sometimes "quick-tempered" and "violent" (1:7). But believers are to be "kind" and not "argumentative" (2:5, 9), "to speak evil of no one, to avoid quarreling, to

be gentle, and to show perfect courtesy toward all people" (3:2).

- *Relationships.* Paul describes unbelievers' attitude toward others as being full of "malice and envy" (3:3), whereas believers' relationships should reflect the "loving kindness of God our Savior" (3:4).

- *Truthfulness.* Paul describes unbelievers as scheming "liars" (1:12) and "deceivers" (1:10), he referred to believers, however, as having a "knowledge of the truth" (1:1) and a devotion to God, who "never lies" (1:2).

I could go on. But you get the point. The distinction between Christians and the world should be crystal clear. Not because we're better people or come from better upbringings. In fact, we're not inherently any different from anyone else. Our hearts would love to march to the same self-absorbed cadence that drives the rest of the world.

The only difference—the *only* difference—is Jesus. The gospel.

But what a difference that makes. What a difference *He* makes!

And the means by which the Spirit keeps loosening our grip on old patterns of behavior, releasing us from the bonds of cultural conformity, and awakening our hearts to the beauty of Christ and His ways, is through the implanted truth of His Word.

Through sound doctrine.

Don't think you can dress up your life with better behavior or become the beautiful woman you're hoping to grow into without grounding your life in biblical truth. If you're not willing to start there and stay there, saturating yourself in Scripture and receiving sound teaching from mature believers, your pursuit of a godly, fruitful life will always be an exercise in frustration.

And if you try to live without paying close attention to sound, biblical teaching, don't think you'll be avoiding an encounter with doctrine. You'll simply be choosing to live by a different kind of doctrine.

Because all of us live (and die) by doctrine.

The Gospel Truth

I have come to believe that every failure and flaw in our lives flows out of some sort of doctrinal deficiency.

Either we haven't been taught and really don't know the truth God has given that enables us to obey and enjoy Him.

Or (worse) we know the truth, but we aren't walking according to what we know.

It's one or the other. Because only sound doctrine, steadily applied, will keep our thinking and our living on the right track.

Sound doctrine is safe. It's hygienic. It's pure. And it's absolutely indispensable to a healthy heart and a godly life.

Now, knowing and embracing sound, biblical doctrine doesn't candy-coat the spiritual warfare we face or guarantee we'll never blow

Our ultimate purpose is to make much of God. We do that as we experience, enjoy, and reflect the loveliness of Christ, making Him known to a world that is starved for true beauty.

it. But when we do fail, it tells us where to turn—it points us back to the cross, calls us to repent and to cast ourselves anew on Christ, and assures us of His mercy.

Again, it all comes back to the gospel. Our purpose for pursuing Titus 2 character, relationships, and ministry is not merely to be better wives, moms, and ministry leaders, to have a better reputation, or to be able to sleep better at night. Our ultimate purpose is to make much of God. We do that as we experience, enjoy, and reflect the loveliness of Christ, making Him known to a world that is starved for true beauty.

You may be concerned—as we all should be—about the rapid moral disintegration around us. Our reflexive reaction is to think the solution will be found in new and better laws, new structures and systems, an overhaul of schools and government. It's tempting to think that a different president, different legislators and judges, or more and better social programs will make the difference.

But what Paul argues in Titus is that what we need first and foremost are disciples who know and live in accord with sound doctrine. Men and women who are grounded in the Scripture and who live out what they believe. Believers who are godly, wise, good, and kind, who have loving, healthy families and relationships.

Our best intellectual arguments alone will never persuade the world at large about the existence of God, the uniqueness of Christ, the way to salvation, the moral rightness of a biblical worldview, or much of anything else. They are far more likely to be persuaded as they see the gospel lived out in our lives and relationships.

As the nineteenth-century German philosopher Heinrich Heine said: "Show me your redeemed life and I might be inclined to believe in your Redeemer."[4]

There simply is no more powerful tool of evangelism, no more effective means of bringing about social or systemic change, than for Christians to believe and demonstrate the doctrine and gospel of Jesus Christ.

That proposition might seem naïve and unsophisticated to some. What difference could a handful of regenerate Christ followers on the island of Crete possibly make in the far-flung, degenerate Roman Empire? What difference does it make if you and I live godly lives in our ungodly world?

You, your family, and your church may be tiny islands of godliness in a vast sea of wickedness. But don't underestimate what God can do to make the gospel desirable to lost souls through those outposts of grace and beauty. That's how the kingdom of God spreads.

So if you're a *younger woman* . . . get started now learning to pursue, grasp, and treasure the sound doctrine of God's Word, knowing it will shape the person you are today as well as the person you will one day become. And be sure you're connecting with godly, older women whose love for Christ and His Word will increase your appetite for sound doctrine and your understanding of the difference it makes in every area of your life.

And for those of us who are *older women*, let's be sure we never leave the basics—the pure, undiluted Word of God. Let's become living epistles of sound doctrine, both learned and practiced. Enough with the allurements and distractions of the world. It's time to show those coming behind us the beauty

When God's Word is learned and lived out by older and younger women together, the outcome will be stunningly beautiful. A mirror reflection of Christ.

of God's truth and its sufficiency for the challenges of our day. I assure you, each time you're obedient to this calling, you'll be able to watch Him paint your life with bigger and bolder gospel colors than you ever imagined possible.

Doctrine is our *what*.

Its application is our *now what*.

And when both are put together, we'll have a strong, level foundation of truth on which to build our lives with confidence.

When God's Word is learned and lived out by older and younger women together, the outcome will be stunningly beautiful. Utterly captivating. A mirror reflection of Christ.

Making It Personal

Older women

1. If a younger woman were looking for a mentor who is solidly grounded in biblical truth and who makes truth beautiful, would she think of you? Why or why not?

2. What practical steps could you take to be better prepared to mentor a younger woman? (Remember you don't have to be perfect to be helpful!)

3. How could you encourage a younger woman in your life to be more intentional about "planting and watering" her heart in the soil of good doctrine?

Younger women

1. Where have you picked up the "doctrines" (teachings) that most influence your life—TV/movies, friends, family members, mentors, books, Scripture, church? Are these wise, godly sources? What is the fruit of these teachings in your life?

2. What qualities in a potential mentor would tell you she has a firm commitment to sound doctrine? What are some possible red flags?

3. What steps could you take to deepen your grasp of God's Word and to saturate your mind, heart, and life with sound doctrine?

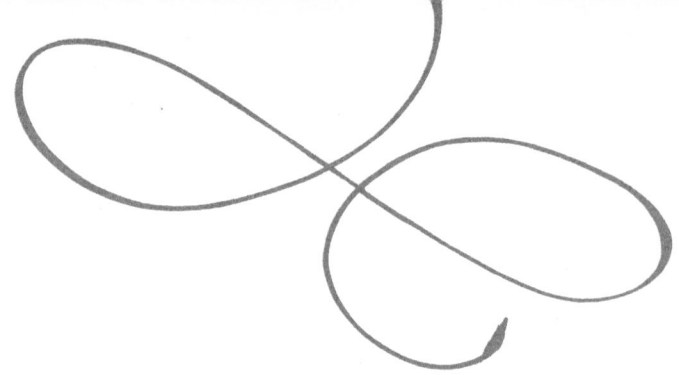

Teach what accords with sound doctrine.

Older men are to be sober-minded, dignified, self-controlled,
sound in faith, in love, and in steadfastness.

Older women likewise are to be reverent in behavior,
not slanderers or slaves to much wine.

They are to teach what is good,
and so train the young women
to love their husbands and children,
to be self-controlled,
pure,
working at home,
kind,
and submissive to their own husbands,
that the word of God may not be reviled.

**. . . so that in everything they may adorn
the doctrine of God our Savior.**

TITUS 2:1–5, 10

CHAPTER 3

Don't Give Up on That Modeling Career

Aging Beautifully—at All Ages

*Somebody old who has walked a long time in the path of righteousness
is a treasure—a treasure of wisdom and a treasure of experience
and a treasure of understanding.*
JOHN MacARTHUR

NOT LONG AGO, A DOCTOR FRIEND INTRODUCED MY HUSBAND and me to a health supplement that has been developed to repair, rejuvenate, and restore the cells of the body at the molecular level. As we get older, these molecules tend to become imbalanced and depleted, and our bodies are no longer able to function at optimal levels.

As we listened to our friend explain the science behind the product and how it could result in increased energy, strength, and health, we looked at each other, both of us thinking: *How can we get it? When can we start?!*

You see, no one had to tell us those cells in our bodies are aging. We know it. We feel it. You do too. And who wouldn't love to slow down that process?

Robert and I are not looking for something that will bring back our twenty-five-year-old bodies. But we would like to have the physical strength to love and serve the Lord, each other, and others for as long as He gives us breath. Even more important, we want to remain spiritually vital—flourishing and fruitful—as we age.

And we're all aging—every one of us. Whether we're twenty or forty or eighty, the years keep ticking off at what seems to be a perpetually increasing rate of speed. None of us will ever be younger than we are now. Yet this reality, inevitable as it is, still somehow manages to surprise us.

Few of us are quite ready to see the characteristics we once noticed in our parents or grandparents now appearing on the skin of our own hands, in the shape of our own bodies, in the graying color of our own hair. When did this happen? Was that dark spot always there? Can I not read anything anymore without these glasses? (If this has not been your experience yet, trust me, it will—and sooner than you imagine!)

How quickly, they told us, the years would sail by.

How right they were.

But in our dismay over life's inexorable effects on our roots, our reflexes, and our recall, let's not lose sight of the fact that the Bible does not view aging as a bad thing. In fact, it *honors* those who have gleaned wisdom over the course of many years.

The aging process can actually be an opportunity for growth and—by eternal standards—for becoming more beautiful, not less.

That's why I love seeing a wide span of ages involved in the corporate worship and ministry of a local church or visiting together over a fellowship meal. We are sure to be diminished anytime the church becomes too homogenous, especially when older (or younger) people are pushed to the sidelines or are simply not sought out as part of the ideal demographic mix of a particular church.

The Lord said to the Israelites from earliest times, "You shall stand up before the gray head and honor the face of an old man" (Lev. 19:32). The Old Testament patriarchs were said to be "full of years," "full of days" (Gen. 25:8; 35:29). And many of the heroes of faith in Scripture flourished in the middle and latter portions of their lives. Job himself pointed out that

> wisdom is with the aged,
>   and understanding in length of days. (Job 12:12)

Even the structure of Titus 2 implies deference toward older believers. Paul spoke first to the older men, then to the older women, followed by his instructions to the younger women and men in turn.

In general, Western culture doesn't think this way anymore. We tend to devalue people as they age, much as we tend to depreciate our own sense of worth as we grow older, becoming unhappy with our appearance and our slower pace and the effort required to stay limber and fit. But the aging process can actually be an opportunity for growth and—by eternal standards—for becoming *more* beautiful, not less. It can lead to increased fruitfulness and a changing but vital role in the body of Christ, contributing to the advancement of the kingdom even as we advance in age.

Please hear me. I'm not suggesting that it's necessarily sinful to be bothered by unattractive changes we see in the mirror or to think back to earlier days with fondness and a fleeting desire to return there.

What I'm saying is that our common experience of getting older, like every other experience in life, should be defined by a biblical paradigm rather than the perspective promoted by the world. Instead of pinning our expectations on what we see in the commercials or hear in conversation or even on research published in scientific and medical journals, we are called to frame our present and our future around the ageless model for aging found in Scripture.

Yes, we are getting older, whether "older" to you means thirty-five or sixty-five or ninety-five.

And, yes, each of these ages brings new challenges, some more acute than others.

But even if you find yourself in the biblical category of "older women" (somewhere beyond the child-rearing years, perhaps far beyond them), your best days as a vital, vibrant model of godliness can still be ahead of you. Each day of life God gives you is an opportunity to continue growing in Christlike character and to recognize in these new lines and creases the makings of a Titus 2 woman.

To Aging Women of All Ages

I've already introduced you to my friend, the late Vonette Bright. I knew Vonette from the time I was a little girl. On numerous occasions, I had the privilege of traveling and ministering with this accomplished woman, the cofounder (with her husband, Dr. Bill Bright) of Campus Crusade for Christ (now Cru). For me, she was one of those people who captured so much of what is beautiful about a godly woman—full of the Word, full of faith, full of spiritual vitality—all the way to the finish line.

Well into her eighties, even long after being widowed, this amazing woman was still traveling worldwide, serving the Lord and others with vigor and joy. Her pastor told me how, busy as she was, she offered to host a weekly small-group meeting in her home. She refused to settle back and live for herself.

In her late seventies, Vonette even took an online course to become a full-fledged member of the Christian Motorcyclists Association—she passed the online test and then went for a ride!—because she loved what they were doing to spread the gospel and wanted to encourage them. One of the most moving moments the day of her funeral was watching an escort of a dozen bikers lead the motorcade of family, close friends, and the hearse that was carrying her casket. What a sight that was—men on Harleys, honoring the memory of an eighty-nine-year-old woman who loved Jesus and loved them.

What came through in Vonette's public ministry was equally evident in her private demeanor and lifestyle. She was a Titus 2 woman all the way through. And it showed.

Vonette and I talked often in the final months of her life, sometimes at length. It gave me great hope to witness the still-full-of-life spirit and the never-ending growth and devotion of this woman more than three decades my senior and to realize, "Yes, this *can* be done!" She offered living proof of what God's grace can bring about in us—in me—as we continue to run the race He has set before us.

But here's the thing we have to remember: Vonette Brights don't just happen. Women don't just wake up at eighty-nine and suddenly find themselves spiritually fruitful and blossoming. This isn't something we can put off thinking about until after we're menopausal.

The challenge for older women may be to think of themselves as still being spiritually vital and relevant. As Vonette faced mounting health issues and her body weakened, she lamented that she was not able to do more for the Lord and for others, and longed to go home to heaven. She needed to be reminded that she had not outlived her usefulness or her calling.

There's a challenge for younger women as well: to make good use of these years when physical strength and beauty and energy come more naturally, so you'll be prepared for the day when your clothes don't quite button the same way and your

> *When you see an older woman who is wise, winsome, grateful, kind, and filled with the Spirit of God—you are looking at character that most likely has been formed over the course of many years.*

joints begin to stiffen—and your modeling career can still go on.

Becoming "a godly older woman" has been one of my goals in life for as long as I can remember. I know that may sound a little strange. But even as a young teen I began to realize the choices I was making then would contribute to my life as a college student and a young adult and a middle-aged woman and, eventually, the little old lady who one day will live at my mailing address. I sensed then, and I know now, that there are no shortcuts to acquiring the traits of a godly, older woman. They must be cultivated over time and slowly seasoned to acquire their taste and savor.

They take life. They take experience.

They take failing, confession, and repentance.

They take intentionality and sacrifice.

They take a lifetime of practice.

I'm not trying to put the pressure of your whole life on top of your social plans for this weekend. Nor am I saying that God can't do anything with you if you fail to be spiritually intentional from a young age. But when you see an older woman at church who is wise, winsome, grateful, kind, and filled with the Spirit of God—a model in every way—you are looking at character that most likely has been formed over the course of many years. And when you notice those older women who appear whiny, narrow, petty, or bitter, they almost certainly became that way over the course of decades.

Here's the truth of it: the most amazing, godly older women you know likely were serious about being godly *younger* women as well.

So the message of Titus 2 is for all of us, older and younger. And as we dig more deeply into its treasures, we'll see how older women in the church thrive by staying attached to the younger and how younger women can find a compelling vision for their long-term character and fruitfulness in the lives and faces of their older spiritual sisters.

That's not to say there are no differences between the various stages of life. Each has challenges and experiences that make Paul's words to each group appropriate. And yet all of us can benefit from reading and applying all of what he wrote.

Including, oddly enough, his opening remarks to the older men.

All-Around Maturity

As we take our first dip into verse 3 of Titus 2, where Paul's instructions regarding older women begin, you'll notice almost immediately a word that causes us to pause before moving on.

"Older women," the verse begins, *"likewise . . ."*

Likewise?

This word leads me to believe that what Paul wrote to older *men* in the previous verse was meant to apply to an older *woman's* character as well. So we need to step back to verse 2 to see what kind of character qualities are in accord with sound doctrine—for both men and women:

> Older men are to be sober-minded, dignified,
> self-controlled, sound in faith, in love, and in
> steadfastness. (Titus 2:2)

These are not cafeteria-style qualities we can pick and choose. No, these are trademarks of all spiritually mature believers. None of them is optional if we are to become Titus 2 models. So let's take time to unpack them briefly.

"Sober-minded"

The most literal application that comes to mind when we hear this term is being free from the intoxicating influence of alcohol. But being sober-minded in a biblical sense has broader implications. It involves not becoming drunk on *any* of the various excesses that are available to us in the world.

It could be a gluttonous appetite for food, medicating your emotions with mindless munching on your favorite snacks, living for the hour when you can go out for dinner and indulge your craving.

It could be a fever for spending money, even if you justify it as a grandma's right to spoil her grandkids with toys and trinkets.

It could be a habit of mindlessly scanning the Internet or binge-watching the newest television series.

From this distance, we can easily see activities like these (and others) as being extravagant, wasteful, self-absorbed, senseless. And yet in a tempting moment, under circumstances that lend themselves toward seeking escape or emotional relief, any of us can fall into overindulgence and excess, stuffing ourselves on short-lived, empty-calorie pursuits that never give us quite enough and always draw us back for more.

A sober-minded woman, by contrast, has learned the soul-satisfying difference between temporary pleasures and eternal pleasures. She recognizes she'll never be entirely immune to the demanding cry of unmet needs and the tug toward fleshly appetites, whether they take the form of extravagant purchases or highly addictive computer games. But maturity has taught her what really matters in life.

And so through a pattern of practiced obedience and surrender to the Spirit, she's experienced the freedom of saying no to indulgences that could eventually leave her defeated, discouraged, and demoralized. And younger women who crave this kind of discernment and strength for themselves will find her example of temperance and moderation— her sober-mindedness—to be appealing and worthy of imitation.

"Dignified"

The NIV translates this term as "worthy of respect." It's the quality of being honorable, reverent, and appropriately serious about life.

Our lives include plenty of opportunities for appropriate fun and laughter, moments that lend themselves to lightheartedness. But not all moments are like that. In fact, I'd say *most* of them are not. Life is to be taken seriously—not gloomily, not unhappily, not devoid of joy and cheer, and yet not flippantly or carelessly either.

That's why Paul urged all believers to "walk properly" (Rom. 13:13), "making the best use of the time" (Col. 4:5). We are called to live in a way that is fitting for those who belong to our God, "who is high and

> *One of the benefits of getting older is a rising awareness of eternity, which ought to color everything about our daily life.*

lifted up, who inhabits eternity, whose name is Holy" (Isa. 57:15).

One of the benefits of getting older is (or *should* be) a rising awareness of eternity, which ought to color everything about our daily life. Things look different when we adopt that long view. We have reason for being less ruffled, less hurried, less dramatic, less inclined to call everything an emergency. We can be more at peace and settled, better able to determine how to handle a given dilemma or dynamic or disagreement. Heaven is near and nearer—enabling us to carry ourselves with quiet confidence and grace and to walk in awe of the One in whose presence we live. And far from making us morose or prudish, this way of thinking and living leads to the highest, purest joy.

Older women are in the best position to model this kind of dignity and poise to younger women, who regularly encounter situations that feel too big for them to handle and who need the calming influence of wisdom and maturity.

Dignity is a beautiful thing to watch.

"Self-controlled"

We're going to devote a chapter to this subject later, since Paul returns to it several times. But let's take a brief look at this important word.

"Self-controlled" comes from the Greek word *sophron*, which derives from two words, one meaning "saved" or "sound," and the other meaning "mind." To be self-controlled is to operate from a "saved mind," a sound mind—to be living in one's right mind.

Interestingly, the last portion of the word—*phron*—is related to the modern Greek word for car brakes. The self-controlled person knows when to stop, when to say no. She knows how to curb her desires and impulses. She is self-restrained under the control of the Holy Spirit. She governs herself and disciplines her mind, her passions, her affections, her behavior.

There are no shortcuts to acquiring this trait. Each of us knows from hard experience how insistent and resistant our human wills can be. We naturally resist not only others' attempts to manage and direct us, but our own efforts as well. That's why younger women need older models who have experienced the challenge of becoming *sophron*, but who can also show by their lives what this quality looks like and how it's cultivated.

"Sound in faith"

Paul ends this list of character qualities in verse 2 with three traits that demonstrate the fruit of sound doctrine in an older believer's character: sound in faith . . . sound in love . . . sound in steadfastness.

The word translated "sound" implies health and wholesomeness, which makes it all the more encouraging when directed to believers in their later years, when health issues tend to worsen. Even while the body may be slowing and sputtering and sagging in various places, spiritually speaking we should be in the best shape of our lives.

"Sound in faith" means to be sound in *the* faith—grounded in the truth of God's Word. And able to affirm from experience the trustworthiness of God's promises.

I think of Joshua, standing before the people of Israel near the end of his life, declaring, "Now I am about to go the way of all the earth, and you know in your hearts and souls, all of you, that not one word has failed of all the good things that the LORD your God promised concerning you" (Josh. 23:14).

These are not the words of a man whose faith was merely intellectual. They reveal a seasoned faith, a faith that's been tested and proven, an unshakable confidence in God and His Word. Even in old age—in fact, *because* of his old age—Joshua could declare his faith with confidence.

Having experienced God's reliable track record over many years and in countless desperate situations, he wasn't merely speaking of something he'd heard, but testifying to something he knew firsthand.

How inspiring such a testimony can be to those who are still running the first laps of their race.

> *The soundness of your faith is based on the soundness of the One in whom you've placed it, not on your perfect record in walking out that faith.*

And yet you may be an older woman who doesn't *feel* "sound in faith." You may not feel qualified to inspire the generation coming behind you. The fact is, we're all still learning. Still growing. Still in need of daily grace. Soundness of faith is not a mountaintop, a finish line. It is a journey. And we each travel imperfectly.

But I promise you, what you have gleaned of God's nature and ways throughout the course of your life, however inadequate you may feel, is worth passing on to others, particularly to those following behind you. Wherever you've seen God prove Himself faithful, wherever His Word has sustained you in weakness and provided needed direction, and yes, even wherever you have experienced the consequences of *failing* to walk according to His Word—there's your story to share.

The soundness of your faith is based on the soundness of the One in whom you've placed it, not on your perfect record in walking out that faith.

"Sound . . . in love"

While sound biblical doctrine is crucial, it can also be complex or even overwhelming. And in the process of trying to get it all straight in our heads, we can miss the heart.

The heart of Christian love.

Increasing age for the believer is to be marked by an ever-increasing capacity for love. Genuine love. Sacrificial love. Patient love. God's kind of love.

I have attended many funerals of people who were well-known for their professional accomplishments or their courageous stand on moral issues or their remarkable public ministry. And I always find it touching to hear these "greats" remembered more for their personal, often unseen demonstrations of love and concern for others.

This character quality can show itself in countless ways, but nowhere does it radiate more beautifully through a person's life or more clearly adorn the doctrine of God than when it is expressed through *genuine forgiveness.*

How many families and family histories and once-close relationships have been destroyed through years of unresolved anger, bitterness, deafening silence, and misunderstanding? A colleague was experiencing this when she wrote and asked me to pray for her mother, who had terminal cancer:

> While I continue to hope that God will do a miracle in her physical body, my main prayer is that He will work in her heart and that she will forgive my father's sister, who has deeply hurt her and my father. She knows she needs to forgive, but she feels like she just can't do it.

Oh, what scars can be left by betrayal and broken trust. But love can help heal those wounds, even years after they were inflicted. Forgiveness in the heart of an older person is among the most compelling modeling performances of all. A person who is sound in love will be familiar with the words, "I forgive you" and "I was wrong, will you forgive me?"

Forgiveness is just one example of the kind of love Paul calls us to model as we grow older. Here are some good questions to ask ourselves periodically:

- Is my love growing—abounding "more and more" (Phil. 1:9)?
- Am I more focused on the needs of others than on my own needs?
- Is my love deeper, richer, healthier than it was a year ago, a decade ago?

"Sound . . . in steadfastness"

Two elderly, godly believers told me recently they are in the midst of the most difficult circumstances they've ever faced. I've been pondering their words, reminded of the sobering biblical observation that

> the years of our life are seventy,
> or even by reason of strength eighty;
> yet their span is but toil and trouble. (Ps. 90:10)

That's not the cynical opinion of a depressed pessimist; it's simply the truth. Life in this fallen world is hard, and it often gets harder as we age. No matter what difficulties we may have encountered already, the worst (in this life) may still be ahead of us.

As older women, we know this. Our own experience confirms it, as does the testimony of others we know. So what kind of people do we want to be for the rest of our lives, realizing that hardship is inevitable and life may get even more difficult?

If our future is to be shaped by the Scripture, then we know what our answer should be: to become sound (healthy and strong) in "steadfastness."

This Greek word is a compound of two shorter words that could be translated literally "abiding under." The idea is that of bearing up under a heavy load—not caving in under the pressure, not being flattened by it, but keeping on despite its weight. And not just surviving, but facing life's circumstances triumphantly, allowing God to use them to mold and shape us, bearing up in a way that glorifies the God we trust.

I love the way one of my heroines of the faith, Dr. Helen Roseveare, put it. In that eloquent British accent of hers, she explained why she preferred the word *perseverance* to *endurance*: "The word *endurance* has a sort of connotation of gritting your teeth, stiff upper lip, getting through somehow. The word *perseverance* refers to steadily going on, refusing to give up, no matter what comes."[1]

This kind of character is found in those who recognize and submit to God's providences. They view even their trials as coming from His hand, which enables them to press on with courage and faith.

That's the kind of woman I want to be.

People who are hurting and those facing trouble ahead need models like that. Younger women with their lives still before them need models like that.

Models of sober-mindedness. Of dignity. Of self-control. Of faith, love, and steadfastness.

And yes, this can be you. It *should* be you. According to the Bible, God *expects* it to be you. And me.

The more we age, the more we can allow God to mold and shape us, to beautify and refine us, to exfoliate the dead, dry skin of impurity and self-centeredness, and to radiate through us with the glow of His workmanship.

Shine On

Everyone is included in the pattern for Christian living found in Titus 2. Older men. Older women. Younger men. Younger women. Each of us has a role to play in adorning the doctrine of God. Whether you're *young* and aging or *not* so young and aging, you can be a vibrant, thriving, fruitful model for as long as God gives you breath—provided you stay sound and constant in your walk with God as your birthdays add up. That's the expectation: chronological maturity accompanied by continual spiritual growth and increasing spiritual health. It's the same vision painted by one of my favorite Scripture verses, one I often include on birthday greetings:

> The path of the righteous is like the light of dawn,
>   which shines brighter and brighter until full day.
>   (Prov. 4:18)

You're not doomed to crest and start heading downhill when you reach your fifties, sixties, seventies, eighties, or beyond. That is the world's perspective on aging, not God's. As we age, our physical bodies and our minds may deteriorate, but our inner spirit (Christ in us) can shine brighter and brighter until we reach high noon—that Day when we enter the endless, shadowless light of His presence and He "transform[s] our lowly body to be like his glorious body" (Phil. 3:21).

One commentator has said, "Old age strips the body of its glamour in order to emphasize the beauty of the soul."[2] It's true. When we're young, we may be able to gloss over some of those pesky character defects with the natural blush of our energy, good looks, and personality. But as we get older, our physical sparkle begins to fade. And those same character shortages, if not dealt with and sanctified, will only become more pronounced and visible.

But if we persevere in the Titus 2 prescription for adorning the gospel, we'll become more and more like the "righteous" people described in Psalm 92, the ones who

> flourish like the palm tree
>   and grow like a cedar in Lebanon....
> They shall bear fruit in old age;
>   they are ever full of sap and green,
> to declare that the LORD is upright ... (Ps. 92:12, 14–15)

Don't you love that? It's a compelling picture of believers who are flourishing, growing, and fruitful—renewed within day by day, to proclaim the beauty of Christ.

Older woman, don't listen to what your feet and fatigue are telling you. Listen to what your faith in God and His Word are telling you. You were destined to be a model, to live a life worthy of respect that is worth following. To become a person of whom others say, "That's what I want to be like when I'm her age." To model the heart and character of Christ.

And *younger woman*, whether you're sixteen or twenty-six or whatever "younger" means in your case, the godly older woman I hope you want to become is not as far removed as you think from the young woman you are now. Begin now cooperating with the Holy Spirit to cultivate these qualities in your life.

Whatever your age, remember we're all aspiring models, following Christ and making others long to know and follow Him. Women of all ages adorned—made beautiful—by the indwelling Christ. And women whose lives adorn the doctrine we claim to believe, making what is already beautiful even more attractive to everyone we encounter.

Making It Personal

Older women

1. Vonette Bright refused to settle back and live her life for herself. She continued to grow and to serve and encourage others until she passed into eternity. How does her life inspire you to be a Titus 2 model until the Lord calls you home?

2. As we get older, many women have a "rising awareness" of eternity. Is this true for you? How does Colossians 4:5–6 encourage you in this area?

3. What can you do to include more of the younger, hungry-hearted women in your church in your times of worship, fellowship, and ministry?

Younger women

1. Have you ever seen age-defying beauty modeled in an older woman? Describe what you see in her.

2. How might the choices you are making today affect the older woman you will someday be? If you can, list some specific examples.

3. What can you do to include more of the wise, older women in your church in your times of worship, fellowship, and ministry?

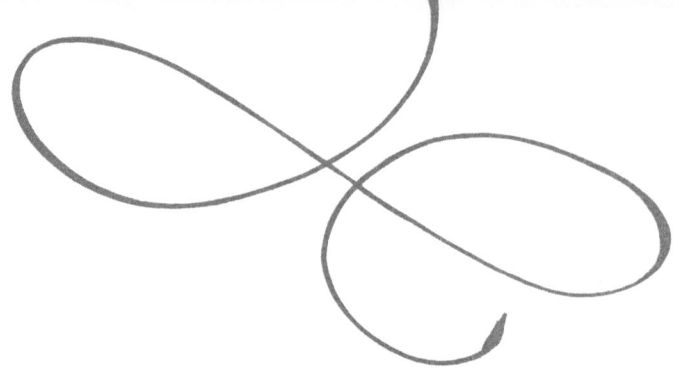

Teach what accords with sound doctrine.

Older men are to be sober-minded, dignified, self-controlled,
sound in faith, in love, and in steadfastness.

Older women likewise are to be reverent in behavior,
not slanderers or slaves to much wine.

**They are to teach what is good,
and so train the young women**
to love their husbands and children,
to be self-controlled,
pure,
working at home,
kind,
and submissive to their own husbands,
that the word of God may not be reviled.

**. . . so that in everything they may adorn
the doctrine of God our Savior.**

TITUS 2:1–5, 10

CHAPTER 4

Grow Up and Step Up

Teaching and Learning— Life-to-Life

Here is the challenge to you spiritual mothers:
Will you allow God to use you to help others learn from your knowledge
and experience, your mistakes and your victories?
CATHE LAURIE

PASTOR TOM NELSON TELLS A STORY ABOUT A WOMAN in his Denton, Texas, congregation. Joy Brown,[1] who at the time was already in her seventies, was known as a godly woman whose life exhibited many of the characteristics we discussed in the last chapter. She had received Christ at an early age and had personally been in attendance to hear some of the greatest preachers of the twentieth century. She had also been an eager student of the Word for years and, through its sanctifying influence, had matured into a true lover of God as well a loyal wife, mother, and friend.

"But Joy," the pastor asked her one day, "are you making disciples?"

"Me?" she answered. "I don't know if I'm ready."

Hearing this, we might wonder, *Ma'am, if you're not ready, who is?* But how many of us, whatever our age or experience, could be asked the same thing and feel the same way?

"Me? I don't know if I'm ready."

Not long after hearing this response, Pastor Nelson pulled aside the church's director of women's ministries. "I don't want Joy Brown enrolled in any more Bible studies. She already knows more than anybody there." He wanted this enormous wealth of knowledge, experience, and perseverance to be shared with a younger generation who could use what a woman like Joy could teach them.

"Get ready," he told Joy. "You're about to go into the ministry."

He assigned her to teach a small group of teenagers. She was scared to death. What would those young people possibly want to hear from an old lady like her? But she dived into the assignment by studying Scripture—filling up notepad after notepad and developing detailed lesson plans.

Six months into her meetings with those girls, Joy had hardly touched her pages of notes. The teens were so full of questions—about life, parents, sex, sin, school, marriage. Joy drew from her knowledge of the Word and the experience of her long life (including her weaknesses, imperfections, and struggles) to respond to their questions, seeding those young hearts with biblical wisdom and perspective.

She continued teaching that way until she was well into her *nineties*. The generations of young women who had sat under her teaching became known around church as the "Brownies," and they tagged around behind her like ducklings following their mother.

Inspiring, right?

But as special as this story is, it shouldn't be all that unusual.

I have watched many friends send the last of their "brood" out of the nest. As their children finish their formal education, get jobs, marry, and start their own families, these moms who have spent so many years caring for their families begin to wonder, *What am I supposed to do now? What is my purpose? My identity?*

Maybe you have asked these questions. Fortunately, Titus 2 tells you exactly what you're supposed to do now:

> Older women . . . are to teach what is good, and so
> train the young women . . . . (vv. 3–4)

In a part of this passage we'll explore later, Paul says that older women are not to be slanderers. That is, we are *not* to use our tongues to spread lies or evil or to wound or tear others down. But here we're told how we *are* to use our tongues: "to teach what is good." We are to speak words that are true and good, words that bless and build others up. And in the process, we train younger women in the life of faith.

That phrase, "teach what is good," translates one Greek word that could also be rendered "teachers of good things." Proverbs 31 puts it this way:

> She opens her mouth with wisdom,
>   and the teaching of kindness [faithful instruction—
> NIV] is on her tongue. (v. 26)

If you're an *older woman*, teaching good things to younger women is part of your job description. God has a purpose for you in this season of life that is vital and that no one but you can fulfill. The assumption is that you have learned how to apply the sound teaching of God's Word to your behavior, affections, relationships, priorities—everything—and that you are committed to take what you have learned and pass it on to others. This should be the norm, not the exception.

And if you're a *younger woman*, this passage raises important questions for you: Who are you learning from? Who are your teachers? Are they mostly your peers? What online communities are saturating your thinking and shaping your relationships? What celebrities are influencing your values, your sense of identity and purpose?

You see, Titus 2:4 is not just a call for older women to teach what is good. It's also a call for younger women to *learn* what is good from their older, more experienced sisters. As we will see, this mandate is a great gift for women of every age.

A Vision and a Calling

If you qualify as an older woman, there's a reason you've been learning about life all these years. More than one reason, actually. One is to help you accumulate godly wisdom—from your mistakes as well as your triumphs—and apply that wisdom to the hurdles you encounter. But equally important is the ability to share that hard-won wisdom with others, especially those who aren't as far along in their journey as you are.

Women who by God's grace have cultivated the fruit of the Spirit in their lives are to come alongside other women who need help developing self-control, kindness, and well-ordered priorities.

Wives who have learned how to love and respect their husbands well over the long haul—"for better, for worse"—are to teach younger women how it's done.

Our job is to embody the wisdom of God's Word in such a way that we can effectively teach it to others—not just out of our notebooks, but out of our lives.

Mothers who have faithfully raised and trained their own children are to use the wisdom they've gained in the classroom of experience to teach younger women who are in the childbearing/child-rearing years.

This is our job whether we're forty, sixty, eighty—whatever. Our job is to embody the wisdom of God's Word in such a way that we can effectively teach it to others—not just out of our notebooks, but out of our lives.

This vision and calling is not just for some supposed class of spiritual superstars or for those among us who possess special teaching gifts. And it's not just for women who are wives and mothers. We are all called to cultivate godly character—to model what it looks like to live out the gospel in every area of our lives. Then we are to teach those women coming behind us how to do the same. As we do this—with our lives, our lips, our labors, our love—our own growth in grace is furthered, the baton of authentic faith is passed on to the next generation, the health of the church is preserved, and its witness to the world is enhanced.

This is a call to grow up and step up. "By this time, you ought to be teachers," God's Word says to believers who have had ample time and opportunity to learn sound doctrine and put it into practice (Heb. 5:12).

But this mandate is not intended to weigh us down with one more obligation, one more burden to be borne. Far from it. God is offering us the incredible privilege and joy of engaging with Him in molding lives (including our own) into the likeness of Jesus, adorned by sound doctrine and ultimately making the gospel beautiful in the eyes of all around. And as anyone who has said yes to this challenge knows, the process itself provides great satisfaction. Unlikely friendships form. Sweet seasons of prayer, Bible study, and spiritual growth are shared.

Why would we not want to be part of that?

Always Teaching

You may struggle to see yourself as a teacher. Perhaps you envision a classroom, PowerPoint slides, two nights every week with commentaries spread out on your kitchen table—a picture that is daunting to you. Perhaps the thought of standing up in front of a group to speak makes you a little queasy.

If so, take heart. I thank the Lord for women He has gifted and equipped to teach the Word to other women in structured settings. I hope your church has women like that. But I don't believe that's the only (or even the primary) kind of teaching the apostle Paul had in mind when he called us to be teachers.

The truth is, you're *always* teaching, simply by the way you live. Your conversation in unguarded moments teaches. Your response to gossip teaches. Your reaction to an unexpected problem teaches. The question is not whether you're teaching; it's whether you're teaching (as Paul says) "what is good."

Many of a younger person's peers, not to mention advertisers who determine what we can't live without, constantly communicate their definition of what's good—good to have, good to do, good to know, good to strive for, good to be involved in.

And most of it, unfortunately, is *not* good.

The younger women in our lives need something to counter those constant messages. They need the voice of someone who teaches them what is truly good. And as a rule, they won't learn the most about goodness—at least not in a way that resonates in their hearts and is reflected in their choices and behavior—by hearing it in a classroom or from some well-known speaker at a conference. They'll hear it and see it best from you, with a cup of spiced tea in front of them, with your hand close enough to reach over and touch theirs, with your wisdom, experience, biblical perspective, and love connecting—one-on-one, life-to-life—with their specific questions and needs.

This is the gift I received from Leta Fischer (or "Mother Fischer," as she was called affectionately) during my last two years of college. I was still in my late teens; Leta's children were all grown. In the church where I worshiped, she was legendary for meeting one-on-one with younger women across a small kitchen table—turning pages in her well-marked Bible, loving, listening, caring, sharing, praying, pouring practical wisdom into open hearts. And today, I have the joy of pouring into the lives of younger women the gifts I received at Mother Fischer's kitchen table more than forty years ago.

A Desperate Need

I find it interesting that Paul didn't assign to Titus this responsibility to teach the younger women. The task of the young pastor was to teach sound doctrine to the church, to keep the gospel and its implications front and center. But the personal discipleship and nurture of younger women was (and is) wisely assigned to the older women. And their ministry is every bit as necessary to the health of the church and to the living out of the gospel as the pastor's ministry is to the whole congregation.

The older women are "to teach what is good," Paul said, "and so *train* the young women" (vv. 3–4). Other translations render this "*admonish* the young women" (NKJV) or "*encourage* the young women" (NASB).

This verb with the complex meaning—which is why one English word can't quite express it—is the Greek word *sophronizo*. It appears only here in the New Testament, and yet it's related to a word we've already seen and will see again: *sophron*. As you may recall, this word carries the idea of a "saved mind" or a "sound mind." Similarly, *sophronizo* means "to make of a sound mind . . . to instruct or train someone to behave wisely and properly."[2] It has to do with bringing someone to his or her senses, so they will live a sensible, self-controlled, sober, spiritually disciplined life.

Sadly, many women today are living lives that are far from self-controlled and sensible. And that's not just true of women you see on reality TV. A lot of women within the church seem to make one foolish, destructive choice after another—choices that result in chronically troubled relationships. Many live shallow lives, spending their time on empty pursuits and vain conversation, carried along by the values of this world.

However, if our reflexive reaction is to regard these women with disapproval or exasperation, we have to ask ourselves: *Have we fulfilled our responsibility as older women?* Have we modeled the beauty of an ordered life, lived under the control and lordship of Christ? Have we been faithful in reaching out to our younger sisters, teaching what is good, and training them to live a life that honors Him?

In some cases, these younger women have never been adequately parented. They have little idea of how to make a marriage work or how to raise kids or how to lead fruitful single lives. Amid the pressures and exhaustion of raising children or building a career, it is easy for resentment, depression, and wrong thinking to creep in. With all the false teaching out there, they are easily deceived, tempted to buy into the world's philosophies.

They need older women in the church to get involved in training them to live self-controlled, wise lives, to show them what that looks like in every area of life and how to fulfill their duty to God, family, and others. They need mothers in the faith to take them by the hand, to encourage and instruct them, and to help them keep their eyes on Christ and maintain spiritual and emotional equilibrium.

They need older women to lovingly teach them what is true and good.

A Ministry of Mentoring

As we've seen, this kind of training usually doesn't happen so much in a formal teaching environment as it does through intentional, nurturing relationships—often called discipleship or mentoring. At times that discipleship may take place in a small-group meeting or a scheduled appointment. More often, however, it takes place organically, in the laboratory of life.

Just this morning I sent a young mom a link to a blog post about her season of life that I thought would be encouraging. Within an hour she wrote back and thanked me for sharing it: "Loved the great reminder of having a Godward focus in my never-ending, mundane, daily responsibilities!"

I also heard this morning from a mom of teens expressing what a lot of moms of teens experience: "I feel like things are moving at warp speed, and I just want everything to slow down." That gave me another chance to encourage a younger woman with a personal testimony of the grace of God I have received in my own harried seasons of life.

But what such mentoring may not require in platform speaking skills, it does require in time. The cultivation of new thinking patterns is not the result of a single get-together. It is the fruit of an ongoing process, a commitment. *I'll be there. You call me. I'm with you. I'm praying for you.*

My sweet friend Sarah recently had her fifth child. She homeschools her three older children. And though she does a wonderful job as a wife and mother, as with every mom, there are times when she loses perspective and thinks she is going over the edge. Sarah's own mother died when she was a teen, and she lives far from family. But she has intentionally cultivated rich relationships with older women like myself—women who have invested in her life and to whom she can turn for wisdom or encouragement when things get crazy in her world.

I got to know Sarah when she and her husband were first married, and I invited them to live in my home. We thought it might be six months or so till they could settle into their own home. Three and a half years and two babies later, they moved out. In the years since, we have remained connected, mutually blessing and encouraging each other as we have opportunity. And now I'm watching with joy as the baton is being passed and God is using Sarah to speak into the lives of women in the generation coming behind her.

I've heard of a church where a group of older women (and their husbands!) throw a bridal shower for couples who are getting married. The main gift they give this young bride and groom is an evening of conversation in which couples who've been married for thirty, forty, fifty years or longer share from their experience what makes a marriage sweet and enduring. How many newlywed women would look back on such an occasion as a defining moment in their preparation for marriage—and would likely find in that group an older woman who could be a great resource down the road?

There are so many other ways this kind of mentoring ministry can play out—in the neighborhood, in the workplace, in gyms and coffee shops. Older women teaching from their lives, investing in those who come after them, training them in what is good. Young women soaking up the help and the advice and learning to reach out in turn to those who come after them.

And no, this kind of mentoring is not easy—for the older woman or the younger.

It requires discipline and planning.

Time and patience.

Willingness to commit to a relationship.

Honesty in opening up our lives to one another.

Nor are we likely to see dramatic results overnight. It's not as formulaic as saying, "Come take my six-week class on how to be a woman of God." This is more a matter of getting next to someone, walking alongside her, going over to see her when you might rather be reading a magazine or watching a movie or taking a long bath. It's costly—the same way anything worthwhile is costly.

But who doesn't want, looking back, to see a legacy of fruitful relationships rather than just a shelf full of used books or a well-worn DVD collection?

Out of Our Failures

"But I've blown it in my relationships."

"I've made so many bad choices."

"I still struggle with this besetting sin."

A sense of personal failure keeps many older women from embracing this kind of ministry and relationships. Your marriage, for example, may still be a battle of wills. Some of your children may be making foolish choices, contrary to what you tried to teach them. An ongoing struggle with anger or addiction or some other issue may leave you feeling disqualified to teach anyone, especially as you look at other women your age who seem to be such models of Christian virtue.

I know. I sometimes look at the inconsistencies and battles in my own life and think, *How in the world could God use me to make a difference in anyone's life?*

None of us measures up to what we long to be. But don't let that stop you. Teach out of your failures. Use them to point others to the amazing grace of God and to a Savior who came to redeem sinners.

> *Teach out of your failures. Use them to point others to the amazing grace of God and to a Savior who came to redeem sinners.*

Teach out of what God showed you when you messed up and didn't trust Him—where you ended up, where God found you. Teach from the addictions you've battled, the choices you should have made, the pain you could have avoided. Open the Word, open your heart, share the hard questions you've wrestled with, and watch God create beauty from ashes right before your eyes.

Perhaps you've experienced a broken marriage. But if you've allowed God to heal, restore, and forgive whatever wounds and failures were involved in the breakup of your relationship, are you not in a prime position to reach out to a woman who sometimes wonders if it's worth hanging in there with her own marriage?

Perhaps you were not sexually pure as a teenager or young adult. Are you not uniquely qualified to counsel a high school girl in your church who doesn't have godly parental support in her life? She needs to know—not from the Internet, the latest cultural icon, or her own best guesses, but from someone who has been where she is—what kind of emotional, physical, and spiritual damage can be done by not treasuring the gift of purity.

Let's admit it: this life-to-life model from Titus 2, the sharing of relationship between older and younger women, would be neither effective nor needful if each of us—if *any* of us—had it all together. The truth is, if we are going to invest ourselves in others or receive the wisdom offered to us by others, some of the most significant encounters will occur within the context of human weakness and inadequacy. Yes, even failure and sin. Because even while we're still in the process of being changed into the image of Christ, He can use us as a means of grace in others' lives.

We're sinners, yes. We're still far from where we ought to be and want to be (and one day will be, praise God!). But this is part of the story we have been given to share with others. Even our failures—humbly acknowledged and redeemed by His mercy and grace—can become a path to a more fruitful life and ministry.

We can't afford to allow past (or current) failures and foolishness to deprive us of the blessings God inevitably multiplies when women come together to draw from one another's wisdom and experience. This is where God makes valuable use of the things we've learned to help others avoid mistakes we have made and to encourage each other to become faithful, fruitful followers of Christ.

Bottom line: God is able to use everything about us—our victories and our defeats. By being open and transparent with the women we influence, we increase our impact in their lives.

No One on the Sidelines

You may be convinced you're too busy to dedicate this kind of time to somebody else, no matter how important the idea sounds in theory. You just can't imagine how to fit it in to an already overcrowded life.

To this, I would gently respond: if you're too busy to do this—to commit to even a single mentoring relationship either as the older or younger woman—perhaps you need to ask yourself if you're too busy with less important things. This generational sharing of life is actually a basic requirement of the Christian lifestyle. It's among the "one anothers" of Scripture—loving one another, serving one another, bearing one another's burdens.

I can't underscore enough how vital this is. In fact, I'm convinced there would be far less need for crisis counseling and treatment if these kinds of woman-to-woman relationships were the norm in the church.

And keep in mind that "older" and "younger" are relative terms. You may only be twenty-three years old, but you're older than that sixteen-year-old in the youth group who has caught your attention because of the things you've heard her say and the way she flirts with the boys. How about approaching her as an older friend who cares enough to teach her what is good? Who knows what tragedy and heartache the Lord might use you to help prevent in that teen's life?

The roles of older woman—lovingly teaching what is good—and younger woman—humbly learning—are for all of us. These connections are not optional for believers. They're what Scripture calls us to. None of us belongs on the sidelines.

Reaching Out — in Both Directions

One summer evening I gathered a group of about twenty younger women in my home; they were all in their late teens or early twenties and serving together in a ministry. After dinner, we arranged our chairs into a circle on the deck, and I asked each of the girls to share a short synopsis of her spiritual journey. As you might imagine, a wide variety of life experiences and issues was represented in that circle. At points I interjected words of encouragement or insight, sometimes sharing out of my own journey. But mostly I listened, my heart warmed by their openness to share their stories and their eagerness to receive the seasoned perspective of the oldest woman in the circle.

Afterward, several of those young women expressed gratitude for the interest I had shown in them and the investment (small as it was) that I had made in their lives. One of them commented how helpful this night had been to her because, as she said, "Our generation is so prone to think we have all the answers, that there's nothing an older person could tell us that we really need to hear."

I believe this sense is a major reason why many older women tend to back away from their role in younger women's lives. *The younger women don't want us,* they think. *If they did, they'd ask.*

So, *younger woman,* let me ask you: How willing are you to seek out and receive the involvement of older women in your life? Do you have a teachable spirit? Or do you leave the impression that you can figure life out on your own?

In His wisdom, God has made a gracious provision that you can't afford to do without. So my challenge to you is to take the initiative. Seek out an older woman who seems to possess the qualities you'd like to embody one day. Ask if she'd be open to visit with you on occasion, fielding your questions and allowing you to learn from her experiences and—together—from God's Word.

Don't be surprised if she says she doesn't know what she could really offer you. But don't be surprised either if she's delighted that you asked.

When you meet, it might help to ask her questions like,

- "Have you ever struggled with _____?"
- "How have you handled _____?"
- "Would you pray with me about _____?"

Don't expect perfectly formulated answers. But do expect to learn from and be encouraged by the experience and hard-earned wisdom of this older sister/spiritual mom.

I believe I can guarantee that, as your relationship grows, you will glean so much from this older woman that you'll wonder how you ever got along without her friendship, prayers, and input. Hopefully you will be inspired to become the older woman in another woman's life—and to never stop pouring yourself into others as long as you live.

I would offer a challenge as well to those who, like me, have reached that *older-woman* season of life. It's easy (and tempting) for us to sit around with our little circle of like-minded friends, talking disapprovingly about how the young women in our church are dressing or behaving. But how much more productive (and biblical) would it be for us to roll up our sleeves and get involved in the life of one or more of those younger women.

I've always realized that younger women need older women in their lives. But now, as an older woman, I've come to realize how much we need younger women in our lives. (One practical perk for me, among many others, has been help with my wardrobe!) You just don't know what you're missing if you don't have these kinds of intergenerational relationships.

These younger women challenge my thinking. They inspire me to press on when I'm weary in the race. They keep me from getting cold-hearted and crusty. They motivate me to believe God for more than I can see or imagine. Today marks another birthday for me. My phone is lighting up with sweet texts, many of them from precious young women I have known and walked with over the years—thanking me for my friendship, encouragement, and influence in their lives. They cannot know how deeply I feel the same way about them.

I assure you, few things in life are more satisfying than watching God work in another's heart through the example of your life, your thoughtful, biblical wisdom, even your humble acknowledgment of regret and lessons learned the hard way.

I realize you may be busier than you ever thought you would be at this stage of life. Many women I know in this post-child-rearing season are working hard to help cover college costs or supplement retirement savings. Others find themselves caught in a whirlwind of volunteerism—activities they always wanted to try but never had time for, as well as new expectations placed on them "now that you have the time."

But these years—when our circumstances and commitments

begin to change and we face new decisions about how to fill our days—can also bring rich opportunities to lean in to our Titus 2 calling. So before dusting off your résumé as an empty nester or filling up your calendar with new commitments, why not at least consider whether you could be of greater kingdom usefulness by freeing up more of your time for a different kind of responsibility?

I sometimes want to say to those moms who are trying to figure out what's next now that their kids are out of the nest: "Look around! You are needed now more than ever. There are younger women who desperately need your love, your time, your encouragement, and your wisdom!"

And what if no one is coming out of the woodwork to sit at your feet for training? Why not begin asking God to bring a hungry-hearted younger woman across your path? Ask His Spirit to show you how to fulfill this biblical mandate. And as He works—He will!—be obedient to follow through, confident that He's paired you with someone who needs what you and your love and life experiences can provide her.

The Power of Availability

I can't emphasize enough that this kind of mentoring ministry does not require advanced degrees or unusual skills. More often than not, it looks quite simple—lingering after a church service, at the kitchen table, over coffee, on the phone, throughout the week. It happens in casual but meaningful conversations that start with showing interest and asking questions and proceed by listening, caring, saying, "Let's pray about that." With even the tiniest bit of intention—a reassuring email or text, a shared link or Scripture verse—relationships grow. Teaching happens. And all it takes is being available, sometimes on the spur of the moment . . .

Several years ago a woman approached me after hearing me speak in another city. She began to pour out her heart about some intense challenges she was facing in her marriage and family. I knew she needed more than what I could offer in the few minutes we had available to talk. Just then, I saw my friend Bonnie out of the corner of my eye. Bonnie was an older woman who lived in that city, a woman I knew to be wise, compassionate, and biblically grounded. I beckoned to Bonnie, introduced her to the younger woman, and encouraged the two to get together in the days ahead.

A short time later, the younger woman and I had occasion to re-connect, and I asked how she was doing. She couldn't say enough about how helpful Bonnie had been to her in the three times they had met. "I've never had anyone do this for me before," she said. "This has been more valuable than nine months of counseling!"

Another woman shared similar feelings with me in a recent email:

> I am twenty-five and have only been a Christian for
> two and a half years. My mentor's name is Carole. She
> is always seeking the Lord, and when she talks about
> the Lord you can see the joy on her face. She has taught
> me so much, been patient, caring, and loving. She
> loves her husband and family, and it is just beautiful.
> She has been a godly example and seeks to do the will
> of God. I was so lost. No one ever taught me about
> Jesus or took time to show me God's love. I will be
> thankful for her as long as I live. *Hopefully I can be a*
> *Carole to someone some day.*

And that's the goal of these mentoring relationships. As the apos-tle Paul said to his young disciple Timothy, "What you have heard . . . entrust to faithful men [and women] who will be able to teach others also" (2 Tim. 2:2).

Over the years, I have watched my friend Holly Elliff become an incredibly effective mentor and discipler of younger women. She has never advertised her services. But younger women flock to her side, eager to learn from the insight she has gleaned through decades of knowing God and walking with Him through a wide variety of seasons and life experiences.

Holly has often shared out of her life and wisdom on the daily broadcast of Revive Our Hearts, the ministry where I serve. Some time ago, one of our listeners—a younger woman—wrote a moving letter, thanking Holly for teaching her what is good:

> When Nancy first had you as a guest on her program, my soul was so famished for help that your calm, seasoned advice brought me out of a deep, dark place.
>
> What helped was my sense that your knowledge wasn't theoretical. It sounded like the words from someone who learned it in the trenches—marrying, raising a family, cooking meal after meal, raising each child, and glorifying the Lord in it.
>
> *Thank you* for giving warm words of godly counsel, for standing on the Lord's commands to us instead of compromising. You cannot know how that has made a real impact on a life and soul so marred and scarred by sin and without any godly women to turn to.
>
> I'm sure when you were changing diapers, or listening to the same story ... again ... you could not have known that those were the very things that would make your advice so weighty and true for me—a single woman. When you speak, it's from the point of view of someone who's lived it, who has raised a family and had to work out the Scriptures in close quarters. The Lord's Word has molded you so your life is sending out such riches.
>
> Please let older women know that the most valuable thing they can do is to develop in *righteousness*, not the

career or beautiful home. It is the life of righteousness that *alone* can help redeem broken lives. I never thought I would come to value God's ways above the world's or actually *see* how beautiful holiness is, but I have, and I thank you for being part of the Lord's way of revealing Himself and His loveliness and the beauty of living a godly life to me.

Older woman, you may never be asked to stand on a platform to speak or to teach from behind a mic on a national radio broadcast, as Holly does at times. But never underestimate the impact your life can have on other women—life-to-life, adorning the gospel, wherever He may have planted you.

And *younger woman*, this is something for you to aspire to—beginning now. As you learn what is good and are trained in righteousness, your life in turn will put the loveliness of Christ on display for those younger women who are coming behind you.

The words Paul wrote to Titus some two thousand years ago are timeless in their impact and relevance. More important, they are God's recipe for the thriving and fruitfulness of His women, essential for the successful passing of truth to the next generation and to our world.

And it starts with you and me—imperfections and all—available to teach and to be taught what is good.

Making It Personal

Older women

1. What does the story about Joy Brown, the older woman in the beginning of this chapter, teach you about what young women really want and need today?

2. Have you ever felt that no one would ever want to learn from your life? What are some of the life experiences you might be able to share to encourage or teach a younger woman more about the ways of God?

3. God's Word calls older women who are not acting as spiritual moms to "grow up and step up." Paraphrase Hebrews 5:12 for these reluctant women. If you are one of these, include your name in the paraphrase.

Younger women

1. Who are you learning from these days? Who are your teachers? Are they mostly your peers? What online communities are saturating your thinking and relationships? What older women are influencing and speaking into your life?

2. A young woman told me, "Our generation is so prone to think we have all the answers, that there's nothing an older person could tell us that we really need to hear." Do you think this is true? What part does humility play in a mentoring relationship? A teachable spirit? The willingness to ask an older woman to invest in your life?

3. What are some questions you could ask to strike up a conversation and encourage a possible mentoring relationship with an older woman?

Teach what accords with sound doctrine.

Older men are to be sober-minded, dignified, self-controlled,
sound in faith, in love, and in steadfastness.

Older women likewise are to be **reverent in behavior,**
not slanderers or slaves to much wine.

They are to teach what is good,
and so train the young women
to love their husbands and children,
to be self-controlled,
pure,
working at home,
kind,
and submissive to their own husbands,
that the word of God may not be reviled.

**. . . so that in everything they may adorn
the doctrine of God our Savior.**

TITUS 2:1–5, 10

CHAPTER 5

Revival of Reverence

Living in Sacred Service

This older woman sees life, all of life, from God's viewpoint
and understands that even the mundane routines of life are important to God. . . .
Watch her walk through her day in order to see what is next to God's heart.
Her life revolves around things that matter to Him.

ROCHELLE FLEMING

THERE AREN'T MANY PLACES YOU CAN GO THESE DAYS without being watched. Consider:

- Traffic cameras monitor your morning commute and stand guard at major intersections, taking careful notice of the precise moment when yellow lights turn red.
- Enormous databases keep tabs on your Internet activity, storing a digital record of every tap or click.
- Street-level images of your home and neighborhood are available for online viewing, all the way down to the cars in your driveway and the doghouse in your backyard.
- And the next time you walk into Walmart or Costco, take a quick look up at the ceiling—and see from the number of

camera portals up there if they can't immediately locate every mother who's scolding her impatient four-year-old somewhere in the store.

I'm not trying to make you paranoid. I'm simply observing that whatever anonymity earlier generations may have enjoyed is no longer available to us. No longer can we control what other people know about us merely by being nice, friendly church ladies and keeping the rest of our lives to ourselves.

And while this erosion of personal privacy is unsettling, I can't help but think it also comes with at least one positive, something we could turn to our advantage. Perhaps the pervasive presence of security patrols, online monitoring, and cellphone cameras can serve as a reminder that as Christians, our lives are always on display. Always. As a colleague of mine sometimes says, "Live like the mic is on—because it is."

Whether we like it or not, as Paul said, we are "a spectacle to the world, to angels, and to men" (1 Cor. 4:9). People are watching. More important, God is watching. This awareness should deepen our motivation to honor and represent Him well at all times.

I recall being at a women's conference where I'd been invited to speak. At one point I was seated in the back row, listening to the speakers who preceded me on the program, when a brightly attired woman was introduced to the stage. I recognized her as a comedian whose routines I had heard before. And though her brand of comedy is advertised as being Christian and family friendly, I knew from experience that she could also drift off-color.

Two men who were part of our ministry team that weekend were seated along with the rest of us. As the speaker made her entrance—to loud hoots and applause—I leaned over to the gentleman nearest me and whispered, "I think you may be uncomfortable with some of this." He nodded and motioned to his colleague and they quietly slipped out.

Unfortunately, I was right. The presentation included lots of body humor and coarse subject matter meant for easy laughs. From my perspective it stretched way beyond the limits of good taste. And yet the women in the audience, who just moments earlier had been praying and worshiping together, were now convulsed in laughter over the crude banter that was being offered up as Christian entertainment.

It saddened me greatly—not that I couldn't see what made the woman's delivery so engaging (she was an exceptionally gifted communicator), and not that I was out to spoil anybody's good time. But we are women who profess to know and love a holy God. We are women redeemed by a Savior's costly sacrifice. We are older women training younger women in what is good. We are younger women desiring to grow in grace and truth, becoming dignified, self-controlled, and steadfast in the faith.

Aren't we?

So with those goals in mind, let's delve more deeply into the nuts and bolts of Paul's challenge to the women of God in Titus' day as well as our own. The ideals contained in verses 3–5 of Titus 2—reverence, love, purity, kindness, and all the rest—are qualities we hope to see cultivated in our lives as God's Spirit works through our surrendered hearts. But they also form a practical discipleship plan for those we're teaching and training in our woman-to-woman, heart-to-heart relationships.

There's a lifetime of wisdom and growth to be gleaned from these few verses, and there's no time like today to begin walking it all out.

Beginning with reverence—the fountainhead from which springs the other graces to which we are called and to which we aspire.

"Older women likewise are to be reverent in behavior," Paul wrote. What does that mean? And what difference should it make in our daily lives?

A Sacred Existence

Various translations capture this exhortation from Paul as instructing us "to live in a way that is appropriate for someone serving the Lord"

(NLT 1996) and to be "reverent and devout in [our] deportment as becomes those engaged in sacred service" (AMP).

Commentator William Barclay's rendering of this verse is similar: "Charge the older women to be in demeanor such as befits those who are engaged in sacred things."[1]

The Greek word translated "reverent" in this passage is a compound word that combines the idea of being sacred, holy, or consecrated to God with that of behaving in ways that are fitting, right, or appropriate. Its root meaning has to do with being "priest-like."[2]

That's supposed to be us! A reverent woman understands that she has been set apart by God for sacred service, and she acts like it.

> *To be reverent means living with the constant, conscious awareness that we are in the presence of an awesome, holy God. God's presence isn't a place of dullness and drabness, with no dessert on the table.*

At all times, day and night, whether on or off the clock, wherever she may be—at church, at work, at home, or online—in public and in private, whether with family, friends, colleagues, or total strangers, she is an example of holiness. It shows in the way she carries herself, in her attitudes and the way she interacts with others. Her daily lifestyle, like that of priests in the temple, is always consistent with her high and holy calling.

Now don't misunderstand this. Being a reverent woman doesn't mean always talking in hushed and somber tones, walking through life as if we were tiptoeing through a European cathedral. It doesn't mean being dour and downcast, always deathly serious, unable to crack a joke with a clear conscience. And it certainly doesn't imply being legalistic and fault-finding. That's not at all what true reverence is about.

To be reverent means living with the constant, conscious awareness that we are in the presence of an awesome, holy God. And God's presence isn't a place of dullness and drabness, with no dessert on the table. Rather, it's a place of abundance, of soul-satisfying pure delight. A place, as the psalmist declared, where there is "fullness of joy" (Ps. 16:11).

And this is where we are to live 24/7—as sacred people in sacred places. Recognizing that all day long we're handling sacred moments and sacred duties.

A young mom and I talked about this the other day. She was feeling stretched, stressed, and scrambled by the demands pulling at her from every direction. When I tried to encourage her by reminding her that she is engaged in sacred service and sacred things, she protested, "But so often all this doesn't *feel* holy!"

I get that. The interruptions, irritations, and interminable tasks that occupy so much of our time and attention don't feel holy—until we recalibrate our focus and remind ourselves that we are in the presence of a holy God.

Wherever we are at this moment is a sacred place, and whatever He has given us to do is sacred service. That means:

- If you're a wife, serving your husband is a sacred duty to be carried out with devotion and intentionality, out of reverence to God.
- If you're a mom, tending to your children's needs is a sacred duty, a daily offering to the Lord in whose presence you serve.
- If you work outside your home, the performance of your responsibilities, however insignificant they may seem in the big picture, is a sacred duty, carried out in plain view of the Lord as an act of worship.
- If you're a student, applying yourself to your coursework is a sacred duty, as is your participation in class, your commitment to integrity, and the sacrifices necessary to make the most of your training.

- If you're retired or unemployed, single or widowed or child-less, your daily tasks and relationships are your sacred duty, to be carried out as a woman who lives and breathes and walks in God's presence.

There is simply no hard dividing line between the sacred and the secular in our lives, no special compartment for those pieces and parts of our lives that pertain to our faith, with everything else in another, separate compartment.

No, it's all a sacred exercise. Each of us, in whatever season of life we find ourselves, is to live in a way that is fitting for "those engaged in sacred service." We each possess a holy calling, a high calling, one worthy of our awe-inspired devotion to God and His will. And we flesh out this calling each day by honoring Him with lives that reflect His character and exemplify our grateful, loving surrender to Him.

Being a Titus 2 woman—and training others to be the same—is not a way of life we can turn off and on. We don't hang up our reverential demeanor in the closet when we come home and change clothes at the end of a long day. We are always serving in His presence, whether we are at home or in church or elsewhere, in our downtime as well as during our tightly scheduled appointments. Yes, we can still have our fun and make the most of each other's company. We can enjoy a good laugh, be silly, celebrate. But the most satisfying enjoyment of all will only come by being aware that we live each moment in His sweet, holy presence.

We become the women we truly want to be by practicing reverence.

Never Out of Style

The prophetess Anna, who appears in one of the earliest scenes of Jesus' life, His presentation at the Temple, provides a lovely example of reverence in action. In the brief biblical snapshot of her life we're allowed to view in Luke's gospel, we see that she was an older woman, a widow for many years. (Her husband, whom she had married as a young virgin, had passed away after only seven years of marriage.) And Anna, even at eighty-four, remained devoted to a reverent lifestyle. "She did not depart from the temple, worshiping with fasting and prayer night and day" (Luke 2:37). Her daily habit, strengthened through years of faithful practice, was just to be with God without distraction, without itching to hurry on to something else more exciting.

Here was a woman with every temptation to slack off in her efforts—a history of aloneness, the onset of advanced age, perhaps the flagging fatigue of unfulfilled dreams. If we were to fast-forward her situation into our day, she might have become someone who spent one mindless evening after another in front of the television, someone who poured forth woe-is-me details of her doctor visits whenever the phone rang, someone who assumed her church didn't really need her anymore except for filling the same seat every Sunday morning.

Anna, however, still spent her hours productively worshiping God. She was prayerful and disciplined, watchful and expectant. Her reverence involved not just camping out for long periods of time in her favorite physical location—the temple—but also an active, everyday awareness that she existed to be in His presence.

I can't imagine Anna turning into a whole other person when she ventured out beyond the temple walls. Can you? And I don't believe her reverence was a recent development either. I see her living this way not just at eighty-four, but even back in her younger days, when she might still have had an active social life and a taste for celebrating and living large.

Reverence wasn't limited to a certain place or time for Anna. It wasn't a certain mood, a certain spiritual routine. It had become the fabric of her life—fashioned over a lifetime of loving and fearing God, trusting Him and savoring His goodness. Whatever else may have competed to occupy her time and attention, she had found her fullness as a woman by recognizing that she was constantly engaged "in sacred service."

That kind of woman is able to experience Christ in ways few others ever enter into. No wonder Anna recognized her infant Messiah so quickly. I love the image of her breaking out in amazed and thankful praise, joyfully announcing the good news to others throughout the city who had long been keeping vigil with her, waiting for God's promised redemption: "He's here! He's here!"

But does this kind of woman appeal to you? Would she fit in well among your circle of friends? Would they admire her brand of perpetual reverence and want to be like her? Or would she be the object of condescending comments and rolled eyes—just a bit too serious about her faith?

I'm concerned that we've lost our appreciation and appetite for a reverent lifestyle—not in theory perhaps, but for sure in practice. I'm troubled by the flippant manner in which so many professing Christian women live today, declaring their *affection* for God but with little if any *fear* of God. Claiming mental assent to His Word but not to the point of actually restraining their impulses and appetites and behaving appropriately before Him. I'm bothered by how prone we are—how prone *I* am—to forget Whose presence we're in, how willing we are to live with a gap between our calling and our character, acting and reacting without recognizing that the moments of our morning quiet time are no more sacred than *this* moment. Than *any* moment.

We need a revival of reverence.

And from what Paul said to Titus, older women in particular need to be mindful of this. As we transition into those stages of life where we are the most tempted to let off the gas, having expended so much energy on conquering the various challenges of young to middle age, we need a reminder that now is not the time to coast.

These days are for yielding ourselves more fully than ever to worship and prayer. To examined lifestyles and consecrated thinking. To God-honoring friendships. To sanctified habits and topics of discussion. To everyday choices that reflect our relationship with this One we revere.

Yes, the house may be a little quieter these days, but not so we can repopulate it with crime-drama characters and Facebook "friends." The body may be more stiff and unresponsive than in our nimbler years, but not so we can spend days on end with our feet propped up. There might be a bit more breathing room in the bank account, but not so we can indulge whatever pleasures and appetites we can afford.

It is not only for our own sakes that we are called to lives of reverence. We are models, remember—for our daughters, our granddaughters, and the other young women we influence. And they desperately need models of reverent living.

You may think they're drawn to those older women who somehow manage to maintain a youthful air of coolness about them, who enjoy playing around the edges of a coarsened culture. But I promise you, what younger women desire most from you as a mentor and model is the fruit of a genuine relationship with God. They're constantly surrounded by coolness, worldliness, and shallowness. What they don't see enough of— what they are suffering from lack of—are mature women who have been with Jesus, what one Bible commentator has described as "life in the presence of the holy."[3]

Young women don't need your perceived relevance as much as they need your reverence.

Young women may laugh loud and long at irreverence, but what they actually long for and need is its polar opposite. They may be enamored of popular trends, but deep down they desire to be rescued from the trivial identities they're experiencing as a result.

They don't need your perceived relevance as much as they need your reverence.

Everyday Reverence

We sometimes reduce reverence to a physical posture: heads bowed, eyes closed, hands folded. But I want to draw you back to the more active meaning of *reverent* that Paul employs in his letter to Titus. He speaks of being "reverent in behavior"—that is, reverent in *everyday actions*, in practice, in our overall character and deportment.

Teachers used to give grades for "deportment" on students' report cards. It's an old-fashioned term for the way we act and carry ourselves. And the way we act, Paul reminds us, is a key indicator of how reverent our hearts truly are. He touched on this same idea in a few instructive passages written to another pastor, Timothy. These passages give us several practical examples of how a heart of reverence shows itself in our choices and our actions.

Reverent in Appearance

> Women should adorn themselves in respectable
> apparel, with modesty and self-control, not with
> braided hair and gold or pearls or costly attire,
> but with what is proper for women who profess
> godliness—with good works. (1 Tim. 2:9–10)

Yes, a spirit of reverence should affect the way we dress and present ourselves. Now, Paul isn't placing a ban on jewelry or makeup or trying to look our best. His point is that these things—the hair, the earrings, the latest cuts and colors and styles—are not meant to be our obsession or to occupy our time inordinately. A woman's physical appearance is only a part of who she is—and not the primary part. So she doesn't need to put excessive energy into adorning her external self. She has more important forms of adornment to focus on.

Also found here is an appeal to "modesty"—which, to take a look around, seems to have gone the way of the wall-mounted kitchen phone. I'm not advocating a rigid and unhealthy preoccupation with measuring necklines and hemlines. But let's at least say that godly reverence should inspire each of us to personal standards of reserve and respectability.

Our selection in clothing and our fixation with the mirror can tell us what our heart is hoping to accomplish through our appearance. Who are we trying to please? Does our appearance draw attention to ourselves? Does it distract others from being drawn to Christ? Or does it cause them to be attracted to Him? These are the kinds of questions that matter to a woman who has a reverent heart.

Reverent in Attitude

> Let a woman learn quietly with all submissiveness.
> I do not permit a woman to teach or to exercise
> authority over a man. . . . She will be saved through
> childbearing—if they continue in faith and love and
> holiness, with self-control. (1 Tim. 2:11–12, 15)

This passage, admittedly, has flummoxed countless commentators and can make women bristle. It's not my intent to explore its full meaning here. But don't miss the timeless principle that speaks to the attitudes of Christian women.

No, we women are not confined to vows of silence, but reverence toward God and His Word does make us teachable and responsive to God-ordained authority. It restrains us from asserting ourselves beyond divinely appointed bounds. And it makes us willing and eager to carry out His sacred calling for our lives.

We cannot afford to pick and choose what situations call for a reverent attitude and behavior. They all do.

As for that statement about being saved through childbearing, it needs to be understood in light of the rest of Scripture. Clearly we are not saved eternally from our sins or justified before God by being mothers and bearing children. And *not* bearing children certainly does not cause us to miss out on salvation. In the context of this verse, I believe Paul is saying women can be "saved" (or as some translations put it, "preserved") from wasted, useless years, simply by being faithful to what God has called us to do, behaving with reverence in whatever season and situation of life we may find ourselves.

Reverent in Lifestyle

> Let a widow be enrolled if she is not less than sixty
> years of age, having been the wife of one husband, and
> having a reputation for good works: if she has brought
> up children, has shown hospitality, has washed the feet
> of the saints, has cared for the afflicted, and has devoted
> herself to every good work. (1 Tim. 5:9–10)

This passage is part of a discussion about women who qualified for financial care by the church. It paints a portrait of an older woman who, even during her younger years, lived with purpose and intentionality before God and others. She served and gave faithfully and sought to bless those around her. She was reverent in her behavior, faithful to her sacred calling. She didn't waste her life on what doesn't matter. And as a result, her life reflected the beauty of the gospel.

That's true for us, too, whether we're older or younger women. We cannot afford to be frivolous or careless with our time, to pick and choose what situations call for a reverent attitude and behavior. They all do.

That's not to say it's wrong to take a break or a vacation. But wherever we go, a reverent heart must travel with us—not just to church, but also to the coffee shop, the gym, the beach, wherever we go. It's who we are. It's the hallmark of the way we live, informing every choice and interaction.

Where Reverence Begins

A nineteenth-century English clergyman, reflecting on what he had witnessed in his childhood home, remembered this:

> My mother's habit was every day, immediately after breakfast, to withdraw for an hour to her own room, and to spend that hour in reading the Bible, in meditation and prayer. From that hour, as from a pure fountain, she drew the strength and sweetness which enabled her to fulfill all her duties, and to remain unruffled by the worries and pettinesses which are so often the trial of narrow neighborhoods.
>
> As I think of her life, and all it had to bear, I see the absolute triumph of Christian grace in the lovely ideal of a Christian lady. I never saw her temper disturbed; I never heard her speak one word of anger ... or of idle gossip; I never observed in her any sign of a single sentiment unbecoming to a soul which had drunk of the river of the water of life, and which had fed upon manna in the barren wilderness.[4]

That, my friend, is a picture of reverence. And it focuses on where reverent behavior begins—with spending regular time alone with God.

"Yeah, but that's just not practical," you may say. "I just don't have room for one more thing in my life."

I know your little ones may be awake and demanding your attention—one needing a diaper change, another needing help finding the shoes he kicked off somewhere the night before, all clamoring to be fed. I understand the phone won't stop ringing and your boss is impatient for you to finish that project and dinner won't make itself.

No matter where you find yourself on the older-younger continuum, life can feel overwhelming.

But ask yourself, *younger woman*: What do your children most need from you as they grow up? What do you want your relationship with God to look like when you're fifty, sixty, seventy, or eighty years of age? And *older woman*, what do the younger women around you most need from you as you teach and train them?

I'm not talking about losing ourselves in prayer and Bible reading every waking minute. That's not the definition of a reverent lifestyle. I just mean staying aware of God, realizing He's here, devoting our worship and attention to Him, until we begin to adjust our thinking, planning, scheduling, and lifestyle to match this glorious, eternal reality.

Until we become what God, through Paul, calls us to be.

Reverent in behavior.

Reverent in worship.

Reverent in lifestyle.

Reverent in what we read and listen to and how we entertain ourselves.

Reverent in where we go, what we do, and who we admire.

Reverent in what we wear and what we love, what we say and what we don't say.

Reverent in a way that adorns our lives and the doctrine of Christ.

Reverent all the time—not just because God's cameras are rolling, but because He is worthy of our wholehearted devotion and obedience. And because He has made pleasing Him the most pleasurable life on earth.

Making It Personal

Older women

1. Christians' lives are always on display—and that's a good thing if we're living to glorify Christ. Is there any attitude or behavior you wouldn't want people to see because you know it wouldn't please the Lord? Something that does not reflect His character? Ask God's Spirit to give you strength to change.

2. Older women are sometimes tempted to sit back and take it easy when it comes to serving the Lord and others. In what ways do you recognize this tendency or desire in your life? Why is this not a time to coast spiritually?

3. Younger women need friendships with older women who model the fruit of a genuine relationship with God. How does your life evidence that you're spending time with Jesus? What could help you grow in this area?

Younger women

1. Is there any attitude or behavior you wouldn't want people to see because you know it wouldn't please the Lord? Something that does not reflect His character? How would an awareness of the presence of God make a difference in that area of your life?

2. What part can friendships play in our desire to live a reverent, holy life—both negatively and positively?

3. What friends (younger or older) inspire you to be "reverent in behavior"?

PART TWO

A Woman under Control

Teach what accords with sound doctrine.

Older men are to be sober-minded, dignified, self-controlled,
sound in faith, in love, and in steadfastness.

Older women likewise are to be reverent in behavior,
not slanderers or slaves to much wine.

They are to teach what is good,
and so train the young women
to love their husbands and children,
to be self-controlled,
pure,
working at home,
kind,
and submissive to their own husbands,
that the word of God may not be reviled.

**. . . so that in everything they may adorn
the doctrine of God our Savior.**

TITUS 2:1–5, 10

CHAPTER 6

You Don't Say

Abstaining from Slander

We are stewards of the treasure of each other's good names.
Let us seek to silence the . . . slanderer within and graciously give
and receive others' help when one of us slips,
perhaps unaware, into slander.

JON BLOOM

"REVERENT IN BEHAVIOR." AS WE'VE JUST SEEN, this should characterize older women in the church. But what exactly does reverent behavior look like? The apostle Paul makes practical application in two specific areas: "Older women . . . are to be reverent in behavior," he says, *"not slanderers or slaves to much wine"* (Titus 2:3).

Sound doctrine in a woman's life produces reverence for God. And that reverence shows itself in a careful use of her tongue and in a temperate lifestyle.

Older woman, this is how we adorn the doctrine of God and make it beautiful and desirable. If we don't have these qualities, we won't have credibility to "teach what is good." We will discredit our own message. We will cause younger women to stray from what "accords with sound doctrine." And the church will fail to reflect the gospel to our world in a compelling way.

Younger woman, this is a portrait of the kind of older woman you want to become; these are the qualities to which you are to aspire. They are worthy of your attention, time, effort, and lifelong pursuit. This kind of Spirit-produced, Christlike character is what will make you truly beautiful.

So let's start with this matter of slander—something God takes seriously for all believers, and, as Paul indicates, for women in particular.

Words That Hurt

Some time ago a listener to our daily broadcast emailed our ministry expressing grave concern about a recent guest on the program. The email included a link to a website she said would provide information to support her concern.

Because I feel responsible for our programming, I decided to check out the site.

What I found behind that single click was a host of online sites, each linked to others, all seemingly devoted to exposing Christian ministries and individuals. I'm talking about reams of personal accusations and biting commentary, including private documents that never should have been made public—church disciplinary proceedings, leaked memoranda, and the like. Most of the material on those pages consisted of petty hearsay related in sensational, scandalous, "he said/she said" fashion, leaving readers to fill in the blanks with their own suspicions.

The site was like a maze of mole tunnels, the kind that run beneath the soil in some of our backyards. Each one that popped up seemed to implicate another person—a pastor, author, speaker, ministry head, or church leader of some sort. It was insidious and ugly—all laid bare in cyberspace for the world to see (and "like" and "share").

The radio guest whose character had been called into question by our listener's email was among those targeted in the feeding frenzy.

Few were left out, it appeared. But when I dug a little deeper into the charges that had been brought to my attention, I discovered a common thread that explained a lot.

The whole thing seemed to trace back to one woman with a vendetta against the spiritual leaders of her local church. They had attempted to confront her about a pattern of disobedience. Unbroken, unrepentant, she had apparently set out on a mission to bring down the people who dared to speak truth into her life, and she had drawn many others into the fray.

If the exposé I was reading had ever been a genuine effort to uncover the truth, it no longer was anything of the sort. It was a hateful, vindictive campaign of division and destruction. And it had all started with one woman whose anger and bitterness gave birth to slander.

As, sad to say, it often does.

In his characteristically blunt way, Martin Luther makes this point in his commentary on the Sermon on the Mount:

Our unleashed words can be every bit as damaging and destructive as any other kind of aggressive outburst.

> It is especially among womenfolk that the shameful vice of slander is prevalent, so that great misfortune is often caused by an evil tongue.[1]

These words are not easy to hear. But if we're honest, we have to admit that women often seem to have particular trouble with this issue. This is not to suggest that men are not just as capable of instigating revenge against others, of getting bent out of shape and wanting to settle their personal scores. But when we hear Paul specifically exhorting Titus to remind the *women* in the church not to be "slanderers" (2:3), we do well to sit up and pay attention.

When men have a dispute with another man, they may resort to getting physical. But we women are more likely to let our tongues do the fighting. When we feel threatened, we can be vicious with our words.

(Do you wonder, as I have, why Paul addresses *older* women about this issue of slander? Perhaps this is a particular temptation for women whose families are grown and who have more time to sit around talking, sharing hearsay and stories about others, without pausing to think: Is this true? Is it benefiting those who are listening? Is it building up those we're talking about?)

As we press into the practical heart of Titus 2, a good place to begin is by realizing that our unleashed words can be every bit as damaging and destructive as any other kind of aggressive outburst.

Sometimes, in fact, they can be worse.

Devil in the Details

Paul's admonition in Titus 2 against slander and sins of the tongue hits close to home for me. Just moments ago, while working on this chapter, I caught myself starting to say something to a close friend about a third party—a report that was unnecessary and would not have put the other person in a good light. This is the very thing Paul says older women who revere the Lord should *not* do. How grateful I am for His Word and His Spirit that restrained me in this instance from passing along the potentially harmful information. I think back with regret to many times when I have not heeded that restraint.

And so I take this seriously.

I hope you do too.

As a clue to how serious this matter of slander should be to us, the word translated as "slanderers" in Titus 2:3—which other translations render as "malicious gossips" (NASB) or "false accusers" (KJV)—is the Greek word *diabolos,* from which we derive our English word *diabolical.*

This word—*diabolos*—appears thirty-eight times in the New Testament. And in all but four of those occurrences, it's used to refer to Satan.

Give that a moment to sink in.

Diabolos. Slander is devilish.

This connection between slander and Satan shouldn't surprise us. The first time we meet him in Scripture, he is slandering God's nature and character to Eve in the garden of Eden. "You will not surely die" for eating fruit from the forbidden tree, he told her (Gen. 3:4). You can almost hear the sound of a snicker in those words. *God said that? No He didn't. If He did, He wasn't telling you the whole truth. Because the truth is . . . well, let's just say there's something He doesn't want you to know . . .*

Slandering God to humans—that's one of Satan's trademark tactics. I'm sure at times he's tried selling you on the notion that "you can't trust God; His Word isn't true; He doesn't care anything about you. If He did, then why did *this* happen? And why didn't *that* happen? God is clearly not on your side, so . . ."

We also know from Scripture that Satan actively persists in *slandering believers to God*. He famously did it in the early chapters of Job, declaring that righteous man's behavior to be the easy response of an easy life. "Stretch out your hand and touch all that he has," Satan said to God, "and [Job] will curse you to your face" (Job 1:11).

See what this Job character is like when You're not paying him to love You, the slanderer sneers.

Diabolical. Do you hear it? And Satan has been slandering us ever since. "The accuser of our brethren"—that's what the apostle John called him in

To be a slanderer is to be like the devil, doing his bidding and fulfilling his purposes.

the book of Revelation (12:10 NKJV). He constantly brings slanderous accusations about us before the throne of God, refuting what Christ's sacrificial death has accomplished in declaring us holy and righteous in the Lord's sight.

He's a liar. An accuser.

Satan (*diabolos*) is a slanderer (*diabolos*).

And to hear Paul tell it to Titus, we should immediately get the connection. To be a slanderer is to be diabolical—to be like the devil. It is to participate in the works and character of Satan himself. When we slander others, we are doing his bidding and fulfilling his purposes.

Interestingly, in two of the three instances where *diabolos* is employed in Scripture to communicate the idea of slander, it is specifically addressed to women. Titus 2:3 is one of these; 1 Timothy 3:11 is the other. In the 1 Timothy passage, the word *diabolos* appears three times between verses 6 and 11, referring to Satan twice and to slanderers once.

As if there's not a lot of difference between the two.

So lest we think of our runaway mouths as inconsequential in the grand scheme of things, let's remember whose acrid, smoke-filled company they place us in. Let's remember, too, that Jesus Himself included the sin of slander in the same list as murder, adultery, and sexual immorality (Matt. 15:19). Are we as concerned and shocked over the sin we commit with our tongues as we are over the evil behavior of others?

May the Lord open our eyes to see how sinister our bent toward slanderous, stinging talk really is.

What Is Slander?

When Paul says, "Let no corrupting talk come out of your mouths" (Eph. 4:29), one of our reactions is to think we'd probably be better off if we never said anything at all.

Yet in that same verse we're exhorted to speak those things that are "good for building up . . . that it may give grace to those who hear."

So before we go off the deep end, taking vows of silence to avoid saying things we shouldn't, let's clarify just what is included in slander (plus some related sins of the tongue) and explore what we need to model and learn in this regard as both older and younger women growing into conformity with Christ.

1. Slander can involve giving a false report.

Saying something that's not true about someone is slander. But this is tricky because we may not intentionally be lying. Perhaps we're just misinformed, or at least *under*informed. We can't know everything that can be known about people's hearts, backgrounds, and circumstances. We rarely have all the facts. And so our version of the truth may be a far cry from what actually happened or what the person really meant. We can give a false report merely because we're not privy to all the information.

So when we're aware of a situation that puts someone in a negative light, we need to be careful not to assume we know all there is to know. If we choose to share what we think we know, we could be passing along lies and misleading conclusions without even realizing it.

And God takes this seriously. It's one of the Ten Commandments: "You shall not bear false witness against your neighbor" (Ex. 20:16). And Proverbs 6 names "a false witness who breathes out lies" among the "six things that the LORD hates" (vv. 19, 16). We must not take lightly what God despises.

2. Slander can involve the spreading of harmful information.

The King James Version uses the quaint but descriptive term *talebearer* to describe one who specializes in this activity. "The words of a talebearer are as wounds," Proverbs 18:8 says—intended to hurt, disparage, malign. In our heart, we know how our harmful words make the other person look. And we'd hate to think people would say similarly unkind things about us. But all too often, to our shame, we go ahead and say them anyway.

3. Slander can include the reporting of truth with harmful intent.

Be sure you don't read too quickly past this one because it's an oft-neglected member of the slander family, one we can easily pass by and rationalize. In order for a word or a story to be slanderous, it need not be concocted out of thin air or delivered inaccurately in the telling. What we say could be 100 percent true and still be a type of slander. So even when we're right, we need to ask ourselves: *What's my purpose in adding this into a conversation? Am I intending to hurt someone? To get back at someone? To put someone down or cast him or her in a bad light? To draw attention to myself as someone in the know?*

"Whoever goes about slandering reveals secrets," Solomon said, "but he who is trustworthy in spirit keeps a thing covered" (Prov. 11:13).

"It is his glory to overlook an offense," he added in Proverbs 19:11.

Just because we know something doesn't mean we need to share it. If part of our motive in telling it is to tarnish what others think about another person, then who cares how true it is? The Lord Himself will bring the truth to light in His own good time without our help.

That is not to say that we should never discuss negative truths with anyone. There are certainly times we need to confront painful realities and perhaps hold someone accountable. But we need to be careful when we do so—praying about the matter, seeking dependable counsel if necessary, and examining our motives. There's a big difference between thoughtful, necessary confrontation about an issue and using that issue to build ourselves up or tear someone else down.

4. Slander is not the same as gossip, but gossip makes slander easier.

By definition, gossip means spreading rumors or revealing personal information about another person. It's not precisely the same as slander, which generally means spreading *harmful* information or lies about the other person. But in the chatty comfort of a gossip session, it's easy to cross the line into speculation, false information, outright lies, or malicious rumors—in other words, slander. Avoiding gossip will help us avoid slander.

Slander Hurts

Slander can be a lie. Slander can be the truth.

But slander always hurts somebody.

That's what makes it slander.

I realize, of course, that our intent is not always malicious. Sometimes the hurtful comment just slips out. It comes to mind, and we can't seem to control ourselves. Before we even know what we're doing, we've already said something slanderous.

Looking back, we see why we did it. People were laughing, our guard was down, and we just went along with the mood around the table. How odd or self-righteous would we have appeared if we'd tried changing the subject?

But that's why James gives this watchword: "Do not speak evil against one another" (James 4:11).

Period.

The Greek word that is translated "speak evil" in this verse contains the idea of "thoughtless words."[2] Casual conversation. Offhand comments. We didn't really mean anything by it—we were "just saying."

But what difference does it make how lightly we say it if reputations are smeared, if trusts are broken, if leaders are trashed and churches maligned, if our children are hardened or our relationships damaged? Are we not still playing into the hands of the Enemy? Is not our fellowship with the Father being hindered? Are we not undoing the unity of the Spirit that is to be a hallmark of God's people?

It may feel good at the moment to make a catty or hurtful comment about someone else. But does anything good come from our having done that? I think we all know the answer to that.

Not only does slander hurt others; it also reveals contaminants in our own hearts such as

- *Pride*—the desire to make ourselves look better, smarter, more together, and superior, if only by making another person look worse by comparison.

- *Envy*—resenting another's position, connections, success, family, talents, possessions, or reputation. We may not be able to speak or sing or entertain guests or quote Scripture like that person can, so we want to bring them down a notch.
- *Critical spirit*—the tendency to be judgmental, to jump to conclusions, to secretly hope others will fail. We can downplay whatever others have achieved by questioning or cheapening how they did it and making them appear "less than."

Scripture warns us that slander divides; it breaks up relationships (Prov. 16:28; 17:9). And slander destroys. Someone has called it a form of "verbal homicide." Proverbs associates it with the imagery of "a war club, or a sword, or a sharp arrow" (25:18). It is heinous. It is vicious. It claws at old wounds. It opens new ones.

Slander hurts.

Unchecked, it will only keep on hurting more.

But you and I can make the hurting stop.

A Plan for Rooting Out Slander

"The bitterness is gone," she told me. "It's all gone!"

I've often witnessed visible relief on people's faces when they are set free from the lies of the devil, from the bondage of sin. That look in their eyes when the weights fall off, when they step into the freedom of surrender, honesty, and forgiveness—there's no feeling quite like it.

And that's what I saw on my young friend's face that day.

She had called and asked if I'd be willing to meet with her that afternoon. I could tell right away something was really disturbing her. She hadn't been sitting there for more than a few minutes before she started sobbing.

It had been a tough season for this young woman and her family. Through no fault of her own, some deeply regrettable things had happened. A conflict had arisen. Several people she trusted and respected had acted and reacted badly. Though she was not responsible for what had taken place, she had picked up an offense for someone she loved and had allowed her heart to become infected with resentment and disgust. Then she had caused the wound to fester even further by talking about it to others. She had let them know what certain people had done and how she felt about it. How she felt about *them*.

But over time, my friend had become saddened and ashamed at how her anger had turned into slander. And now she was broken— right there in my living room. She couldn't have taken her role in the fallout any more seriously.

I listened carefully. We talked and we prayed. And then, sensing a prompting from the Lord, I asked if she'd like me to call the person she felt she had wronged the most—a local pastor. "What if he were to come over here," I said, "and you could talk with him right now?"

Less than an hour later, my friend was pouring her heart out to this man who had been an object of her anger and venom: "I've sinned against you. I've said unkind things about you to others. I've undermined your leadership, and I hope you can forgive me. I'm truly sorry." More tears. More prayers all around.

What took place that day was so beautiful. So redemptive. Exactly what God instructs us to do when we've caused harm to another person.

That's the kind of thing that happens when we get before the Lord and discover how *He* feels about what's going on in our lives. Instead of being stuck with how we feel and what we want, we can begin to face and confess what our own words have done—how they've injured other people, poisoned others' opinions. And then, with all our pride and envy and criticism and contention pulled up by the roots, we also might be able to say, "The bitterness is gone. It's all gone!"

As God does His healing work in your heart (and mine), let's take advantage of the opportunity to root slander out of our lives. As repentant people, as women who know we've been loose with our tongues and are serious about not inflicting verbal damage on our homes, our relationships, and the body of Christ, let's turn to the Word for our way out.

Here are seven practical helps to putting a halt to slander.

1. Humble yourself.

Breaking free of the diabolical grip of slander in your life begins with facing your own involvement—acknowledging that you have spoken falsely or passed along hurtful "news"—even under the pretense of a prayer request or personal concern. Then, once you've admitted it to yourself, confess this hurtful behavior and ask forgiveness.

Start with God because, first and foremost, you've sinned against Him (Ps. 51:4). Confess your sin in speaking rashly as well as the root issues behind it, those hidden attitudes that have been like silent partners in the process. Receive and begin to rest in the forgiveness He's purchased for you by His saving grace.

But you've not only sinned against God. You've also sinned against other people. So if you truly want to experience release, you may also need to confess your slander to others—those to whom you've spoken words of slander as well as those you've slandered—and seek their forgiveness.

There are times, of course, when the act of apologizing for what you've done might injure the victim further, especially if they aren't already aware of what you've said. But if we would purpose in our hearts to humble ourselves and confess and ask forgiveness for the negative things we say about other people, we'd think twice about saying them in the first place.

2. Stop it!

Scripture tells us, "Let all bitterness and wrath and anger and clamor and slander be put away from you, along with all malice"

(Eph. 4:31). All of it. Impose a zero-tolerance policy concerning the sharing of unkind, untrue, unhelpful information about others.

Notice the first sin listed in this verse—*bitterness*. Think how often our divisive words are fueled by a bitter spirit. If you are harboring resentment in your heart, if you can hardly think of this person or of certain people without reeling off your list of charges and accusations, realize you will never be able to control what crosses your lips until you've crimped off the oxygen line that feeds life to it. Bitterness, wrath, anger, clamor, slander, malice—get rid of it all. Do whatever is necessary to stanch the flow at the source.

I understand you may be dealing with situations where people have truly sinned against you. They may still be doing things that harm you or others. Your husband may be passively delaying decisions and not seem to care how you're affected by his procrastination. Someone you considered a friend may be undercutting you at the office. Name a relationship, name a setting, and you can probably find a good reason for commiserating with someone about what's going on.

But before you air your grievances, take a minute to check your motivation. Is it to see the offender exposed? To punish him or her? To gain an outside ally who'll sympathize and feel sorry for you? Are you as concerned about the people you're criticizing as you are about how their actions are affecting you?

And then consider: have you prayed for the person who is hurting you? And have you gone to that person directly, not in a shouting match but in a genuine appeal for his or her personal welfare and restoration?

Some situations—I'm thinking in particular of abusive relationships, or perhaps a rebellious teen, something involving criminal behavior—do call for outside intervention. You need to report what is happening to the appropriate authorities and seek guidance from a pastor or wise counselor. But whatever you share in such an instance ought to be meant as a salvage operation, not sabotage. When it becomes necessary to expose the sin of another, be sure the exposure comes from a heart that is genuinely concerned for the other person and wants to see him or her restored to a right relationship with God. And be sure to pick your confidants carefully. A good rule of thumb I heard many years ago has been helpful to me: If the person with whom you're sharing this concern is not part of the problem or the solution . . . don't say it.

3. Speak well of others.

Commentator William Barclay rightly observes, "It is a curious feature of human nature that most people would rather repeat and hear a malicious tale than one to someone's credit."[3]

Perhaps the best way to curb our bent for picking at others' faults is simply to go out of our way to say *good things* about them—not by being insincere or buttering people up, and not by being blind to their imperfections, but simply by paying attention and making the effort to voice what we notice.

You might be surprised how many opportunities present themselves to pay a compliment, brag on the good work someone else has done, or express gratitude for a lesson you've learned from observing the other person's demeanor and character. If you're married, you might be amazed how taking the time to express admiration to your husband or tell a friend what you admire about him can enrich your relationship.

How much slander could we displace if we were more intentional about speaking words of grace and encouragement?

As the wife of an intense, busy pastor and the mother of eleven children, Sarah Edwards (1710–1758) certainly faced temptation and opportunities for slander. But she was known for just the opposite:

> Sarah made it her rule to speak well of all so far as she
> could. . . . She was not [prone] to dwell with delight
> on the imperfections and failings of any; and when
> she heard persons speaking ill of others, she would

say what she thought she could with truth and justice in their excuse or divert the [slander] by mentioning those things that were commendable in them.

Thus she was tender of everyone's character, even of those who injured and spoke evil of her. . . . She could bear injuries and reproach with great calmness, without any disposition to render evil for evil; but on the contrary, was ready to pity and forgive those who appeared to be her enemies.[4]

What a commitment—to speak well of all. And what a calling—to reflect the kind, gracious heart of Christ to those around us.

4. Rein in your thoughts.

Much of what eventually becomes slander is born and nourished when our unbridled thoughts are given free rein. That's why we need to be careful what we choose to let our minds dwell on. We need to squelch that unholy curiosity of ours, the kind that loves hearing dirt about others and then adds our own commentary as we reflect on it later in the day.

A commitment to "take every thought captive to obey Christ" (2 Cor. 10:5) requires conscious, disciplined effort. And it takes time spent at the feet of Jesus—fixing our eyes on Him, being "transformed by the renewal of [our minds]" (Rom. 12:2) as we meditate on His Word.

When we bring our thought life under the control of the Spirit, we can enjoy the sweet fruit of words that are acceptable to Him and nourishing to others.

We would all do well to make the psalmist's prayer our own:

Let the words of my mouth and the meditation of my heart
  be acceptable in your sight,
  O Lord, my rock and my redeemer. (Ps. 19:14)

When we bring our thought life under the control of the Spirit, we can enjoy the sweet fruit of words that are acceptable to Him and nourishing to others.

5. Talk less.

How often do we engage in conversations we just don't need to be part of? We inject ourselves into a discussion. We impulsively reach for our phone. We ask questions that probe more deeply than we ought to go. Cutting back on the quantity of our words lessens the opportunity for and temptation to slander.

Again, I'm not saying we need to go stoically silent or feel guilty for being friendly. But there is wisdom in the words of Proverbs 10:19:

> When there are many words, transgression is
>   unavoidable,
> But he who restrains his lips is wise. (NASB)

For several years I had a walking partner. Over the course of that time, we walked some 1,500 miles together. And while we enjoyed the chance to chat and catch up, even to pray and quote Scripture and encourage one another in the Lord, we also had to guard against idle talk, sharing gossip, and even slandering others with our words.

It's so easy. It comes so naturally. It breeds in constant conversation and can quickly grow into slander.

Of course, we ought to speak *more* words that bless and encourage and strengthen others. But if there's nothing needful to say at the moment, nothing kind, uplifting, encouraging, or helpful ... *fewer* words may be just what is needed.

6. Think before you speak.

Are you one of those people who doesn't really know what you think until you've said it aloud? Do you tend to blurt out your thoughts and impressions? If so, you may be in greater danger of falling into slander than a more reflective person—although quiet folk are not immune from sinning with their tongues.

If the person being talked about were here in the room with us, would I say the same thing?

I'm not trying to inhibit effervescent, spontaneous speech, but I do think this is something to consider, especially for those of us who possess a quick and eager tongue. How often do we get ourselves in trouble by failing to think about what we're saying while we're saying it?

When people ask our opinion, sometimes the best answer we can give is, "I don't really know enough to have an opinion." And when we find ourselves in the middle of a group discussion, sometimes the wisest thing we can do is say nothing at all. Do the people we're talking to really need to know what we think—especially if our assessment of another person is less than positive?

I try to ask myself: if the person being talked about were standing or sitting right here in the room with us, would I say the same thing? In the same way? Would I be willing to say it to his or her face? If not, I likely shouldn't be saying it behind their back.

7. Don't even listen to it.

I don't mean making a big show about leaving the room whenever talk turns to other people. That's pride of another color. But where gossip and slander are starting to flow, we can graciously try to steer the conversation to another topic or to say something positive about the one who's being talked about. In some situations, we may need to gently ask our companions if we really ought to be talking this way.

You may remember that the apostle Paul—before he became an apostle—once watched over the coats of those who stoned the Christ follower Stephen to death. Although he may not have thrown the rocks, he was as much a part of the scene as those who did. And so are we, whenever we listen greedily to slanderous conversation.

Just as we have an "advocate with the Father, Jesus Christ the righteous" (1 John 2:1), we as beneficiaries of His unmerited mercy should be quicker to advocate for our brothers and sisters than to debase them—or to *hear* them being debased.

Bookends

Humble ourselves. Stop speaking ill of others and speak well of them instead. Control thought patterns. Talk less. Think before we speak—in fact, don't even listen when others are speaking slander. Doing these things will go a long way toward eliminating slander from our lives. Better yet, as women joined together in this commitment, we'll adorn the gospel by keeping slander out of the church. And in the process, we'll help each other develop the hallmarks of an abundant life spelled out in Galatians 5:

> The fruit of the Spirit is love, joy, peace, patience,
> kindness, goodness, faithfulness, gentleness, self-control;
> against such things there is no law. (vv. 22–23)

Did you notice the two bookends of Paul's famous list? *Love* and *self-control*. Between these two lie all those other qualities that characterize a fruitful life—joy, peace, patience, kindness, goodness, and faithfulness. I'm convinced the order of this listing is no accident. Wherever we lack love and self-control, we invite all manner of breakdown and discord to take up residence in our midst. Bitterness and anger in our hearts, expressed in evil speaking, vengeful words, malicious gossip, and talebearing—these are the telltale signs that love and self-control are in short supply among us.

I imagine that Satan watches and cheers as we bite and devour one another, rather than being like our reconciling, life-giving Father. So let's join together as women in shutting down the slander machine—the one we've used to chew up far too many people, damaging reputations, wounding spirits, and fracturing relationships (even entire churches) in the process.

Instead, "let us pursue what makes for peace and for mutual upbuilding" (Rom. 14:19). And let's pray earnestly with the psalmist:

> Set a guard, O Lord, over my mouth;
> keep watch over the door of my lips! (Ps. 141:3)

If you and I will adopt a "don't say it" policy when the Spirit tries to restrain us or we're not sure what's motivating our drive to speak, we will be in a position to make peace and to make a difference where we live. People will know from experience, "That woman can be trusted with my heart, my vulnerabilities, my confessions, and my imperfect story, because I know she would never slander me to others."

The groom in the Song of Solomon praises his bride for how she blesses him and others with her words:

> Your lips drip sweetness like the honeycomb, my bride.
> Honey and milk are under your tongue. (4:11 hcsb)

This woman doesn't babble on and on like a flowing brook. She doesn't gush everything she thinks. Her words, like honey, are measured. They are thoughtful and sweet. Her tongue has a filter. It has a governor—much like the safety mechanism that limits the speed on a car or boat. And her words strengthen and encourage the hearts of those who hear them instead of causing harm and contention.

I want to be like that woman, don't you? I want my words to minister grace to others, starting with my heavenly Bridegroom.

With God's help, let's use our tongues to build up those around us rather than tearing them down. Above all, let's speak words that make much of Christ. Words that adorn His gospel and put His loveliness on display. Words worthy of women whose hearts have been won by His amazing grace.

Making It Personal

Older women

1. What kinds of speech and behavior evidence the quality of reverence in our lives? Why is this especially important for mature Christian women? Are there any changes you need to make in this regard?

2. Jesus included the sin of slander in the same list as murder, adultery, and sexual immorality (Matt. 15:19). Do you tend to be as concerned about the sin you commit with your tongue as you are about the evil behavior of others?

3. Which of the seven practical steps from this chapter do you especially need to put into practice? Which are the most challenging for you?

Younger women

1. How does social media contribute to sins of gossip and slander? Why is it easier to share hurtful information on social media?

2. Much of what eventually becomes slander is "born and nourished" when our thoughts are unbridled, unrestrained, not under the control of Christ. How can Psalm 19:14 help you train your heart against gossip and slander?

3. Which of the seven practical steps from this chapter do you especially need to put into practice? Which are the most challenging for you?

Teach what accords with sound doctrine.

Older men are to be sober-minded, dignified, self-controlled,
sound in faith, in love, and in steadfastness.

Older women likewise are to be reverent in behavior,
not slanderers or slaves to much wine.

They are to teach what is good,
and so train the young women
to love their husbands and children,
to be self-controlled,
pure,
working at home,
kind,
and submissive to their own husbands,
that the word of God may not be reviled.

. . . so that in everything they may adorn
the doctrine of God our Savior.

TITUS 2:1–5, 10

CHAPTER 7

At Liberty

Experiencing Freedom from Bondage

*Looking this addiction straight in the eye
has brought me to my knees—
To the cross.*
RENEE JOHNSON

IF EXCESSIVE DRINKING ISN'T AN ISSUE FOR YOU, you may be inclined to skip this chapter.

Finally (for once!) a Titus 2 directive that doesn't step squarely on your toes.

Well . . .

Regardless of whether you drink or not, I hope you'll hang in with me here, because this is not just about alcohol—though we will definitely touch on that in this chapter.

It's not just about older women, either, although I believe there's a reason Paul specifically cautions older women about this issue. We will touch on that as well.

In this passage, Paul specifically pinpoints the issue of alcohol abuse—a warning that was needed by Christian women in his day and is no less needed in ours. But I believe the heart of this text goes beyond dealing with a single behavioral issue. It seeks to plumb and expose the hidden depths of our hearts, the chains that keep us from being free to portray and proclaim the gospel.

We live in a highly addictive culture. At some level, most of us struggle with some kind of enslavement or sinful bondage. The prohibition against being "slaves to much wine" could more broadly include any behavior, practice, or craving that we have allowed to enslave us.

Indulgence and Excess

We've seen the apostle exhort older women to be "reverent in behavior"—to live in a way that "accords with sound doctrine," as those who are engaged in sacred service (because we are!).

And what does that look like? What are the implications for everyday life? Paul identifies two marks of reverent behavior in older women: we are not to be "slanderers," and we are not to be "slaves to much wine" (Titus 2:3). Our reverence for God is to be reflected through our tongues and our temperate lifestyles. We looked at the first mark in the previous chapter; now we turn our attention to the second.

At one level, being "slaves to much wine" represents a mindset of overindulgence that leads invariably to bondage. It is the natural, human bent that is perpetually in pursuit of whatever brings us pleasure or eases our pain. It's the "eat, drink, and be merry" mentality. The tendency to pursue a life of ease and comfort, pampering the flesh and—whenever the flesh experiences physical or emotional discomfort—doing whatever is necessary to make that discomfort go away. Now. At any price.

Are older women the only ones who fall into such a mindset? Of course not! But apparently the apostle Paul, under the inspiration of the Spirit, knew that older women particularly needed this word of exhortation. And indeed, as I grow older, I find I'm often tempted to seek pleasure and ease in excess. It can be a subconscious, unspoken attitude: "I've paid my dues. I deserve a break today. I'm going to do something that makes me feel good. And if it makes me feel good . . . maybe I'll do it some more."

Note that emphasis on *more.* Paul tells us not to be slaves of "*much* wine." That's an important part of this all-too-human tendency. If we have a little of something, even something good, we tend to want a *lot* of it. Indulgence turns to *over*indulgence. In particular areas of our lives, we may find ourselves wanting more and more of something until we reach the point that we depend on it—we must have it.

Being "slaves to much wine" (or "slaves to much" of anything else other than Jesus) is the opposite of being sober-minded—temperate, self-controlled—a virtue Paul upholds repeatedly in this short epistle (1:8; 2:2, 5, 6, 12).

So in considering what the Spirit is saying to us through this phrase, we might begin by asking whether there are any areas where we are given to indulgence and excess. Are we driven to have too much of anything?

Is our life temperate? Is it fruitful and productive and bounded by godly ways of thinking? Or are we just taking our ease, indulging ourselves, mindlessly doing whatever brings us pleasure or numbs our pain?

Can't Get Away

But Paul is speaking about something even deeper than overindulgent lifestyles. He's concerned about our tendency to become *enslaved* to certain substances or habits or activities—anything—that we deem essential to our happiness, sanity, or survival.

That word *slave* in Titus 2:3 means "to be held and controlled against one's will."[1] And that's exactly what happens when we are enslaved by a substance or a behavior. We can't stop. We can't do without it. We cannot get away.

We call such slavery by many names—habit, obsession, compulsion, dependency, addiction, stronghold. Each term has a specific nuance, but they're all about slavery—and we're all prone to it. It's hardwired into our human nervous system—the brain's tendency to create habits out of repeated actions and its drive to seek pleasure and avoid pain. It's part of our spiritual DNA as well—our natural propensity for turning even good gifts or neutral activities into opportunities for sin.

Consider some of the common compulsions that enslave many women today—including Christian women:

- *Food.* Binge eating is the most common eating disorder in the US. A CNN.com report called it "a way to numb feelings."[2] Research suggests that while one in ten women who attend church is likely to have a problem with drugs or alcohol, as many as one in four possesses an abusive relationship with food.[3]

- *Diet and exercise.* Have you ever spoken to someone who talked of nothing but carbs, calories, heart rates, and repetitions? It really is possible to get hooked on being healthy!

- *Shopping.* According to one report, compulsive shopping affects up to 8 percent of the U.S. population, and 90 percent of those shopaholics are women.[4] What starts as a way to meet legitimate needs becomes a relief from pent-up pressure. And before we know it we're hiding credit card receipts and paying exorbitant interest rates on overdue bills.

- *Television.* American households overall watch far more TV each day than families in thirty-four other countries surveyed.[5] Soap operas continue to be a popular "drug of choice" among women. Author Shannon Ethridge writes, "It's no coincidence that I was experiencing the most extramarital temptation during the days that I watched *All My Children, One Life to Live* and *General Hospital* while my children were napping."[6]

- *Screen time.* The panic you feel if you lose or break your phone is evidence enough that phone use can have addictive qualities. That goes for other forms of "screen obsession"—computer games, social media, or the like.

- *Work.* Workaholism is sometimes thought of as primarily a male addiction, but women can also become obsessed with either paid or unpaid "productivity."

- *Romance novels.* A woman writing under the pseudonym Lindsay Roberts describes a time in her life when she became "addicted to romance." "Feeling trapped," she remembers, "I escaped by reading romance novels. . . . Since I worked only in the mornings, I'd spend afternoons reading one or two novels before the children came home from school. In the evenings, after the kids went to bed, I even progressed to a third. But . . . after a while it wasn't enough to just read about romance. Long, solitary walks or drives blocked out the real world, enabling me to conjure up my own fantasies."[7]

- *Sex.* Whether it involves illicit sexual activity, marital infidelity, or pornography, a compulsive desire for sex (even legitimate sex) can be deeply destructive and especially hard to shake. A woman who ministers to college students wrote to me: "During our recent women's retreat, I was up till 4 a.m. talking to young women addicted to Internet porn and self-stimulation. Help!"

- *Prescription meds.* Abuse of prescription drugs such as stimulants, painkillers, sedatives, and tranquilizers is the fastest-growing category of substance abuse among women. Beyond that, millions of women are dependent on psycho-therapeutic drugs to function.

Masters and Minions

Some experts reserve the term "addiction" for the abuse of substances such as alcohol and narcotics. However, so-called behavioral addictions (most of the items on the above list) share some common characteristics with chemical dependencies.

First, they all involve something that lifts our mood or changes the way we feel. Desiring God's Jon Bloom observes that it is this good feeling that initially lures us in:

> At the moment of indulging, it doesn't feel like an
> enemy. It feels like a reward that makes us happy.
> And it feels like a relief from a craving that insistently
> begs for satisfaction."[8]

Second, all such dependencies can eventually compromise our physical health, our emotional and spiritual well-being, and our relationships—sometimes all three. They're bad for us and for others.

And third, they are extremely difficult to stop, even when we desperately want to.

Slavery indeed. And it happens so easily.

Whether it's so-called innocent pleasures (the kinds that aren't likely to send us into rehab for treatment) or the more destructive habits of drug use, pornography, gambling, and alcohol addiction, they all begin with a choice. Then the body's mechanisms and our sinful desires kick in, and before we know it we're hooked.

If you don't believe me, I challenge you to an experiment.

Over the next thirty days, why not intentionally abstain from anything you think *might* be controlling you? See if you can say no to it for just those few short weeks. If you find that you can't, then ask yourself who's in charge here. Who's the master, and who's the minion?

More likely, though, you don't need any convincing that your heart has been hijacked by one or more controlling passions or habits. You may have given up hope that your life could ever be different. Maybe you've concluded you're just going to have to live with this.

Or maybe you're fed up to the point where you're ready to take any action you can to break free.

Either way, when the Scripture says we should not be "slaves to much wine" (or anything else that might enslave us), implicit in this text is an invitation to be set free from addictive cravings and lusts. That should give us hope. And it should motivate us to pursue deliverance from anything and everything that controls us apart from Christ.

Not just for our own sakes, but for those who may be patterning their lives after ours.

And for the sake of adorning the gospel in their eyes.

A Worship Issue

Paul reminds us that prior to being saved by the grace of God, we were all "slaves to various passions and pleasures" (Titus 3:3)—that is, to sinful desires and satisfactions. By contrast, he writes, godly women are to be known for *not* being slaves to much wine or by implication, to any other substances or practices that do not honor God.

Because we can't do both.

We cannot be servants of God while at the same time bowing and scraping to the demands of some other substance or influence. Jesus Himself said it is impossible to serve two masters (Matt. 6:24).

So we have to choose.

And how do we choose? By obeying. As the apostle counsels in another place, "You are slaves of the one whom you obey, either of sin, which leads to death, or of obedience, which leads to righteousness" (Rom. 6:16).

In other words, we are either slaves to ourselves, to our sin, to Satan and his deceptions, or we are slaves to our loving God, trusting that His "wages" are "eternal life in Christ Jesus" (Rom. 6:23). I think we'd all agree this beats the payback we get for hiring ourselves out to other masters.

Another way of putting this is that addiction is a worship issue.

We are slaves to what we worship.

Now, admittedly, a lot of factors come into play when we feel powerless to stop engaging in harmful or unhealthy activities. There's guilt, there's history, there's a desire to meet what we feel to be unmet needs and to dull or anesthetize our pain. There's the urge to escape our relational problems or financial pressures or other unsolvable issues. There may be anger toward God, toward life, toward others who have contributed to the difficulties we face and the ways we instinctively react to stress and adversity. And even when there are no chemical substances (such as drugs or alcohol) involved, physiological factors or changes in our bodies can render us more susceptible to dependency.

And yet . . .

Our addictions reflect our heart's inclination to kneel before other gods that can do nothing for us, dissatisfied with the one true God.

Above and underneath it all, when we become dependent on a substance or an activity, we're yielding our willing *worship* to it. We are offering it the first-fruits of our time, our love, and our energy. We are saying through our actions—the most telling language of all—that we choose sin's rule over us rather than that of our wise, loving, heavenly Father.

So we more accurately describe our addictions when we think of them as what they truly are: *idolatry*. They reflect our hearts' inclination to vacillate in our allegiances, voluntarily kneeling before other gods that can do nothing for us, dissatisfied with the one true God to whom we owe our lives.

That's the exact opposite of what we're called to be as Titus 2 women. Our mission and our privilege is to yield ourselves fully in service of the Lord Jesus. To turn from our idolatrous habits and experience together the joy, the freedom, and the pure, sweet worship that flow from being wholly His.

Freedom Fighters

"But it's not that easy!" you might say.

And of course you're right.

I hear from so many women—younger, older, married, single—who feel enslaved to sinful habit patterns and destructive compulsive behaviors. They thought their faith in Christ would be enough to drive these intruders away. They hear stories and testimonies of people set free from horrible lifestyles by the rescuing power and mercy of Christ, but that's not been *their* experience. Instead they keep giving in, keep going back, keep falling under the weight and pressure, surprised at how they can still feel so pulled toward something that leaves them feeling so guilty, hurt, ashamed, and unhappy.

Those unrelenting obsessions feel to them like the enemies David describes in Psalm 59:

> Each evening they come back,
>   howling like dogs
>   and prowling about the city.
> They wander about for food
>   and growl if they do not get their fill. (vv. 14–15)

They may have experienced seasons of victory, hoping that perhaps they'd put this thing away for good: this indulgent escape, this private embarrassment, this sexual sin. But then one day, under a certain alignment of circumstances, with their guard down and their emotions on edge, a familiar temptation came sneaking back in. It seemed

Our enemy would have us believe we can't be free, that we'll always be prisoners to our habits and addictions. The Word of God declares that no matter how enslaving your sin has been, it is no match for the overcoming power of the Spirit of God.

so harmless. So deserved, in fact. And before they knew it, they were enslaved again.

And that's just what life is like for them now. Even when they work hard to resist the temptation—gritting their teeth and sitting on their hands—they still don't feel free. Just tired. Torn. Like they're trudging through.

Our enemy, of course—*diabolos*—would have us believe we *can't* be free, that we'll always be prisoners to our habits and addictions, that even God Himself is not strong enough to help us conquer what we've obviously not been able to overcome in all these years of trying.

But, let me remind you, the Word of God is filled with promises intended to fuel hope, expectation, perseverance, and triumph. Repeatedly it declares that no matter how enslaving your sin has been (and can sometimes continue to be), it is no match for the overcoming power of the Spirit of God.

Now, this doesn't mean that God will wave some cosmic wand and instantaneously remove all desire for every harmful practice that calls to us. Of course, He is able to do that—and sometimes chooses to do so. But our experience will likely be more like that of the Israelites in relation to their enemies in the Promised Land:

> The LORD your God will clear away these nations
> before you little by little. You may not make an end
> of them at once, lest the wild beasts grow too
> numerous for you. (Deut. 7:22)

God could have supernaturally wiped out all the opposition His people would face in Canaan. But He knew that would cause more difficult circumstances, so in His mercy He promised to give them victory "little by little"—the same way He helps us conquer our idolatrous, enslaving dependencies.

We know from His Word that our fight against sin will not be completely won until we are at Home with the Lord. And what He wants us to learn through the sometimes grinding battle is that this gospel that saved us can also *keep on saving us*, delivering us moment by moment, even as the daily war between flesh and spirit wears on. This onslaught can keep us continually turning to Christ, His cross, His power, and His grace. And when we do, we discover that He is actively at work within us "both to will and to work for his good pleasure" (Phil. 2:13).

It is actually His love for us, then, that causes God to lead us down this long, hard road, putting to death all our unwholesome substitutes one obedient choice at a time. He enlists us in the battle so we can learn to fight His way.

After all, we were the ones who made the choices that led us into this bondage in the first place. We played an active part in our enslavement. And now we can play an active part in our liberation— by choosing to set our affections on Christ, believing that we've been set free "from the law of sin and death" (Rom. 8:2) and taking "every thought captive to *obey* Christ" (2 Cor. 10:5). As we persevere in these spiritual tactics, we begin to experience a richer, more satisfying, more enduring victory over our habits and addictions than any divine snap of the fingers could provide.

That's because our goal is not merely to get better, to be able to say we've quit doing this or that or whatever thing we've done a thousand times before. The goal is to draw near to our God, who is more desirable, attractive, and fulfilling than any excess of food or drink. Than any forbidden relationship. Than any pleasurable, exciting, yet enslaving enticement.

Than anything.

Fighting Together

Part of the beauty—and the power—of a Titus 2 lifestyle is that we're not in this battle alone. We tend to think of our compulsions and addictions as a personal issue—something that's mainly about our individual health, growth, and desire for change. But the directives we're exploring in this book—such as not being "slaves to much wine"—are not just about us as individuals, but also about how we live out the beauty of the gospel—*together*.

God has given us each other, remember. We do this in community with others, and we do it for the sake of others. What a joy—and responsibility—it is to fight together for grace and freedom in Christ and to take others with us into a place of victory where together we can worship in full surrender at the feet of Christ.

This Titus 2 mandate is about sharing and receiving from one another the gifts of transparency, accountability, mercy, and encouragement, reminding one another who our Master really is.

And it's about teaching one another as well—which brings us back to why Paul addressed his "not slaves to much wine" admonition to older women in the church.

In much the same way that a pregnant mother is said to be eating for two—and should view her daily choices in that context if she wants her child to be healthy—we cannot think of our secret sins and excesses as being mere private indulgences. They are not. If left unchanged and unchallenged, they will not only continue to discourage and defeat us personally, but will also hinder what God has called us to do for others.

By God's grace, being a slave to "much wine" has not been an issue in my life. However, as I have shared elsewhere, I have faced a recurring battle with being a slave to "much food." I am committed to keep pursuing freedom in this area—and in *every* area of my life that threatens to enslave me—for the sake of my own walk with God, yes, but also for the sake of my sisters and daughters in Christ.

I know that being enslaved to anything other than Him makes it more difficult for me to speak words of encouragement and hope to other strugglers in the battle. It diminishes my confidence in the gospel and my ability to proclaim it passionately. It causes me to shy away from certain topics of discussion, leaving younger women to fight their battles alone and thus perpetuating the shame and defeat into the next generation.

I've tried to stress that we don't have to conquer every weakness before we can speak into the lives of other women. We'd all be disqualified if this were the case. But we'll be far more effective in leading them through struggles similar to ours when we are experiencing freedom in our own lives.

Just think what life could be like with all of us running together, fighting together—rather than shadow boxing all alone with such stubborn opponents.

And Now . . . About the Wine

Thus far, our consideration of this portion of Titus 2 has focused on the need for vigilance in the battle against all kinds of overindulgence, excess, and anything that enslaves us. But Paul's challenge to the older women of the Cretan church specifically addresses the issue of being "slaves to much *wine*."

You may wonder if this issue affects enough women to warrant giving it more than a passing mention. The fact is, this is a significant and growing issue among women. Journalist/author Gabrielle Glaser sheds light on the little-known epidemic of female drinking in her book *Her Best-Kept Secret*. She points out that

> by every quantitative measure, women are drinking more. They're being charged more often with drunk driving, they're more frequently measured with high

concentrations of alcohol in their bloodstreams at the scene of car accidents, and they're more often treated in emergency rooms for being dangerously intoxicated. In the past decade, record numbers of women have sought treatment for alcohol abuse.[9]

And it's not just a concern outside the walls of our churches, as I was reminded when a mature Christian woman confided in me recently that she had found herself returning to some destructive patterns that had plagued her before coming to know Christ, including "a super unhealthy coping mechanism of relying on alcohol at certain times and in response to certain emotions."

So I think we would be remiss not to address more specifically the use and abuse of alcohol, as Paul does in Titus, and to examine what the Bible as a whole has to say about it. Three recurring admonitions in Scripture can serve as a starting place.

1. The Bible condemns drunkenness.

There's not a positive word in Scripture about the overuse or abuse of alcohol. To the contrary, drunkenness in the Bible is associated with sensuality, immorality, carousing, violence, works of darkness, and sinful, pagan behaviors.

That, of course, raises the question of when drinking crosses the line into drunkenness. People I've known who have battled alcoholism confess they were the last ones to recognize they'd had too much. They generally couldn't tell when they were heading out of bounds. And, as there is no standard consumption level that defines being "drunk,"[10] it is difficult if not impossible to know how much is too much until that line has been crossed.

2. The Bible counsels us regarding the consequences of abuse.

Cautions regarding alcohol use and warnings against its abuse are frequent in Scripture. Proverbs 20:1 pulls no punches about this:

> Wine is a mocker, strong drink a brawler,
> and whoever is led astray by it is not wise.

And Proverbs 23 expands on the theme, describing the symptoms and effects of excessive drinking:

> Who has woe? Who has sorrow? [*emotional effects*]
> Who has strife? Who has complaining? [*relational effects*]
> Who has wounds without cause?
> Who has redness of eyes? [*physical effects*]
> Those who tarry long over wine;
> those who go to try mixed wine. (vv. 29–30)

So what are the wise to do? How can these destructive effects be avoided? The writer's counsel (at the very least, for the person described in the preceding verses) is straightforward:

> Do not look at wine when it is red,
> when it sparkles in the cup
> and goes down smoothly. (v. 31)

This passage, which continues through the end of the chapter, paints the picture of a person who takes a dangerous moral path and ultimately reaches the point where he wakes up each morning saying, "I must have another drink" (v. 35). He (or she) is enslaved. His drink of choice may look good, and it may feel good as it goes down. But he is urged to carefully consider the consequences (the ones the ads don't mention) and to stay away from the intoxicating substance (vv. 31–35).

3. The Bible charges those with greater responsibility to exercise greater restraint.

Several chapters later, the royal mother who gave us the description of the Proverbs 31 woman instructs her son, who will one day rule the land, with these words:

> It is not for kings, O Lemuel,
>> it is not for kings to drink wine,
>> or for rulers to take strong drink,
> lest they drink and forget what has been decreed
>> and pervert the rights of all the afflicted. (Prov. 31: 4–5)

Knowing how strong drink can dull the senses, slow the mind, and cloud good judgment, this mother warns the young prince about anything that could render him ineffective or cause him to become an oppressive, insensitive leader.

"Remember who you are," she says in effect. "You're destined to be a king! You can't govern others if you're a slave to your appetites, passions, and lusts."

She acknowledges that, for some, "strong drink" might be a means of dulling physical or emotional pain or drowning out problems, and it might be helpful as an end-of-life palliative:

> Give strong drink to the one who is perishing,
>> and wine to those in bitter distress;
> let them drink and forget their poverty
>> and remember their misery no more. (vv. 6–7)

But the royal son needed to be clear-headed, in full control of all his faculties, able to focus on his responsibilities and to be a wise, good leader.

And who were the people Paul challenged to a temperate lifestyle in his letter to Titus? The elders of the church (1:7) as well as, of course, the older women—groups of people who were particularly influential and whose example would be closely watched and followed.

Considerations for Titus 2 Women

So the Bible makes clear that the *abuse* of alcohol is to be avoided. However, before leaving this subject, I feel constrained to raise the question of the *use* of alcohol. I do so, with the realization that sincere believers who love God's Word hold quite different positions on this topic. After all, there are some verses that represent wine as a gift from God intended for our enjoyment (for example, Ps. 104:15; Isa. 55:1; John 2:1–11), while others, some of which we've just seen, focus on the potential dangers of drinking.

I believe this is one of those gray-area issues on which Scripture gives no explicit command. That means Christians have freedom in this matter. No one position necessarily makes us more spiritual than another. Neither do we have license to tear down those who disagree with us. Paul, in fact, addressing a similarly contested subject from the first century, warned specifically against passing judgment on a brother who is "convinced in his own mind" that he is staying true to the Lord in his thinking and practice (Rom. 14:5–12).

That said, here are several questions I have found to be helpful in determining our practice in this matter—considerations which can and should be applied to other potentially enslaving behaviors as well:

1. Is it harming my body?

Scripture declares that the body—the corporal, flesh-and-bone part of us—is a "temple of the Holy Spirit" (1 Cor. 6:19). In the context of this verse, Paul was warning specifically against sexual immorality, but the same warning could be applied to any misuse of our physical bodies.

The physical risks associated with drinking too much—whether on a single occasion or over time—are well documented. According to the National Institute on Alcohol Abuse and Alcoholism, these potential effects include interfering with the brain's communication pathways, heart damage (strokes, high blood pressure), liver damage (fibrosis, cirrhosis), increased risk of certain cancers, weakened immune system, and more.[11] Pregnant and nursing women are warned against any consumption of alcohol because its presence in the bloodstream elevates the risk of physical or mental birth defects in their unborn children as well as spontaneous abortion.

This is not to say that occasional or moderate drinking will ruin your health. Still, in light of its potential for abuse and addiction, I believe it's a mistake to downplay the physiological risks of excessive alcohol consumption—which leads us to the next, more important, question.

2. Does it—or could it—enslave me?

One woman told me that in her drinking days she would call her husband before leaving work and promise to come straight home, which she fully intended to do. But a local bar was also on her way home, and "I couldn't drive past it without stopping," she told me. "I tried. I just couldn't."

Obviously, this woman was not free. She was a slave.

Drinking, of course, is not the only habit that can have this kind of effect on a person. But the nature of alcohol—which the American Medical Association classifies as an addictive drug—is that it can take us and hold us. Ironically, many people who drink to escape some sort of pain in their life, all too often end up imprisoned by their habit.

In 1 Corinthians 6, Paul quoted the popular slogan, "All things are lawful to me," as a way of establishing common ground with his audience in the city of Corinth. But though "all things are lawful to me," he added, "not all things are helpful." Sure, he was at liberty to enjoy earthly blessings with a clear conscience. But he would not allow himself—even in his freedom—to "be dominated by anything" (v. 12).

Here's what I gather from these words of Paul. When choosing whether or not to drink, we must consider what alcohol can do to challenge the limits of our self-control and take away our freedom.

As a young man, prior to coming to faith in Christ, my dad demonstrated a propensity toward addictive behavior as a gambler and in his use of alcohol. That history, coupled with knowing my natural bent toward compulsive patterns when it comes to simple pleasures, has caused me to suspect that if drinking were a part of my life, I could well be among those who have a predisposition toward excess. So years ago, I decided that was a risk I would rather not take.

3. Is alcohol an idol in my life?

We hear sometimes of people being "driven to drink," perhaps by the stress of marriage problems, work difficulties, depression, or other challenges. God wants to use such eye-opening bouts with adversity to teach us just how fully we can rely on Him—how faithful, caring, and redemptive He is. But when things aren't going the way we want, our hearts often go searching for substitutes. And the calming, diffusing effects of alcohol can seem like exactly what we need to help us cope.

Liquor is quicker, in other words. (Or so we think.)

And it does something for us that prayer can't do. (Or so we think.)

And what do we call a substitute for God?

An idol.

As you think about your drinking habits, ask yourself whether you're turning to alcohol for comfort He wants you to seek from *Him*. In processing how you respond to life's hardships and disappointments, consider: Are they driving you to drink, or are they driving you to Christ? Are you trying to fill a place in your heart that was made for God? Are you looking to alcohol (or anything else) to provide relief and answers to problems such as anxiety, guilt, boredom, rejection, or loneliness? Have you embraced a false, substitute god in your life?

Of course, the "bad guy" here is not alcohol (or food or whatever), but our own, sinful hearts that are bent to seek substitutes for God. You may never touch alcohol and yet have other false gods in your life. It's wise, however, to consider how any substance or thing could become an object of false worship.

4. Could my drinking cause spiritual damage to others or lead them into sin?

This question invokes the law of love—our responsibility to love others more than we love ourselves and our liberty.

In Romans 14 and 1 Corinthians 8 and 10, Paul addresses various lifestyle issues that are not clearly spelled out in Scripture—issues in which some believers feel they have liberty and in which others cannot partake in good conscience. The apostle lays out two principles for how we should deal with such matters, the first of which we've already talked about. Both of these principles are applications of the law of love:

- Don't pass judgment on others when debating questionable topics. (Rom. 14:1–12)
- Don't place a stumbling block or hindrance in the way of a Christian brother or sister. (vv. 13–23)

This second principle is a key checkpoint in thinking about such matters as alcohol use. Which trumps the other—my freedom to drink, or the possible negative effect my example of drinking may have on others? What does the law of love require?

You may have heard it said, for example, that what parents tolerate in moderation, their children often excuse in excess. I have seen this illustrated by women who've shared with me about their nightmarish ordeals with alcoholism. Many could trace their first taste of liquor back to the readily available stock in their childhood homes. I'm not talking about parents who were alcoholics, but those who simply enjoyed a beer with their football games or a glass of wine with dinner.

Were the parents doing anything wrong? Not necessarily. Did they have a personal drinking problem? Maybe not. But did their example help ignite the spark that set a curious teenager on the path to becoming a forty-year-old alcoholic? All too frequently, yes.

I watched one husband's eyes fill up with tears of regret as he realized—too late—that in the exercise of his liberty to drink socially and moderately, he had failed to consider the weakness (and the family history) of his wife, who along the way had fallen prey to a dependency on alcohol.

To limit your liberty for the sake of others who may be led into sin as a result is not to capitulate to legalism, as some would suggest. It is to exercise a greater liberty—to live by the law of love.

There are many devoted followers of Christ who believe they are being faithful to Scripture by exercising the liberty to drink in moderation. And that may be where you land in good conscience before the Lord.

However, in our day—and in a culture where addictions are so epidemic and destructive—my personal opinion is that it is the better part of wisdom to voluntarily choose to limit rather than exercise our liberty to drink.

Admittedly, my thinking has been influenced by seeing the horrific toll taken on the lives of men, women, and young people—including many believers, even pastors—by the intemperate use of alcohol. It has always struck me as unwise (at best) that some Christian leaders would be so keen to celebrate the liberty to drink without being equally earnest about stressing the potential physical and spiritual dangers of excessive drinking, for the sake of those who are less mature in their faith or who battle strong temptation in this area.

Once again, however, this is an issue each of us must decide thoughtfully and prayerfully, with a sincere desire to honor the Lord and to bless and serve others.

In fact, I would encourage you to read or listen to a trusted Bible teacher who has a different view than mine. Then ask God for wisdom and clarity about your own life, considering your circumstances and proclivities, seeking to walk in the Spirit.

For Love's Sake

After reading a draft of this chapter, my husband came up to my study and (ever the encourager) said, "This is terrific, honey! And so greatly needed." Then he wondered aloud if I should include "our story" about this issue. So with his blessing I share a personal, unforgettable account of a conversation we had that gave me an important glimpse into the heart of the man I would marry nine months later.

One evening, on one of our first dates, when we were just getting to know each other, Robert asked, "Would it be okay with you if I were to have a glass of wine before dinner?"

"Of course, feel free," I responded.

He apparently suspected or assumed that I don't drink. So he pressed, to be sure I would not be offended by his having a drink. "That's totally between you and the Lord," I assured him. "But at some point I would love for us to discuss this further so we can hear each other's hearts on it."

We added it to our growing list of "things to talk about." He brought the subject up when we were together again later that week.

Robert shared with me that for years he and his first wife had enjoyed a glass of wine each evening after work. It was a way of relaxing and transitioning into the evening. He knew of others who had struggled with drinking to excess, but that had never been a temptation for him.

When he asked about my thoughts on the matter, I explained that I did not see this as a matter of clear-cut right or wrong or a measure of spirituality. But I also shared about my dad's issues with addictive behaviors before he came to Christ. He knew from firsthand experience both the attraction and the potential risks of drinking. So after he became a Christian, he resolved to abstain from alcohol. He was not self-righteous about his position or condemning of those who did not share his views. But we did not have alcohol in our home, and we knew he believed it was, at best, unwise to drink.

As I grew to adulthood, this is one of many areas where I took to heart the exhortation of Hebrews 13:7—I remembered the way my parents had taught me the Word of God, considered the outcome of their way of life, and set out to imitate their faith. It was not a hard decision for me not to drink. I saw it as a way of honoring my parents, as a protection from any genetic predisposition to dependency I might have inherited from my dad, and as an opportunity to find my soul's greatest satisfaction in Christ.

I shared all this with Robert, as well as my desire as a ministry leader not to exercise any liberty that could possibly cause spiritual harm to others.

Our conversation on this topic was not a long one. He listened intently, and within a matter of minutes said, "This is a no-brainer. If alcohol is something I have to have, then I have a problem. And if it means more to me than you do, how foolish would that be? You're worth far more to me than the freedom to drink could possibly be."

He thanked me for sharing my heart and then said tenderly, "This is not a big deal to me. I'll never drink again."

End of conversation.

In that moment, my heart was touched at a level Robert could not possibly have realized at the time. The issue wasn't really about alcohol—to drink or not to drink. Far greater than that, I knew this was a man who loved the Lord supremely and who was willing to surrender any pleasure or habit for the sake of another.

For love's sake.

And isn't that to be the driving force behind all our decisions? Love . . . and the true liberty Jesus offers from our self-indulgent and addictive tendencies.

Liberty for Captives

It happened on a sleepy Sabbath in Nazareth. Jesus, fresh from His experience of being tempted in the wilderness, had stopped by His hometown and decided to visit the synagogue. He stood up to read from the Scriptures, and someone handed Him a scroll. There was a pause while Jesus found His place. Then He read this passage from the prophet Isaiah:

> "The Spirit of the Lord . . . has sent me to proclaim liberty
>   to the captives
>   and recovering of sight to the blind,
>   to set at liberty those who are oppressed,
>   to proclaim the year of the Lord's favor." (Luke 4:18–19)

The words were familiar. Everyone in that Nazareth synagogue had heard them before. But something seemed different this time. Nobody spoke as Jesus rolled up the scroll, returned it to the synagogue attendant, and then sat down. Every eye was fixed on Him.

Then came the words that transport the writings of an Old Testament prophet right into the living rooms and bedrooms and other places where we've all experienced the chafing restraints of sin's enslavement.

"Today," the Lord Jesus said that afternoon in Galilee, "this Scripture has been fulfilled in your hearing" (v. 21).

And on this day—today—wherever you happen to be reading, know that this Scripture can be fulfilled for you too. Through the presence and power of Christ in your life, you can be free from whatever holds you captive.

Free from the "innocent" pastimes that have you hooked.

Free from the substances and behaviors that have lured you into idolatry.

Free from bondage to (so-called) pleasures that can never truly satisfy.

That freedom comes not by willing yourself to obedience, but by yielding yourself to your Master.

It probably won't happen in an instant. In fact, escaping your enslavement may be the hardest thing you've ever done—though God's deliverance is available to you on a moment-by-moment basis. And chances are it won't happen in a vacuum, without the help of other Christians who know you well and pray for you and hold you accountable—especially other Christian women who have experienced the liberating power of the gospel and are eager to help you know the same.

Jesus came to earth to set the captives free. May one of those captives be you. And another, me. And being liberated from every earthly enslavement, may we become wholehearted, grateful, adoring slaves of Christ. There is no greater liberty.

But it can happen. It does happen. And that's the word we all need to hear when we're struggling with our temptations and our obsessions.

Jesus came to earth to set the captives free.

May one of those captives be you. And another, me.

And being liberated from every earthly enslavement, may we become wholehearted, grateful, adoring slaves of Christ. There is no greater liberty .

Making It Personal

Older women

1. In what areas of your life do you tend toward indulgence and excess? Are you driven to have *too much* of anything?

2. How could your transparency about your own struggles with areas of bondage encourage a younger woman and give her hope? How much "victory" do you think an older woman needs in one of these areas to be helpful to a younger woman?

Younger women

1. Are there any substances, habits, or activities that you consider essential to your happiness, sanity, or survival? What lies are you believing about these issues?

2. How might seeking out a godly, older accountability partner help you in your struggles with habits that enslave you? Can you think of some precautions that should apply in doing so?

Teach what accords with sound doctrine.

Older men are to be sober-minded, dignified, self-controlled,
sound in faith, in love, and in steadfastness.

Older women likewise are to be reverent in behavior,
not slanderers or slaves to much wine.

They are to teach what is good,
and so train the young women
to love their husbands and children,
to be self-controlled,
pure,
working at home,
kind,
and submissive to their own husbands,
that the word of God may not be reviled.

. . . so that in everything they may adorn
the doctrine of God our Savior.

TITUS 2:1–5, 10

CHAPTER 8

A "Sophron" State of Mind

Developing Self-Control

Without self-control, we become the slaves of all our enemies
(the world, the flesh, and the devil) and become incapacitated,
unable to serve God and one another or even our own best interests.
We end up not only serving ourselves, but we become slaves to our appetites.

J. HAMPTON KEATHLEY III

IT WASN'T THAT BIG AN ERUPTION, AS VOLCANOES GO. But the disruption it caused was unbelievable.

It started in March of 2010. Seismic activity around the Icelandic volcano Eyjafjallajökull began to spike. Fire fountains spewed from a dozen or more vents along its rocky surface, but those slender openings could not accommodate the vast amount of raging magma underneath. By April 14 the lava had boiled its way toward the summit, melting the glacial ice before finally blasting out an explosive plume of ash that mushroomed to a height of more than thirty thousand feet.

The event continued for six days. Falling debris threatened farming and livestock operations in the surrounding areas, contaminating water sources and coating everything in its path under a gray-black layer of ash. More notably, the massive cloud of particles in the atmosphere grounded air traffic in twenty countries across northern Europe. Hundreds of thousands of travelers were stranded, and the delays cost an estimated billion dollars. It was the greatest disturbance of its kind on the European continent since World War II.

As I followed the news reports about this event, I began to realize that something all too similar had been taking place a lot closer to home.

My emotional gauges had been spiking for a number of months. Organizational and financial pressures in the ministry. The stress of an unsettling move. Hormonal changes. Just a lot of things. And over time, the pressure building inside had pushed its way to the surface.

I had grown increasingly tense and tightly wound. I often found myself on edge, reacting instead of responding to circumstances, snapping at people who were trying to be helpful, micromanaging our team, and being generally uptight, negative, and difficult to please. I felt out of control—like an emotional pressure cooker threatening to explode. And though I was aware that I was demoralizing even my closest friends and coworkers, I couldn't seem to stop myself.

But all the hubbub about that eruption in Iceland strangely exposed me. In its angry, fuming face, I could see the cauldron of my own heart. And in the swath of volcanic ash that spewed out across the European continent, I could see something of the damage my erupting spirit was doing to those around me.

Early one morning I confessed to the Lord in my journal that I had "spread a toxic, ashen cloud over the lives of countless people, among them dear staff and friends," and had "caused the light to go out from the eyes and souls" of some of my closest ministry colleagues. I had been allowing my emotions to dictate my behavior—to the detriment of my friends, my ministry, and my own soul.

That's just one of many personal examples I could share. I'm definitely a "work in progress" when it comes to the difficult challenge of becoming a woman of godly self-control. I suspect you've faced it as well.

The single word from Titus 2 we're looking at in this chapter represents a daunting requirement—an impossible one, apart from the gospel of Christ. It is this gospel and this Savior we seek to adorn; and it is the same gospel and Savior that empower us to "live *self-controlled*, upright, and godly lives in the present age" (Titus 2:12).

A Life of Self-Control

Lest we become so immersed in these individual chapters regarding slander and enslavements—or, later, in chapters dealing with our homes and family relationships—that we lose sight of the big picture, let's remind ourselves of Paul's reason for giving us this character curriculum.

To older women, Paul is saying that the grand goal of our lives on earth is not to reach some point of sit-back, feet-up ease. We're called to know, love, and serve Christ our entire lives, even when confronted with joint stiffness or back pain or the nagging fear that our best days might be behind us. This calling requires us to keep ourselves spiritually healthy. It also involves investing in younger women and serving as mentors and friends, as women who have a track record with God and know what it is to be recipients of His amazing grace.

And to younger women, his message is that a beautiful, blessed, bountiful life begins *now*, not decades from now. The woman you will be in ten or twenty or fifty years is being determined by the woman you are this week. And by joining hands with older women who model truth and encourage and guide your growth, you can become a mature, fruitful follower of Christ who will do the same for the women coming behind you.

Put it all together, and we're becoming what God intended His people to be. We're adorning the gospel by living out His Word—together—in dependence on His Spirit.

And in few places do we need the Spirit more consistently than in cultivating self-control.

Self-control is both a lifetime need and a lifetime pursuit.

The idea of "self-control" is a thread that runs through Paul's message to Titus. Paul mentions it six times in this short pastoral epistle and applies it to all varieties of people in the church.

Elders, he wrote, are to be self-controlled (1:8). The older men are to be self-controlled (2:2). Older women are to train the younger women to be self-controlled (2:5)—something they can't do effectively if they themselves aren't self-controlled! Younger men, too, are told (in the only line that's written specifically to them): "be self-controlled" (2:6).

The clear implication is that self-control is both a lifetime need and a lifetime pursuit.

We're all in this together.

And we're in it for the long haul.

What I hope we *don't* take away, however, is that this lifelong battle is a perpetual breeding ground for discouragement, defeat, and weariness. Constantly beating ourselves up. Living with that scolding voice of shame and inferiority in our heads.

For while self-control is indeed hard work, it's not God's plan to torture us with this lofty demand from Scripture. When seen rightly, against the backdrop of His grace and His gospel—by which, we're told, we are *still* "being saved" (1 Cor. 15:2)—the rewards of self-control become a sweet, soul-satisfying experience. And they make us instruments of goodness and grace in the lives of those around us.

There is *hope* for us, in other words. You and I can actually be self-controlled women in a world that is spinning wildly out of control, in a way that beautifully adorns both our own lives and the doctrine of Christ as we share it with others.

To help us begin moving together in that direction, I want you to let a strong but beautiful Greek word start rolling off your tongue and into your life. We've already introduced it briefly, back in chapter 2.

The Beauty of Sound Thinking

Sophron. (Pronounced *so-phrone.*)

What does that word sound like to you? Maybe it brings to mind the aromatic, orangey spice saffron, which is prevalent in much Indian and Mediterranean cuisine. You may think exotic. Earthy. Colorful and flavorful. Hold on to that association because we need a fresh appreciation of the beauty and fragrance of *sophron* in our lives.

Sophron, as we have seen, comes from two other Greek words— *soos*, meaning either "sound" or "saved," and *phren*, meaning "outlook" or "mind." When we put the two together, it means to have a "sound mind" or a "saved mind."

It's tough to come up with one English word that conveys the full meaning of this word. In many modern translations it's translated "self-controlled." Other translations render it as "discreet" (NKJV) or "sensible" (NASB). In a few instances it is rendered "sober" or "temperate."

Here's what some Bible dictionaries and commentators have to say about *sophron* and related words in this Greek word group:

- "the exercise of that self-restraint that governs all passions and desires, enabling the believer to be conformed to the mind of Christ"[1]
- "habitual inner self-government, with its constant rein on all the passions and desires"[2]
- "one who has a sound mind; a person who limits his own freedom and ability with proper thinking, demonstrating self-control with the proper restraints on all the passions and desires; one who voluntarily places limitations on his freedom"[3]
- "that cleansing, saving strength of mind which has learned to govern every instinct and passion until each has its proper place and no more"[4]

As I mentioned in chapter 3, the second part of this word is related to the modern Greek term for car brakes—conveying the idea of being able to slow down or stop. If you're headed down a steep mountain incline or zipping along on the freeway when a truck pulls in front of you, you want to know that your brakes work. If they don't, you're going to be in trouble. And that's exactly the reason a lot of women are in trouble today: their "brakes" don't work. Their thoughts, their attitudes, and their tongues are always racing full speed ahead with no way of stopping.

A *sophron* lifestyle begins with a *sophron* state of mind—a way of thinking that affects everything about the way we live. A sensible, sound, self-controlled mindset will result in sensible, sound, self-controlled behavior.

By the same token, irrational, impulsive, undisciplined, out-of-control behavior is evidence of thinking that is not *sophron*.

Now, I understand the language lesson can get a little confusing here. But I don't want you to miss the huge meaning compressed inside this handful of letters. Learning to be *sophron*—self-controlled, sensible, sober, able to "put on the brakes" when appropriate—is vital to the process of becoming an adorned and adorning woman.

As I've pondered this word and its meaning, I've come to see it as one of the most practical and vital aspects of my personal walk with the Lord. My reactions to everyday or unexpected circumstances can often be explained simply by asking one basic question:

"Is it *sophron*?"

Are my words, actions, or reactions excessive, compulsive, or unstable? That's a dead giveaway that, at least in that moment, I am not *sophron*. I lack the self-control that flows out of having a "sound mind." My thinking is not in accord with "sound doctrine" as found in God's Word.

And that's true for all of us. When we consider some of the foolish, destructive, out-of-control choices we've made in life—or when we hear others trying to figure out how they've gotten themselves into some of the fixes they're currently experiencing—most of them can be traced back to times when we weren't thinking or reasoning clearly, when we were basing our actions on faulty thinking or simply reacting without any thought at all.

In other words, when we weren't operating from a sound mind. When we weren't *sophron*.

The devil delights in perpetuating the kinds of unsound thinking we addressed in the last chapter, the kind that leads us to excesses and indulgences and eventually to compulsion and addiction:

- "That box of Christmas candy will make it all better."
- "I just need one drink to settle my nerves."
- "I can't help myself. He makes me so mad!"
- "Just one more handful of chips. I'll fast tomorrow." (Or "I'll run an extra mile tonight.")
- "Just one more computer game and I'll get back to work."
- "But it was on sale!"

On and on it goes—giving in to excuses, distractions, substitutes, and temporary idols, all because a lack of sound thinking leads to out-of-control actions.

The ramifications of self-controlled, sound thinking and living (or the lack thereof) are deep and wide. Notice how Paul's reference to self-control sits right in the middle of his curriculum for young women:

"Train the young women," he says, "to love their husbands and children, *to be self-controlled* [*sophron*], pure, working at home, kind . . . that the word of God may not be reviled" (Titus 2:4-5).

In other words, if you don't have a self-controlled, sound mind,

- You won't be able to *love your husband* when he's not lovable.
- You won't be able to *love those children* of yours amid all the laundry and lunches and trying to get everybody to bed on time.
- You won't be able to sustain *purity* in your habits and relationships.

- You won't be able to see the value or the necessity of *caring for your home.*
- You won't be able to show *kindness* toward those who are unkind to you.

You'll storm out and check out and flame out and wimp out on every bit of resolve you can muster. And ultimately your life will cause others to reject the very gospel you claim to believe.

Unless you're *sophron.*

The Goal Is Transformation

Too often, I believe, we focus on trying to change or stop our behavior—"I won't," "I'll quit," "I promise"—without understanding the real trigger behind our actions. That's because those actions originate not in our wills or our stressful circumstances, but rather in our minds.

In what we're thinking—or *not* thinking.

The reason you lashed out at _____ again (insert name of husband, child, mother-in-law, coworker) is not that he or she did something to hurt you. Not really. It's because in that moment when the frustration and anger erupted in impatient, fiery words, you weren't operating from a sound mind.

The reason you polished off that whole bag of chips or went out and bought six new pairs of shoes or couldn't stop checking your Facebook page every five minutes—even though you were telling yourself the whole time to quit—was that you weren't thinking sensibly about what you were doing.

You thought you'd never hear such nagging and venom coming out of your mouth. You never *dreamed* you could act the way you've been acting.

Or you look up one day, sick from the bitter consequences of a reckless, shortsighted decision, and you wonder, "Why did I *do* that? Why didn't I stop before it came to this?"

Here's why.

It's because you weren't *sophron*. You weren't self-controlled. Your thinking wasn't sound.

This is a grid that can be applied in countless situations in the laboratory of life:

- The way I talked to that person—was it *sophron*?
- The way I ate today, or exercised today, or managed my time today—was it *sophron*?
- Was that a *sophron* response?
- Was I *sophron* in that situation?

We're talking about a virtue that is as foundational for living the Christian life as are the ABCs and times tables for a child's education. If we don't master this, we will struggle with every other virtue and spiritual discipline. To be self-controlled—to have a *sophron* mind—is basic to every believer in every season of life.

The Sophron *Woman*

To help you understand the impact that a sound—*sophron*—mind has on every area of our lives, I'd like to paint a portrait of two kinds of women. The chart on pages 170–171 lists tendencies and characteristics that indicate a woman is *not sophron*—that she doesn't have sound thinking and is not self-controlled. On the right side are corresponding qualities that characterize a woman who *is sophron*.

Of course, no woman falls entirely on one side or the other. Within the course of a single day, we may demonstrate qualities from both lists. But thinking about these characteristics has helped consider whether I am being a *sophron* woman in any given moment or situation. I hope it will help you do the same.

I would encourage you to set aside some time to go through the chart prayerfully, with a pen or highlighter in hand. Make a notation next to those qualities that are often characteristic of your life. Then ask yourself:

- Am I generally a *sophron* woman?
- What are the areas of my life where I need greater *sophron* thinking and living?

Godly examples and personal encouragement can be a great help in becoming more *sophron*. *Older woman*, are you a model of self-control? We can't lead others where we've not been ourselves. How could you use your personal experience and what you have learned about developing a *sophron* mindset and lifestyle to help the younger women in your life cultivate greater self-control?

And *younger woman*, is this something to which you aspire? Then don't wait until you're sixty years old and your lack of discipline and self-control have worn deep ruts in your character that are oh, so tough to change. The time to start developing this kind of thinking and lifestyle is now. Find an older woman who demonstrates self-control in her attitudes, emotions, words, and behavior. Ask her to pray for you, encourage you, and walk with you as you seek to cultivate the kind of sound thinking and self-control that result in sound living.

> *If I could somehow wind the clock back thirty years or so, this is one area where I wish I could have a do-over.*

Please hear my heart on this. *If I could somehow wind the clock back thirty years or so, this is one area where I wish I could have a do-over.* There are areas of my character and my walk with God today that would be more fruitful and blessed, battles I might not have to fight so vigorously, if I had been more intentional about developing a *sophron* mind as a younger woman. How I would love to be an older woman in your life who helps you make those choices now.

Now, perhaps this self-controlled, sober-minded woman sounds to you like someone who never has any fun. Someone who is boring, rigid, uptight. You've probably known some women like that. I've been that kind of woman more often than I care to admit.

But the woman with Spirit-produced, grace-enabled self-control is anything but boring. Unlike other women around her, she is not a slave to her passions and impulses. She is free to love and serve God and others, free to enjoy His greatest gifts. Her life is a winsome, compelling reflection of the goodness and loveliness of Christ.

Or maybe this way of thinking and living sounds exhausting to you—always struggling to rein in your flesh—kind of like playing whack-a-mole at the county fair. No sooner do you strike one "mole" down into its hole than two more pop up.

But thankfully, God hasn't left us to acquire *sophron* by sheer willpower and determination. As Paul makes clear in his letter to Titus, this *sophron* mindset is initiated, produced, and enabled by His Spirit and His grace.

> For the grace of God has appeared, bringing salvation
> for all people, training us to renounce ungodliness and
> worldly passions, and to live self-controlled, upright,
> and godly lives in the present age . . . (Titus 2:11–12)

That said, to be a *sophron* woman does require effort and vigilance on our part. And we tap into the enabling grace of God as we take advantage of the means He has provided for our transformation and growth.

Renewed by His Word

Consider how you've felt at times after you've lost control, after your emotions rose up and sloshed over their banks like a river at flood stage.

Are you *Sophron?*[5]

Non-*sophron* Woman	*Sophron* Woman
HER MINDSET AND ATTITUDES	
1. Impetuous, impulsive	Exercises restraint and self-government
2. Easily taken in by unbiblical ways of thinking and ungodly philosophies	Brings every thought captive to the obedience of Christ; processes everything through the grid of Scripture
3. Overly concerned about what other people think	Fears the Lord; lives for His approval
4. Lacks discernment; not careful about what influences her; lets anything in	Careful/discerning regarding what she reads, watches, listens to
5. Feeds the flesh; flesh controls the spirit	Feeds the spirit; restrains the flesh; spiritually/mentally/morally vigilant—heart and mind are grounded and guarded
6. Seeks escape from pressure and problems	Willing to endure hardship for the sake of ultimate gain/reward
7. Victim of her circumstances and past	Uses her past as a stepping-stone to greater fruitfulness
8. Self-centered—"How does this affect me?"	Others-centered—"How does my behavior affect others?"
9. Consumed with externals	More concerned about being godly than looking fashionable, beautiful, or youthful
10. Mentally unstable	Healthy, stable; mind fixed on the Lord
11. Has good intentions but doesn't follow through; commitments are short-lived	Follows through on commitments; develops godly disciplines
12. Discontented; entitlement mindset: "I deserve better"	Contented, humble, grateful; gives thanks in all things
13. Manipulative; takes matters into her own hands	Surrendered; waits for the Lord to act
14. Focuses on the here and now; little or no thought for eternity	Has an eternal perspective; views the here and now in light of eternity
HER EMOTIONS	
15. Emotions controlled by circumstances; lives on emotional roller coaster	Emotionally stable; remains calm/doesn't lose it under pressure
16. Choices driven by feelings, external pressure, circumstances	Choices driven by the Word of God
17. Falls apart in a crisis	Heart is steadfast, trusting in the Lord; responds in faith rather than fear when facing challenges; confident in the Lord; has presence of mind and knows what to do in a crisis
18. Easily provoked/irritated; flies off the handle quickly	Slow to get angry; not easily provoked
19. Fearful	Trusts in the Lord
20. Moody, sullen, temperamental	Peaceful, joyful; the joy of the Lord is her strength
21. When life doesn't work, becomes angry, resentful, depressed, loses hope	Hopes in the Lord; trusts Him to write her story; waits on Him to right all wrongs
22. Fretful, anxious	Prayerful, trusting

Non-*sophron* Woman	*Sophron* Woman
HER TONGUE	
23. Says whatever comes to mind without hesitating	Slow to speak; words are measured; thinks first
24. Talks too much	Good listener
25. Quick to vent frustration/anger	Quick to praise, give thanks
26. Wounds/belittles/tears down others with her words	Words minister grace/blessing/encouragement to the hearer
27. Exaggerates	Careful with the truth
28. Speaks roughly, uses profane or crass talk	Gracious, pure words
29. Argumentative—has to get the last word	Humble; yields the right to be right
30. Excessive shyness; fearful to talk	Blesses others by speaking good words in due season
HER BEHAVIOR	
31. Life is out of order—chaos, confusion, perpetual drama; out of control	Well-ordered, peaceful life; controlled by the Spirit and convictions vs. circumstances and emotions
32. Instant gratification—must fulfill cravings now!	Willing to delay gratification; can say "no" now for future benefits
33. Impulsive spender; buys things she can't afford or doesn't need; temporal values	Wise, restrained spending—doesn't spend money she doesn't have; lays up treasure in heaven; generous
34. Eats whatever she feels like eating when she feels like eating it; lives to eat	Temperate, balanced eating—eats to live versus living to eat
35. Unpredictable	Consistent
36. Rash—acts without thinking about the consequences or impact	Stops and considers the potential consequences of her choices before acting
37. Morally careless—lacks discretion; flirtatious, sensual, easily led astray; seductive; leads others astray	Modest in dress and behavior; morally chaste/pure
38. Yields easily to temptation; in bondage to fleshly, sinful desires	Resists temptation; servant to God and righteousness
39. Frivolous; lover of vain pleasures; lives for temporal pleasure	Eternal values; finds joy in the things that bring God pleasure
40. Procrastinates—puts off hard or unpleasant duties; play now, work later	Diligent and faithful in her responsibilities—worship and work first, play later
41. Struggles to maintain consistent disciplines and routines	Develops and maintains healthy, consistent disciplines and habits
42. Given to excesses and extremes	Temperate, moderate lifestyle
43. Makes foolish decisions; lacks wisdom to deal with difficult issues	Shows good judgment; has the ability to solve difficult problems
44. Wasteful	Wise steward of the resources God has entrusted to her
45. Silly, vain, trite, foolish	Sober-minded, wise
46. Loves mindless entertainment; life's a party	Enjoys wholesome recreation for the glory of God
47. Fritters away time; lives for the moment	Uses her time purposefully; considers long-term results of her choices
48. Easily distracted—flits from one thing to another; inability to focus, concentrate, or finish a task	Focuses on what God has given her to do at the moment; brings tasks to completion
49. Makes decisions based on personal feelings or what is easiest or most comfortable	Makes decisions based on biblical principles, even if that requires difficult choices

You were desperate to stop, to change, to get yourself back under control.

But what you and I are *most* desperate for in such moments is not just more restraint and self-control, but more of Jesus. More of His Spirit. More of His power to live with a saved and sound mind.

It is the Word that will restrain your flesh, renew your mind, strengthen your resolve, and give you an appetite for those things that bring God pleasure.

And to get more of Him, we need more of His Word. I think most of us underestimate just how much we need it. This is why Paul's exhortation in Romans 12 is so vital:

> Do not be conformed to this world, but be transformed by the renewal of your mind, that by testing you may discern what is the will of God, what is good and acceptable and perfect. (v. 2)

That's the goal—being transformed by the renewal of our minds. And the proven means of this renewal is time spent in the Word. Reading it. Studying it. Discussing it. Meditating on it. And obeying it.

It is the Word that will restrain your flesh, renew your mind, strengthen your resolve, and give you an appetite for those things that bring God pleasure. It is His Word that will fortify and prepare you for troubles that may lie around the corner.

Many years ago my longtime friend Susan gave birth to a son with multiple, serious, life-threatening defects, including having no esophagus. Susan hardly slept for the first four years of her son's life because she had to watch through the night to make sure he did not choke or stop breathing. But during that season this young mom was driven to the Word. When some might understandably have gone crazy with sleep deprivation and worry, Susan developed a sound mind, grounded in the Word, the character, and the ways of God. That is where she found perspective, comfort, and strength; this daily manna from the Word became her sanity and her sustenance.

Years later, when another one of her children was facing a prolonged health crisis with a child of her own, Susan (now the older woman) was able to walk her daughter through that difficult season with wisdom and grace—taking the younger woman to the Word, helping her cultivate a *sophron* mind. In God's providence, Susan has also been used to minister to and mentor hundreds of other young moms, passing on to them what God taught her in that stressful season years ago.

This is the dynamic Paul had in mind when he wrote Titus 2. *Older woman*, the younger women in your life need your example. They need your encouragement and your prayers. And they need you to help them get into the Word and get the Word into them.

There is no substitute.

There are no shortcuts.

By choosing to let Scripture reshape our thinking and redirect our choices, we can become *sophron* women of God.

Inspired by Eternity

A little later in Titus 2, Paul gives us another important key to cultivating a *sophron* lifestyle. He calls us to

> live self-controlled, upright, and godly lives in the
> present age, waiting for our blessed hope, the
> appearing of the glory of our great God and Savior
> Jesus Christ . . . (vv. 12–13)

In other words, our ability to have godly self-control in the here and now is tied to our *future* hope. Those who look forward to the return of Christ can say no to their flesh now in anticipation of the eternal rewards that await them in glory. They can endure the difficulty of delayed gratification—they can *wait* to have their longings fulfilled—knowing that what (Who) lies ahead is far better than anything this "present age" has to offer.

The apostle Peter echoes this truth:

> Therefore, preparing your minds for action, and being sober-minded, set your hope fully on the grace that will be brought to you at the revelation of Jesus Christ. (1 Pet. 1:13)

Peter's concept of "preparing your minds for action," by the way, is what the King James Version describes as "gird[ing] up the loins of your mind." This refers to the ancient practice of gathering up the folds of one's robes when needing to take off in a hurry, tucking them inside a belt or gripping them with a fist. No one who needed to run from danger or dash into battle wanted to trip over his own hem while doing it.

Those who think eternally will live this way—mentally prepared, looking forward, ready to go. The more we keep our minds "straining forward to what lies ahead" rather than being encumbered by "earthly things" (Phil. 3:13, 19), the less likely we'll be to stumble in this area of self-control. Our thoughts and behavior will become more heavily influenced by the hope-filled promises of heaven than by the pressing issues of the moment, no matter how tempting or upsetting those issues may be.

Think of it this way. In a moment of weakness, you might be tempted to pull off the next exit and into the drive-through of a fast food joint to buy a burger that looked irresistibly big and juicy on the billboard you just passed. But then you remember you have reservations that night at Ruth's Chris Steak House. You think of that luscious steak you're going to sink your teeth into shortly. And all of a sudden, that fast-food burger seems cheap, mass-produced, and tasteless.

You can wait. You can say *no* to the drive-through because you're going to get to say *yes* to an amazing feast just ahead.

Later on in his first epistle, Peter again stresses the importance of being self-controlled in light of what is yet to come:

> The end of all things is at hand; therefore be
> self-controlled and sober-minded for the sake of your
> prayers. (1 Pet. 4:7)

If we don't have sober, sound, self-controlled minds and lives, we'll have difficulty praying (I get that!), and we won't be ready to face the Lord when He returns.

The solemn reality of giving account on That Day for every thought, word, and deed, and the joyous expectation of spending all eternity with our Savior—these are cause and motivation to cultivate a *sophron* lifestyle now.

We can wait! There's an amazing feast prepared for us just ahead.

In Christ Alone

When I think of having a "sound mind"—a *sophron* state of mind—I'm taken back to a tranquil scene from Jesus' ministry that is all the more remarkable in light of the intense turmoil that immediately preceded it.

Jesus had just disembarked from His disciples' boat, having miraculously calmed their "spirit of fear" by rebuking the winds and waves of a severe pop-up storm at sea. "Peace! Be still!" He'd commanded (Mark 4:39). And in so doing, by His confident, capable power, He had enabled His followers to regain their shattered self-control.

But no sooner had Jesus set foot on dry land than He encountered a man possessed by a multitude of demons. (The man identified himself as "Legion," the term for a large contingent of soldiers.)

The three Gospel accounts of this event (Matt. 8:28–34; Mark 5:1–20; Luke 8:26–39) paint a disturbing picture of a deranged lunatic whose strange, erratic behavior included running around naked and prowling among the dead bodies buried in the seaside ledges. Because of his violent nature, people had tried to restrain the poor man with chains, if only to keep him from slashing his bare skin with sharp rocks and other available implements of self-torture. Yet he'd always managed to snap the shackles people placed on him.

His condition was chronic ("a long time"..."night and day"..."always"). His behavior was dangerous to himself and others. As a result, he was isolated, lonely, cut off from relationships. Here was a man in deep mental and emotional anguish, extremely out of control. And to greater or lesser degrees, he bears a resemblance to many people today.

I think of women I've known who live with varying degrees of mental or emotional torment. Some of them (some of us!) act out in ways that endanger themselves and others. One woman poured out to me in an email her frustration with herself:

> I just had an outburst with my preschool daughter. I have lately found myself unable to control my communication with her or my other children.
>
> I grew up in a home where my mother was always raising her voice about her frustration with things I did. I am catching myself doing the very thing that I hated receiving from my mother. But for some reason I get really angry.
>
> I read about parents who have abused their children and wonder if I am also capable of that. I don't want my children to feel like they are always walking on eggshells ... wondering when the volcano will erupt again.

And this man wrote to our ministry, asking us to pray for his wife:

> The ups and downs are mainly where she lives—
> constant panic attacks, anxiety, hurtful actions and
> attitudes toward herself, me, and the family.
> Throughout our marriage there have been short times
> of peace; but the majority of the years have been
> filled with spiritual turmoil and trouble, like living
> with the enemy—almost as if having to daily talk
> someone down off the ledge. It breaks my heart.

Undoubtedly this is how the family of the demonized man in Jesus' day felt. Heartbroken. Powerless. Fearful.

And just as no one was able to subdue or help the man, so many women (and men) today—Christians included—are being treated with a lot of different methods, but not really being helped. Not changing.

But the man Jesus encountered was changed. Dramatically changed.[6]

By the end of his dramatic confrontation with Jesus, we get a completely different picture of this man. Instead of thrashing and cutting himself and behaving in the wild manner that had scared people away, this former lunatic is sitting quietly with Jesus, "clothed and in his right mind" (Mark 5:15).

In a *sound* mind. *Sophron.*

In both of these biblical instances—the disciples in the storm as well as the possessed man on the seashore— the common denominator in their recovery of self-control was a first-hand encounter with the living Christ.

Unless we lean on Jesus for the power to put these truths into practice, we will not be able to find sustainable victory over our rogue thoughts and emotions.

He was their only hope.

Just as He is *our* only hope.

We can do everything conceivable to force mature behavior from ourselves. We can make promises and mean well. We can get eight hours' sleep a night and maintain a healthy blood pressure and pay attention to our hormone levels. We can even cram Scripture into our heads on a daily basis. But unless we lean on Jesus for the power to put these truths into practice, we will not be able to find sustainable victory over our rogue thoughts and emotions.

Spirit-produced self-control will elude us unless we're continually calling out to Him for the transformation He alone can bring about.

When the man once known as Legion—the one who'd lost every vestige of self-control—saw Jesus at a distance, "he ran and fell down before him" and cried out for help (Mark 5:6). A short time before, in their storm-tossed boat, Jesus' disciples had done the same, crying out, "Save us, Lord; we are perishing" (Matt. 8:25).

In both cases, Jesus heard their cry and stepped into their crisis. And when all was finished, order had been restored. Peace and quiet had replaced panic and chaos. Once there was bondage—to an unsound mind, to emotions out of control. Now there was *sophron*. And as you might imagine, it didn't take long for news about the transformation in the demonized man to spread throughout the region!

The enemy of our souls is doing a number on the minds of women today. And only the presence and power of Christ can restore us to our right minds. Only He can make us *sophron*. And to be *sophron* is to be adorned with the mind of Christ.

Not By Ourselves

Decadence, perversion, rampant substance abuse, and immorality—this was the prevailing culture of the Roman Empire in the first century, when Paul wrote to Titus. In the midst of that darkness, followers of Christ were called to be *sophron*—sober-minded, self-controlled. They stood out. They made a difference. They reflected the beauty, balance, and stability that the gospel brings to a mind, a life, a culture.

It's fair to say—judging from the frequent refrain of "self-control" found in Titus 2—that this particular trait is sort of a hub from which all the other pursuits and principles flow. And if so, few things should be of higher priority to us than the development of a clear-thinking, gospel-saturated, sound mind.

The change is not always as dramatic as the one that took place among the tombs in Jesus' day. It often occurs in the simple, everyday spaces and places of our lives. Such was the case with a woman who wrote to share with me how the Lord had exposed her non-*sophron* thinking and was in the process of replacing it with a *sophron* mind and heart:

> My husband was called into ministry about nine months ago and moved our family to another state. We took a pay cut of 50 percent, a space cut of 50 percent, and I took a joy cut of 50 percent or more.
>
> For the last nine months I have grumbled in my heart and often out loud about the things we no longer have or that I wish I had. I have coveted nearly every possession imaginable and been completely miserable.
>
> You have helped me realize that my ingratitude and grumbling spirit really is an attack on the life God has chosen for me—and that I have been detesting it. Thank you for bringing me to my senses and showing me once again the goodness of the God we serve.
>
> This little apartment will now be filled each day with joy as I thank the Lord for all He has chosen for me.

Don't you love that? What a great picture of the beauty of being *sophron*—our minds renewed by the truth, freed from the shackles of our peevish, demanding selves, living under the control of the Spirit of God. And joy filling the space invaded by His grace.

Making It Personal

Older women

1. What has been most helpful to you in learning habits of self-control and sound thinking? What has *not* helped?

2. What examples of not "thinking sensibly" can you think of from your own experience that you might share with a younger woman to help her with her own thought processes?

Younger women

1. Think of a recent time you weren't "thinking sensibly." What was the result? How might operating from a *sophron* mindset have changed that?

2. Identify an area in your life where you need to be more *sophron*. What practical steps could you take (including asking another woman for counsel) to acquire more self-control in this area?

Teach what accords with sound doctrine.

Older men are to be sober-minded, dignified, self-controlled,
sound in faith, in love, and in steadfastness.

Older women likewise are to be reverent in behavior,
not slanderers or slaves to much wine.

They are to teach what is good,
and so train the young women
to love their husbands and children,
to be self-controlled,
pure,
working at home,
kind,
and submissive to their own husbands,
that the word of God may not be reviled.

**. . . so that in everything they may adorn
the doctrine of God our Savior.**

TITUS 2:1–5, 10

CHAPTER 9

Passionate about Purity

Pursuing Holiness in an Unholy World

O Lord, keep our hearts,
keep our eyes,
keep our feet,
and keep our tongues.
WILLIAM TIPTAFT

THANKFULLY, SHE MADE ONE MORE PHONE CALL.

The first one had been to a cruise-ship captain, a dashing man she had met while working on a special ministry assignment, coordinating an evangelistic campaign in various port cities in the Caribbean. Though her husband of five years was also onboard, most of his time was tied up with the project. In the course of her own work, "Kaylee" had often found herself in close proximity to the captain. And increasingly—despite the red lights and warning signs flashing in her mind—she found herself looking for ways to "accidentally" be alone with him.

The captain respected Kaylee's husband and knew he needed to tread carefully. But he also enjoyed Kaylee's company. So when she just "dropped by" to talk or eagerly accepted his invitation to go scuba diving or pointed out how many interests they shared in common, he was more than willing to go along.

Nothing physical had happened between them. Not yet. But their discussions had grown more and more personal, less and less reserved. When Kaylee dared to hint at how she felt about him, his warm response had sparked a tingle that enlivened her waking hours with romantic daydreams. The scenarios kept playing in her head—the dashing sea captain, the adventurous lifestyle, the thrilling possibilities.

One afternoon about two months into this multistop journey, with the ministry project about to end, Kaylee phoned the captain from a remote location. She had been off the boat for several days attending to her responsibilities and found herself thinking of him during a stretch of unoccupied hours. So she called "just to talk"—and maybe to wonder. Was he as saddened as she by the prospect of their parting ways in a few more weeks? Somewhere in the course of that two-hour conversation, those seed thoughts took root and began budding into potential plans—plans to leave behind her married life in Colorado and set permanent sail on the Caribbean with this seafaring man.

Talk about your exotic romance.

But as soon as Kaylee ended the call, the dizzying emotions she had been fueling were suddenly invaded by the conviction of the Holy Spirit piercing her conscience, reminding her of her commitment to Christ and to her husband. When she got back to her room that night, she placed another call, this one to a longtime friend and mentor back in the States.

The two had developed a relationship over the years, sometimes meeting regularly, sometimes more sporadically. This older woman had always been a voice of reason, encouragement, and wisdom for Kaylee. And at this critical juncture, when Kaylee's once strong convictions had been eroded by deception and confusion, she felt herself being drawn toward a woman who was sure to tell her what she needed to hear, even if she wasn't so sure she wanted to hear it.

And that is why these cords of connection between us women are so important—because they're more than just standing appointments every other Tuesday. They're more than structured mentoring programs in our churches. As these relational ties are strengthened by time and life experiences, they provide spiritual protection and reinforcement. They become the personal touch that brings truth back into focus when it's been blurred into so many shades of gray.

And sometimes, at just the right time, a relationship like this may be the last available lifeline that pulls a disoriented swimmer back to shore, tugged to safety from the powerful undertow.

This is especially true, it seems, when it comes to issues of purity.

So much so that one of the core courses in the Titus 2 curriculum for women is "to be . . . pure." Along with the other courses Paul lays out, this is foundational if we want to adorn the

This call to purity touches every part and particle of our lives.

doctrine of God. It is one of the "good" things older women must teach young women if the church is to be a beacon for the gospel in the world and the baton of faith is to be handed off from one generation to the next.

Of course, it's not just *young* women who need to be pure. *Be holy* is one of the great, recurring themes of Scripture—and a calling for every believer.

This call to purity touches every part and particle of our lives— what we do, what we say, how we think, our attitudes and motives. "Let us cleanse ourselves from *every* defilement of body and spirit," Paul urges in 2 Corinthians 7:1. No type of impurity is insignificant— hidden, "respectable" sins of the spirit are no less defiling than more obvious sins of the flesh.

Defiled and Unbelieving

Christian purity stands in stark contrast to what is characteristic of the unbelieving world. Paul describes the latter in Titus 1:

To the defiled and unbelieving, nothing is pure; but
both their minds and their consciences are defiled.
They profess to know God, but they deny him by
their works. They are detestable, disobedient, unfit for
any good work. (vv. 15–16)

These unbelievers are, Paul says, "slaves to various passions and
pleasures" (3:3). They are not free, but are bound to fulfill the lusts of
their flesh. We see this everywhere we turn today. It's hard to overstate
how mainstream impurity has become in our culture.

And I wonder: Have we lost our capacity to be shocked and
grieved by sin? Are we so accustomed to raunchiness, filth, and
viciousness on the public airwaves that we've become immune to its
deadening effects in our own hearts? Have we become desensitized
to unholy language and images that pass through our eye gate and
ear gate into our mind and heart? Are our heroes the kind of people
David called the "saints in the land," the "excellent ones" (Ps. 16:3), or
are we more taken and enamored by the worldly and the provocative,
the best dressed and most widely photographed?

After compiling an eighty-two-page document of research related
to impurity in our culture, one of my colleagues wrote to me: "I feel
like I need to take a mental bath. So much trash." Our world is awash
in moral trash. And this is not something we can simply blame on "the
culture." In one way or another, we are all contributors to the garbage,
which flows out of contaminated hearts. We all need to take a mental
and spiritual bath.

And that is exactly what Christianity offers. This is good news
indeed.

Women Called to Purity

In the face of a culture where the most base, fleshly instincts were
unrestrained and promiscuity was pervasive, Paul wrote,

We ourselves were once foolish, disobedient, led
astray, slaves to various passions and pleasures. . . .
But when the goodness and loving kindness of God
our Savior appeared, he saved us . . . by the washing
of regeneration . . . (Titus 3:3–5)

Did you get that? We who belong to Christ have been saved—
rescued—from our former life. We have been *washed* from sin—
cleaned up, purified. We are different from unbelievers, and that
difference should be obvious to everyone. It shouldn't be hard to
identify whether we are really a Christian.

This thread runs through the book of Titus and, indeed, the entire
New Testament. The unbelieving world is characterized by impurity,
but followers of Christ are supposed to be pure. This is the reason He
died a sacrificial death on our behalf:

[Christ] gave himself for us to redeem us from all
lawlessness and to purify for himself a people for his
own possession who are zealous for good works. (2:14)

And in light of the price He paid to redeem us, believers are to
be "above reproach" (1:6–7), "to renounce ungodliness and worldly
passions, and to live self-controlled, upright, and godly lives" (2:12).
Pure lives.

This applies to all Christians, of course. But Paul makes the
particular point that Christian *women* are supposed to stand out by
being "pure" (2:5)—or as some translations render it, "chaste" (KJV,
NKJV). According to one Bible dictionary, the original Greek means
"pure from every fault, pure from defilement, immaculate . . . not
contaminated."[1] Another defines it as "without moral defect or
blemish."[2] Warren Wiersbe describes it as "pure of mind and heart."[3]

This is no insignificant—or easy!—calling for women in a raunch
culture that celebrates "girls gone wild" and sexual promiscuity.

Now the topic of purity is broader than sexual purity. But Scripture makes clear that sexual sin has particularly serious implications (1 Cor. 6:12–19). When God's good design for sex is thwarted and distorted, the damage can be devastating. That's why a discussion of purity has to include this vital issue.

The assumption used to be that immorality was mostly a men's problem. However, that notion is no longer valid (if it ever was). Take, for example, the fact that one in six women regularly views some type of online pornography and the vast majority of these women—something like 80 percent, a much larger ratio than men—will eventually follow up their virtual activity with actual, face-to-face relationships.[4] (I read of one marriage counselor with twenty years of professional practice who says that at one time, almost 90 percent of the infidelity she encountered was initiated by men. But these days, she says, it's closer to half and half.)

Regardless of the escapes and delights it promises, an impure life does not satisfy. In fact, it does the exact opposite.

As we explore this whole issue, I want to do so with both passion and compassion, because I realize the tender, sensitive places in a person's heart that my words can touch. They can stir up old regrets. They can expose hidden secrets. They can even be used by the devil to instigate waves of guilt and shame that can bury a woman in depression and despondency rather than lead her into the light of freedom.

But the pain and brokenness I've seen resulting from impure choices, particularly in the sexual realm, compels me to speak up.

Regardless of the escapes and delights it promises, an impure life does not satisfy. In fact, it does the exact opposite. Our communities—yes, even our churches—are littered with broken hearts that have been chewed up and spit out by the monster of impurity. They desperately need to see women whose lives show forth the beauty of God's purity and love, the difference His grace can make.

And, oh, the need for older women who have observed or experienced this fact and who will obey the Titus 2 appeal to speak into the lives of younger women, whether to help deal with the consequences of past choices or to help avert further fallout in one more life, one more marriage, one more family . . . one more time.

The apostle Peter—speaking specifically to wives in relation to their husbands, and yet establishing a principle that has broader application—said others can be won over to the truth "without a word" when they see "respectful and *pure* conduct" (1 Pet. 3:1–2).

According to one theological dictionary, the word translated "pure" both here in 1 Peter 3 and in Titus 2:5 suggests something that "awakens awe,"[5] the kind of life that inspires notice and creates an impact. Christian women who have pure hearts and lives become a walking advertisement for the truth and power of the gospel. Others can see that it really does change lives. In a dark, unholy world, those transformed lives will expose the darkness and draw sinners to the light of Christ.

"Teach what is good," Paul commanded the older women in Titus' city, "and so train the young women . . . to be pure."

Yes, pure.

And contrary to what the

The more pure we become, the more beautiful our Savior appears in the eyes of those who see His beauty reflected in us.

world would have us believe, this is *good*. So older women, if we really believe that, why would we not want to do all within our power to help the young women in our lives to be pure?

The more pure we become, the more beautiful we become . . . and the more beautiful our Savior appears in the eyes of those who see His beauty reflected in us.

The Hard Work of Staying Pure

If we are in Christ, of course, we have been declared "positionally pure." His righteousness has been credited to our account. And He has promised that one day we will be clothed in white with Him in glory (Rev. 7:9).

This is the great hope and longing of every child of God. But what about right now? Is it really possible to be pure when we are surrounded by such muck and corruption?

My dad thought so.

Before he came to know Jesus, being pure was the furthest thing from his mind. But all that changed in his midtwenties when the Spirit captured his heart and he became a follower of Christ. From that point on, he was passionate about holiness.

And that is what he wanted for our family, as well. I can recall him telling my siblings and me that he desired for us to be "as pure as the driven snow"—not just in heaven someday, and not just when sitting in a church service, but even when just sitting at home or interacting with friends or choosing entertainment options or being alone with our thoughts at the end of the day.

Not just *positionally* pure, but *practically* pure.

The Bible says that's what God wants for us too. The Scripture urges us to pursue purity:

> The aim of our charge is love that issues from a pure heart and a good conscience and a sincere faith. (1 Tim. 1:5)

> Having purified your souls by your obedience to the truth for a sincere brotherly love, love one another earnestly from a pure heart . . . (1 Pet. 1:22)

And it repeatedly calls us to be sexually pure:

> Sexual immorality and all impurity or covetousness must not even be named among you . . . (Eph. 5:3)

> Let marriage be held in honor among all, and let the marriage bed be undefiled, for God will judge the sexually immoral and adulterous. (Heb. 13:4)

> For this is the will of God, your sanctification: that you abstain from sexual immorality. . . . For God has not called us for impurity, but in holiness. (1 Thess. 4:3, 7)

If we want to enjoy the freedom and joy of walking in purity, we do well not only to ponder these kinds of passages frequently, but to consider what it will take to follow their direction in our daily lives—because, as we've seen, practical purity isn't easy. This part of our Christian walk requires focused, ongoing effort and training as well as the watchful encouragement of these crucial Titus 2 relationships.

We need women we can call on the phone who will go to their knees and call out to God on our behalf. We need friendships with those who understand that the most godly or well-intentioned woman is never immune to temptation or failure. We need intentional, mutually invasive relationships with truth-telling friends.

And yes, I meant *invasive*—in the sense that we allow these friends to step into our lives and we are willing to move into theirs. These kinds of relationships don't settle for staying on the surface where everything appears to be just fine. They don't stand on ceremony or hold back for fear of rejection. We don't refrain from asking tough questions and saying things that need to be said.

Of course we should do this "in a spirit of gentleness . . . [keeping] watch on [ourselves], lest [we] too be tempted" (Gal. 6:1). Of course we should act in true concern and humility, not jealousy or judgment. And this should generally take place in the context of established relationships, where genuine love and care are already a given.

We can look to Him to transform us by His grace — no matter what we've done, no matter where we've been — until our lives ultimately mirror the gleaming whiteness of His purity.

But we all need people in our lives who love us enough to probe our hearts, who will hold us accountable to walk in the light. And we need to be willing to be that kind of friend to others. There is a time when it's necessary to lean in, to say the hard things, to not be silent when one of our sisters is teetering toward compromise. This is how we "bear one another's burdens, and so fulfill the law of Christ" (v. 2). This is how we live out the beauty of the gospel—together.

In all of this, we must let God's Word reveal and determine what our hearts are meant to love, what our minds are meant to dwell on, what our relationships are meant to be like, and what our habits are meant to avoid. We can look to Him to transform us by His grace— no matter what we've done, no matter where we've been—until our lives ultimately mirror the gleaming whiteness of His purity.

Hints and Hedges

Ours is obviously not the first period in history to experience the intense battle involved in maintaining a pure heart and walk. Extended portions of the book of Proverbs, in fact, focus on this battle and warn about the damaging, deadly consequences of sexual sin (see chapters 5–7).

Or listen to Paul, in the first century, urging the believers in Thessalonica to take these matters to heart, to walk in God-pleasing, Spirit-empowered purity "more and more" for the health of their bodies and spirits, of their families and worship (1 Thess. 4:1). And in Ephesians 5:3 (NIV) he urges, "Among you there must not be even a hint of sexual immorality, or of any kind of impurity...."

Not even a hint? Not "any kind of impurity"? To modern ears, that may sound antiquated, extreme—just not realistic in today's world. But consider the upside of pursuing a lifestyle of purity:

- the joy that comes from being fully surrendered to God, satisfied in Him alone
- the freedom that comes from living inside His loving borders of protection
- the depth of relationship with others that is possible when the barriers of impurity and impropriety are removed
- the unity that takes place within marriages when honesty and transparency replace secrets
- the impact in the lives of sons and daughters who witness their parents actually living what they claim to believe
- the opportunity to point others to Christ and the purity that is available through Him

Surely it's worth any price to obtain and maintain a life that is pure and above reproach. But is it really possible?

Purity can indeed feel like an unattainable standard. And in fact, it is—apart from the indwelling, enabling power of the Holy Spirit. But the very fact that Paul urges older women to *teach* younger women to be pure suggests that purity can be *learned*—by watching the example of these mentors and by listening to what they have learned in their pursuit of purity.

In that spirit, let me share with you several practical day-to-day strategies I have found to be helpful in my own life as well as the lives of others when it comes to sexual purity. Hopefully you'll find these ideas helpful and can use them as a springboard for discussion in your Titus 2 relationships with other women.

I think of these practices and commitments as "hedges." Picture the rows of manicured shrubbery a person might place around his or her property, establishing a ring of privacy, a barrier to unwanted intruders. Hedges help keep things out, and they help keep things in. That's what these habits can do in your life. And while these practices don't make us holy in themselves or render us less dependent on the Lord for the desire and the power to be pure, they can help us as we wage war against the lure of the world and the cravings of our flesh. They contribute to our sanctification as the Holy Spirit motivates and animates our practical purity.

Hedge #1: Choose discretion.

We don't hear much about discretion any more. This important quality has to do with being discerning and prudent in our interactions—our speech and our behavior—with others.

Discretion is what restrains a woman from confiding personal marriage problems to a male friend or colleague or from having deep, private, spiritual conversations with another woman's husband. It makes her careful about how she meets a man's gaze or responds to flirtation or inappropriate words or behavior on his part. It helps her avoid settings and situations where the natural thing would be to do something wrong.

Hedge #2: Value modesty.

We looked briefly at this topic in chapter 5 in regard to reverent behavior, but it certainly applies in terms of purity as well. I don't want to minimize a man's responsibility to maintain his own purity of thought and eye control. But the dress and demeanor of many women and teenage girls today leaves so little to the imagination, it can cause a man's temptation meter to spike.

Godly men who desire to have pure thoughts and behavior toward women have implored me to help women understand the power they wield and how much they need our support and assistance in their battle for purity.

As Christians, one of our chief commitments should be not only preserving our own purity, but also protecting and honoring the purity and morals of others. And when we behave or dress in a fashion that competes with a man's affections for his (present or future) wife, we work against the purity of his heart as well as our own.[6]

Hedge #3: Check your emotional attachments.

It never fails to undo me when I hear of another woman (married or single) whose heart and emotions have been drawn into relationship with a man who is another woman's husband. It happens in the workplace. It happens at the fitness center. It happens in the stands at their kids' ball games. Sometimes it even happens in the church and with men in spiritual leadership.

In many cases, the woman is as surprised as anyone. She didn't intend to go there. But she arrived at that point one careless step—one incremental compromise—at a time. One thought at a time that she nursed and gave free rein to rather than taking "every thought captive to obey Christ" (2 Cor. 10:5).

Before she knows it, she is in emotional and moral quicksand.

The fallout and unintended consequences of tasting forbidden fruit are always messy and painful. In the end, sin—alluring as it may be—never pays what it promises. Never.

You belong to a God who raises the dead.

So this needs to be zero-tolerance territory. When the first of these thoughts comes in, it needs to be the next one going out. No flirting with it, no toying with it, not even for a second.

Here's what you need to do, instead: If you're married, determine to put that emotional energy into lavishing your own husband with love and interest—even if you feel your marriage is dead. You belong to a God who raises the dead.

If you're not married, invest your mental and emotional focus into cultivating a more intimate relationship with the Lord. The moment you sense the smallest flickering desire drawing you into an intimate, imaginary circle with another man—desire that cannot be righteously fulfilled or acted on—redirect your attention and your affection toward an object you can rightly desire. Otherwise, you are setting yourself up for disaster—and the longer you give it to build up, the harder it will be to deal with it.

Hedge #4: Guard your electronic communications.

Texts, emails, and social media provide a fertile context for developing inappropriate relationships. Even though you may be miles apart and your interaction can feel completely harmless, it's amazing how quickly an "innocent" exchange on our electronic devices can pick up steam.

Carelessness on this front is a huge contributing factor to the break-up of marriages today. I heard it once again recently as a woman poured out her heart to me about how her husband is mired in an emotional (at least) affair with an old girlfriend he connected with on Facebook.

Secrets and clandestine communications have no business passing between married men and women (who are not married to each other) in electronic or any other form.

Scripture doesn't lay down specific ground rules for our digital communication, of course. But it does provide foundational principles we can apply to help us make wise choices and guard our hearts.

I want to honor the Lord and have a pure heart and walk. And I know I am no less vulnerable than anyone else to be deceived or led astray. So when it comes to electronic communications I have chosen to err on the side of caution.

For example, when it comes to personal text or email exchanges with a married man, I generally copy his wife or a mutual friend. And now, as a married woman, I am purposeful about not having exchanges with other men that I would not want my husband to see. I want to be vigilant to protect the marriages of my friends and colleagues as well as my own heart and marriage.

Hedge #5: Don't forget to lean on your trusted female relationships.

As we've seen, this is at the heart of the message of Titus 2. It's worth mentioning again here because it's such an important hedge against impurity. The power of sexual sin is often found in secrecy. When we get honest about our secret temptations and failures—whether sexual or in other areas—and bring them into the light, they lose their power. And when we get in the habit of sharing them with a caring older woman who has a track record of faithfulness and obedience, God can use her to steer us back in the direction of purity.

And here's another benefit of these woman-to-woman friendships. Many women, whether single or married, are drawn into inappropriate relationships because they are lonely and lack fulfilling, caring relationships. Healthy, caring relationships among women can be a means of grace to help meet those needs in legitimate ways.

If we aren't deliberate about pursuing purity, the natural bent of our hearts and the breakneck pace of life make it easy to cut corners, compromising for the sake of convenience.

And don't forget that mentoring can go both ways. As an older woman, I have found that developing these kinds of relationships with younger women can serve as a hedge in itself—providing reminders and an incentive to persevere in the pathway of purity.

Taking Purity Seriously

To some, these kinds of cautions may seem over the top, especially by modern standards. But if we aren't deliberate about pursuing purity, the natural bent of our hearts and the breakneck pace of life make it easy to cut corners, compromising for the sake of convenience.

It's a mistake to see these practical "hedges" as putting us in some sort of legalistic straitjacket. In reality, true freedom for ourselves and for others, exists only within purity's well-hedged borders.

Listen, if I'm driving on a narrow mountain road with hairpin turns, peering out my window at steep cliffs below, I sincerely hope that road has guardrails. I will not resent those barriers as inhibiting my freedom. Instead, I will be deeply grateful for the freedom they give me to navigate the road without driving over the edge and plummeting to my death.

It's the *absence* of guardrails ("hedges") that poses the real threat.

I can attest to this personally, having been single until my midfifties. As a woman with normal longings for intimacy and companionship, there were occasions and circumstances in which it was tempting (and would have been easy) to veer off the path of purity. How I thank the Lord for the protection and freedom these kinds of practical hedges afforded me in those years. And for how He satisfied my longings day after day, with His promises, His presence, and His precious love.

Now, as a married woman, it is even more apparent to me that God intends not to restrict or limit our happiness through His precepts, but to *bless* us—whether married or single—with the rich, sweet fruit of purity.

A woman who desires to be pure will not consider wise, practical hedges to be a hardship or a burden, but rather will see them as a means of grace to help her navigate life with freedom and joy.

I find that when women begin to take purity seriously, their consciences become sensitized to things they might once have dismissed. Off-color humor. Sexual innuendoes. Questionable entertainment. Flirtatious behavior. Indifference or resentment toward their husband's sexual needs. As they deal with these and other issues the Spirit brings to their attention, the thoughts and practices that once crowded out God's ways in their lives begin to be displaced, making room for pure thoughts, pure worship, and a purer freedom than the world's ways can possibly provide.

Pure desires.

Pure satisfaction.

In place of their short-term, misplaced emotions and attractions, they begin to see God's holiness, His covenant-keeping love. That's because for every hint of compromise we avoid, we experience greater freedom to draw near to God. Carefully maintained, Spirit-directed hedges do more than just keep out unauthorized intruders. They also provide a border within which a lovely garden can be planted.

God's desire—and it's important to keep this in mind as we interact with other women—is to give us so much more than our modest, careful interactions appear to take away.

Life played on the edges is a date with disaster.

Life spent pursuing the Lover of our soul and, for those who are married, pouring ourselves into the husband we can love without restraint is the path to life's purest pleasures.

The Scripture says of Jesus that He "loved righteousness and hated wickedness," as a result of which God "anointed [Him] with the oil of gladness beyond [His] companions" (Heb. 1:9). The same will be increasingly true of those who love and follow Jesus. And to the extent that we love purity and loathe sin (starting with that in our own hearts), our lives will point people to Him.

The Promise of Purity

Kaylee didn't go through with it.

When she hung up from the second phone call with her longtime friend "Rebecca," she knew what needed to happen next. She needed to wrap up her work responsibilities, get back on a plane, and apply the cleansing agent of confession to her resistant, runaway heart. Her husband had to be told. Healing had to begin. Purity had to become her new home.

Again.

"Do you remember the letter that's here in my files?" Rebecca asked her that day. She was referring to a commitment Kaylee had written out and signed and left in her friend's keeping years earlier.

Kaylee's past had included a moral failure during her college years. So more than five years earlier, at Rebecca's suggestion, she had written a letter expressing her commitment to pursue purity and inviting accountability.

Yet when Rebecca brought up that promise on the phone that day, Kaylee's first reaction was to resist it. This situation was different, she said. She had her reasons, she said. This relationship was not out of God's will for her. It was making her happy, she insisted.

But there's something about a promise—a solemn, sincere vow—that's able to block off a road that appears to head off into the sunset but actually leads off a cliff.

And there's something about that older woman we've allowed into our lives to "teach" us and to "train" us in purity. She holds us back. She holds us up. She holds us close when temptation is circling in the water, just as she holds us when condemnation is circling back to confront us over our failures.

You need a woman like that.

And you need to become a woman like that.

When she was in danger of making the biggest mistake of her life, when she was about to dishonor the Lord and perhaps throw away her marriage, there was a woman like that in Kaylee's life. A woman who pleaded with her to remember her vows and remember her God. By God's grace, Kaylee listened to the older woman's appeal. She came to her senses, realized what she was about to do, and repented. As a result, the course of her life was forever changed.

Today, nearly twenty-five years later, Kaylee is experiencing the blessings and the fruit of that watershed moment. She and her husband have a terrific marriage. They are serving the Lord together. And God is using her to speak into the lives of younger women, helping them avoid the same pitfalls Rebecca helped her avoid falling into decades ago.

Personal willpower simply isn't enough to sustain our vows to our holy God. If we are to mirror His purity to our generation in a way that truly makes a difference, we mustn't attempt to make it alone. We must do it together.

Together, in dependence on the power of the indwelling Holy Spirit, our struggle with temptation can yield to the joys of personal, practical purity.

The snow-white beauty of His purity.

Making It Personal

Older women

1. "Christian women who have pure hearts and lives become a walking advertisement for the truth and power of the gospel." Do you see yourself in this statement? Why or why not?

2. Do you have any "intentional, mutually invasive relationships"? Are you a "truth-telling friend," or do you hesitate to say the "hard things" to someone who is struggling in the area of purity? What holds you back? How can you speak truth effectively while remaining loving and gracious?

Younger women

1. Kaylee called Rebecca when she was battling moral temptation. Who would you call if you were in a similar situation? Do you have any "intentional, mutually invasive relationships with truth-telling friends"?

2. Personal, practical "hedges" can be a means of grace to help you navigate life with freedom and joy. What hedges do you have in place to help guard your heart and protect you from unwise, impure choices? Are there additional hedges that need to be put into place?

PART THREE

A Woman under Her Roof

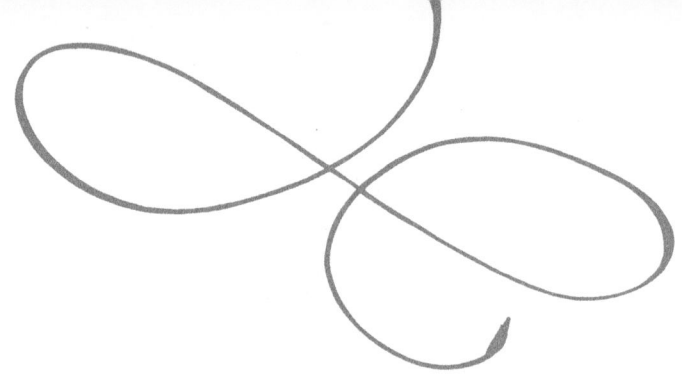

Teach what accords with sound doctrine.

Older men are to be sober-minded, dignified, self-controlled,
sound in faith, in love, and in steadfastness.

Older women likewise are to be reverent in behavior,
not slanderers or slaves to much wine.

They are to teach what is good,
and so train the young women
to love their husbands and children,
to be self-controlled,
pure,
working at home,
kind,
and submissive to their own husbands,
that the word of God may not be reviled.

**. . . so that in everything they may adorn
the doctrine of God our Savior.**

TITUS 2:1–5, 10

CHAPTER 10

Taste of Heaven

Cultivating a Heart for Home

Love and labor, home and work—
these concepts need an eternal perspective.
CAROLYN McCULLEY

IT WASN'T ANYTHING FANCY—BUT WHAT A SWEET GIFT IT WAS.

My husband and I joined our sweet friends "Gretchen" and "Alex," along with their four children and another family member, for an evening in their home. We gathered around their dining-room table to feast on savory chicken-vegetable soup and fragrant bread. We talked, laughed, and played a spirited game of Toss Up. Then we closed the evening with an extended time of prayer around the circle. Surrounding us on the walls was beautiful original artwork that depicted biblical themes—just one way that Gretchen, who left a career in marriage and family counseling to minister to her own husband and children, uses her gifts to worship Christ and point her family and friends to Him.

This generous-hearted wife and mom is being pulled in many directions these days—juggling the needs of her husband, home-schooled children and teens, aging parents, a disabled sister who has come to live temporarily in her home, and a steady stream of college students who find a home away from home under her roof. And yet she intentionally makes her home a place of outreach and welcome.

She doesn't typically offer gourmet meals or Martha Stewart table settings. What she—along with her husband and children—does offer is extravagant love, warmth, acceptance, meaningful conversation, and smiles. Her home is not an idol or an end in itself. It is a tool, a means of putting the gospel and the grace of God on display.

My friend is giving those who come through the front (or garage) door a taste of heaven.

Because she—like all true Titus 2 women—has developed a heart for home.

A Home-Based Curriculum

Let's take a quick step back and pause here for a little refresher:

> Older women . . . are to . . . train the young women
> to love their husbands and children, to be self-
> controlled, pure, working at home, kind, and
> submissive to their own husbands . . . (Titus 2:3–5)

Paul truly said a mouthful when he outlined this curriculum for the "women's ministry" of the church in Crete roughly twenty centuries ago. Before we dive into these individual qualities, I'd like to make a few observations about this list as a whole.

For starters, I think you'd agree this list flies in the face of what a lot of people think these days. It was radically countercultural in Paul's day, and it is no less so in our day. But those who trust the wisdom of God and who are willing to swim upstream against the culture to embrace this timeless calling will find it a way of great beauty and joy.

Next, it's worth noting what is *not* on this list. Notice, for example, that Paul doesn't mention anything about the women's prayer life. There's nothing about their knowledge of Scripture or their evangelistic fervor.

That's not to say that these areas are unimportant. Every believer, man or woman alike, ought to pursue and embrace them, and Paul makes that point in other letters. But they aren't Paul's focus in this particular passage. Nor does he include instruction about a woman's vocational life or her personal ministry activities.

It's also interesting that Paul apparently assumes the qualities he highlights don't come naturally. He says younger women need to be *trained* in these important areas. They are skills to be taught and learned—one generation passing them on to the next.

And finally, Paul's list reminds us of the priority God places on the home. Four of these instructions for women in the church relate directly to the domestic sphere:

> *Our home life—far from being a separate compartment from our spiritual life and witness—is a foundational way we express the love of God and the beauty of the gospel.*

- loving our husbands
- loving our children
- working at home
- being submissive to our husbands

And while the rest—purity, kindness, self-control—are broader topics, all are certainly vital within the context of home and family relationships.

So one important takeaway from this passage is that God cares about what happens inside the walls of our houses. Our home life— far from being a separate compartment from our spiritual life and witness—is a foundational way we express the love of God and the beauty of the gospel.

Home, as God designed it, is not a cultural convention or a matter of pragmatic convenience. It is intended to be a parable of the redemptive storyline in which He is intent on restoring Paradise, establishing His dwelling among men, and making beloved sons and daughters out of prodigals. Christian homes are meant to tell that story.

That is not to say that those who do not marry or bear children are excluded from this story—or that a discussion of the responsibilities and blessings of home leaves them stranded on the sideline.

No, at some level, Paul's home-based curriculum applies to all of us.

So if you're tempted to skip over these chapters because you're not in the "young wife and mom" demographic, I hope you'll hang in there with me as we explore how all of us can live out and adorn the gospel of Christ on the home front.

Not an Add-On

If you're anywhere close to my age, when you read Paul's prescription for young women, you may picture the *Ozzie and Harriet* generation of the 1950s. And you might consider that a good thing—*ah, those were the days!* Or you might recoil at the thought—*can you say "barefoot and pregnant"?* For sure, it would be a mistake to idealize that period or to try to return to another time.

It would also be a mistake to write off this portion of Scripture as being archaic and irrelevant.

All of God's Word is inspired and intended to be taken seriously. We must wrestle with how to apply its enduring truth to our own era and cultural context—including that little phrase in Titus 2:5, "working at home."

The phrase Paul uses here is rendered a bit differently in other Bible translations. Those of us who grew up with the King James Version remember it as "keepers at home." Still other translations read:

- "workers at home" (NASB)
- "busy at home" (NIV) .

- "homemakers" (NKJV)

The main reason for the difference is a disagreement regarding the actual compound word that is used in the original Greek. Ready for a little language lesson? The oldest Greek manuscripts use the word *oikourgos*, a compound word that combines *oikos* ("home" or house") with *ergos* ("work")—literally, "one who works at home." This suggests a woman who is not idle, who is busy at home and active in caring for her household duties.

Other manuscripts, however, use a slightly different word: *oikouros*, from *oikos* ("house") and *ouros* ("keeper" or "guard").[1] This is where we get the rendering "keepers at home"—suggesting one who cares for the home, taking care of household affairs.

Some scholars favor the first as the more accurate reading, while others think it should be the latter. Thankfully, for those of us who are not Greek scholars, it doesn't matter a whole lot. In fact, both words shed helpful light on our mission and calling.

In either case, the general sense of the word is that of a woman who's devoted to her home, who has a heart for it. She's actively engaged and involved in its life on a high-priority basis.

Today it's common for homes to be little more than physical structures where people park their bodies at night, take their showers in the morning, and then disperse in a hundred different directions as they start their day. The clock ticks on the mantelpiece, the thermostat cycles off and on to regulate the temperature, the microwave dings as residents run in to grab a snack and then run out again, but there's little shared life.

And that's the *best*-case scenario. At *worst*, our homes are in utter disarray, characterized by active hostility and oblivious neglect. They may be decorated to the nines and obsessively up-to-date with seasonal front-door hangings, yet the relationships within the walls are seriously fractured—or at least emotionally distant and dishonest.

And this—or something like it—is what far too many women today have grown up with. It is their concept of "home."

Then here comes Titus 2 into this messy reality, reminding us that home is not an add-on to our "spiritual" life. It is part and parcel of our discipleship and our calling as children of God.

We can know the Bible backward and forward. We can have the whole neon rainbow of highlighter colors at our side, ready for study. But if we are not practicing *self-control* at home, if our children or husbands (or roommates or guests) wouldn't describe us as *loving* and *kind*, then something is off.

We can't separate our home life from our Christian life without missing something that is critical to our fellowship with God and our usefulness to His mission in the world. When we minimize the role of wife and mother or the importance of establishing and maintaining Christ-centered homes that put the gospel on display—or even when our main goal is just to keep everybody in line and on schedule—we shortchange the enormous kingdom impact our life at home is supposed to have.

Remember Paul's reference in Titus 1 to false teachers who were "upsetting whole families"? He didn't elaborate about what these people were saying, but he did indicate they were doing it for "shameful gain" (v. 11). That probably means their teaching was quite popular. It was selling well. So it's possible to imagine, from what we *are* told, that some of what these individuals were peddling was subverting God's design for families.

We see the same thing happening today. A young woman whose primary ambition is to be a godly wife and mother—as opposed to, say, a physical therapist or an architect—is treated as if she doesn't have a brain in her head or any ambition in her soul.

Several years ago, the announcement that a leading evangelical seminary planned to offer an undergraduate degree in humanities with a concentration in homemaking caused no small stir. One pastor, responding on his blog, characterized the degree program as "frivolous and foolish." He wrote, "A seminary degree in cookie-baking is about as useful as an M.Div. [master of divinity degree] in automotive repair."[2]

In light of such attitudes and assumptions, even among Christians, what are we to make of the fact that Scripture includes "working at home" in the core curriculum for the training of young women? A look back at the history of work and home can shed some light on the subject.

Ancient Realities and Modern Eyes

For longer than you or I have been alive, there has generally been a clear-cut division between what happens at work and what happens at home. Most people who "work" get up, leave their house, and go to another location (the public sphere) where they do the tasks they are paid to do before they return to their home (the private sphere), spend their paycheck, and start the process all over again.

But this now-familiar model is relatively recent. Prior to the Industrial Revolution, which spanned the eighteenth and nineteenth centuries, there was no such separation of work and home. The *home* was the economic engine of society, a place of productivity. Families— men, women, and children—all pitched in to produce goods that made it possible for their needs to be met and enabled them to care for others in need. Both the home itself and the work that took place in and around it were considered essential and highly valued.

By the twentieth century, however, all of that had changed. Rather than being a place of productivity—all hands on deck—the home had become a place of consumption. Today we decorate our homes to express our unique personality and style. We showcase them on Pinterest and Instagram so they can be admired by others. But for the most part, our "work" and our homes tend to run on separate tracks. And in general the public sphere—the marketplace where one is paid for one's labors—has become the more highly valued realm. The private sphere—homes that are outposts for nurturing loving marriages, discipling and training children, caring for disabled or elderly family members, and extending hospitality and care to friends and neighbors—has been devalued.

In the eyes of the world, as well as in their own eyes, women often derive their sense of identity and status from productive work done outside of the home, work for which they are financially compensated. Less status is conferred on daily labor that takes place in the home and is not rewarded monetarily. This division between the private and public sphere has given rise to heated debates (think "Mommy Wars") about the place of women and the meaning of home.

Far from demeaning women, Paul welcomed the participation and partnership of women in the ministry of the gospel.

However, when Paul exhorted older women to train young women to be "working/keepers at home," he was living in an entirely different setting than this post-Industrial-Revolution world of ours. It is important that we understand this in order to avoid interpreting passages such as Proverbs 31 and Titus 2 only through the lens of our modern cultural context.[3]

To our twenty-first century ears, it could seem that by urging women to be workers at home, Paul was diminishing their worth—implying that they were less important than men because, after all, unpaid "home work" is not as important as work done in the marketplace (the public sphere). We could conclude that Paul was discouraging women from contributing to their church, community, or culture. But to do that is to misunderstand the intent of this injunction.

Far from demeaning women, Paul was actually progressive for his time and culture. He called Christian women to be intentional about employing their heads, hearts, and hands for the sake of the gospel. The apostle worked with Priscilla and her husband in their tent-making business, remember, and his ministry in Philippi was supported by the business successes of Lydia. He welcomed the participation and partnership of these and other women in the ministry of the gospel (see Romans 16:1–16) and he never disparaged their work or their contributions. Rather, he encouraged them to utilize their skills and maximize their assets for the advance of the kingdom of God.

As I have meditated on and grappled with Titus 2 in the light of the whole of Scripture, I've come to believe that when Paul instructs women to be "keepers/working at home," there are some things he does *not* mean:

- He is not mandating that women are *only* to work at home or that the home is to be their only sphere of influence or investment. He is not saying that their domestic activities are to be their sole focus or that their home requires 24/7 attention at all times.
- He is not saying that women are singlehandedly responsible to do all the work that needs to be done in the home or that it is inappropriate for children, husbands, and others to help.
- He is not prohibiting women from performing tasks outside the home or from being compensated financially for such work.
- He is not implying that women have no place in the public arena or that they should not contribute to their church, community, or culture.

So what *does* Paul mean to say in this passage, and what do his words imply for Christian women?

For starters, the phrase *"working at home"* makes clear that women are to *work*. They are to be gainfully occupied. They are not to be like the young widows in Ephesus that Paul referred to in his letter to Timothy: "idlers, going about from house to house, and ... also gossips and busybodies" (1 Tim. 5:13). Rather, they are to live honorably and to faithfully carry out whatever work God has given them to do.

As we have seen, the home in Paul's day (and in most eras prior to our own) was a place of employment and the small business unit of the local economy. And within this system, it was important for women to be productive and not idle. Although our twenty-first-century homes are not the center of productivity they once were, it should still be true of every woman who fears the Lord that

> She looks well to the ways of her household
> and does not eat the bread of idleness. (Prov. 31:27)

The alternate rendering, *"keepers at home,"* highlights the importance of preserving and prioritizing our homes. As we have seen, that doesn't necessarily mean it's the only or number one priority at all times. But he is saying to women, "Don't drop the ball!"

The apostle's instruction affirms that the work we do at home matters—not just to ourselves and our families, but to the wider community and to the cause of the gospel. Paul is not calling us just to feather our own nests and make ourselves comfy. As my friend Carolyn McCulley reminds us, our work at home is "a co-labor of love with our Creator *for the benefit of others*."[4]

Even if our culture does not validate the significance of that work, God values it. And even though we may not be rewarded tangibly for it, God will reward our labors. The work we do in our homes has eternal value. So Paul is being strategic for the gospel when he says to women, "Don't fumble what matters in eternity."

This passage also implies that "young women"—that is, women in the child-bearing, child-rearing season of life—have a distinct responsibility to prioritize their homes and children. This is not to say that home and children do not matter in other seasons or that childless or unmarried women do not need to be concerned about their homes. But no woman (or man) has unlimited bandwidth; we all have to make choices. And younger women with children need to be particularly careful that other activities—even good ones—don't cause them to neglect their children and homes.

It seems to be the norm rather than the exception today for women to be chronically overwhelmed from overcrowded, margin-less schedules. Now, being busy isn't necessarily a bad thing—Jesus Himself worked hard and had some filled-to-the brim days. But in my personal experience, much of the stress and strain are the result of attempting to take on activities and responsibilities that compete with my core commitments and my priorities for that season (or that moment). Periodically we need to push the pause button and ask ourselves if some of those activities (jobs, hobbies, even ministry involvements) would be better postponed for another time when we can undertake them without violating other God-given responsibilities.

As the Scripture reminds us, "For everything there is a season, and a time for every matter under heaven" (Eccl. 3:1).

A Matter of Priority

So, does having a heart for home mean every woman needs to grind her own wheat and bake her own bread? Line her cellar with canned fruit and vegetables from her (organic) garden? Knit a quilt for her husband's easy chair? Put wall art decals on the walls of her children's bedrooms?

I've heard women mock and exaggerate such stereotypical "homemaking" activities as a way of dismissing—and thereby *missing*—the whole point.

What matters—particularly for married women and moms—is not what a woman's home looks like or what she does there, but whether she is giving it the appropriate *priority*. Is she fulfilling her God-given calling in her home and in the lives of her husband and children? Is she giving them more than just the leftovers of her time and attention? Is she investing her heart and best efforts in these priceless lives? Is she being diligent, productive, and intentional in the care and oversight of her home and in meeting her family's needs?

There is no one-size-fits-all, cookie-cutter approach to how this works. Having a heart for home will look different for different women, depending on the configuration and particular circumstances of their family and what best serves their needs at any given time.

I have friends and acquaintances who have chosen to be full-time "workers at home," at least while they are rearing children. This choice often requires significant sacrifice, but those who are willing and able to make it stand to gain many potential benefits and blessings.

Recently I had a spellbinding conversation with "Anna"—a bright, lovely twenty-two-year-old woman who reflected on her upbringing. Her mother, a gym teacher and basketball coach, returned home when God blessed her and her husband with children. "We didn't have cable TV and didn't go out to eat a lot," this daughter told me, "but we didn't suffer. I believe it was better for us this way." She shared how her mom had been involved in various types of activities, relationships, and ministries in the neighborhood and at church.

Now that the children are grown, Anna's mother considered going back to work outside the home. But as she prayed about this option, she realized it would limit her flexibility and availability. Now she is free to help her aging parents with unexpected medical needs that are beginning to arise. She leads Bible studies, helps neighbors with gardening, and is on call for blessing those around her in many practical ways.

I don't know this mom, but I see her reflection in her daughter—a deeply caring young woman who loves and serves the Lord and others, and hopes to follow in her mom's steps. And I see great value in Anna's mother's decision to dedicate her primary attention and effort to being a "keeper/worker at home." Such a choice should be supported and affirmed. Many women like her, while forgoing paid employment, engage in work that is nevertheless of great eternal value for the Kingdom—work such as caring for children, ministering to the poor, sick, and needy, extending hospitality, and volunteering in schools and at church.

Having said that, I could also introduce you to a number of other women whose hearts are no less at home, but who have chosen—for a variety of reasons—to work outside the home. Some hold down regular nine-to-five jobs. Others have found different ways to contribute to their family's financial well-being. I'm thinking of

- moms who run a small cleaning business in which they can involve their kids
- women who work from their home to give piano lessons, alter clothes, provide accounting services, or offer daycare
- a single mom who works tirelessly to support herself and her teen kids, but whose business allows her to set her own schedule so she can be with her kids as much as possible (From the time her husband left her, she has lived in an apartment in the home of close family members, providing an extra layer of "family" for her children.)
- a colleague whose husband was diagnosed with severe early-onset dementia while still in his forties and who juggles his care with freelance contract work to meet their financial needs
- women who have worked hard to provide for their family during their husbands' incarcerations while courageously striving to shepherd their kids' hearts in the absence of a dad in the home
- women who work alongside their husbands in family businesses, arranging their schedules to be able to tend to the needs of children, grandchildren, and elderly parents
- two nurses who work two or three shifts per week and swap childcare with each other

Is life a juggling act for these women? Absolutely. Do they sometimes lose their balance and feel their priorities are out of whack? No doubt. But each one has a heart for home. And each one is asking the Lord for wisdom to make the choices that would best honor Him in their current circumstances.

I realize there are many women who feel they don't have an option about whether to work outside their home or how to arrange that work. We live in a broken world, so the picture is not always ideal and the choices are not always easy. We are not called to determine or legislate specific life/family/work choices for others. But we cannot escape the fact that we are called to have a heart for our homes—to recognize the priceless value and the strategic importance of the eternal investments that are being made there.

> *We will diminish the impact of our ministry as believers if we allow home to become an afterthought.*

Again, how this all plays out may change according to the different phases and changes of a woman's life. There may be seasons when a woman can have extensive pursuits outside her home without neglecting the priority of her home. Being a "keeper at home" looks different for me today than it did during my decades as a single woman. It will look different for a mom with preschoolers than it does for an empty nester or an older widow. Our responsibilities may change, our control over our time and schedule may be greater or less than what we've had in other seasons.

But no matter what our circumstances or season of life, home still matters for us women. And we will diminish the impact of our ministry as believers if we allow home to become an afterthought or resist God's call to be workers/keepers at home.

Resisting the Call of Home

I don't believe it's any coincidence that the adulterous woman in Proverbs 7 is described as "wayward; her feet do not stay at home" (v. 11). By neglecting the God-given priority of her marriage and home, she becomes more vulnerable to temptation and to dishonoring the Lord.

That was the case with a friend whose disdain for her home nearly cost her a marriage. In an email exchange, "Ellen" shared with me that her views on "homemaking" had been skewed from the time she was a child:

> The very mention of the word "domesticity" used to practically make me shiver. It spelled out a life of boredom, drudgery, thanklessness, and even slavery. It certainly wasn't anything I ever envisioned myself doing, much less desiring.
>
> Even though my mother and both grandmothers were "at home" mothers, I never witnessed the joy and freedom this calling can be for a woman. What I recall seeing was service done out of duty, not delighting in serving. My mother was a horrible housekeeper—cleaning only when the dirt was unbearable, washing the dirty dishes only when they outnumbered the clean ones, and doing the laundry only when we ran out of clean clothes. . . .
>
> When "Joe" and I married, I still had all of this damaged thinking inside me. . . . I didn't enjoy serving him or caring for our home. I do remember trying, but it was only out of a sense of duty, rather than with a heart that delighted to serve the Lord and bless my husband.

When her daughter was around seven, Ellen was asked if she'd be interested in helping out part time at a local ministry. Eager to escape the frustration she experienced at home and to find another outlet for her energies, she quickly accepted the opportunity. This was going to be great.

"I instantly fell in love with my job," she wrote. "I only worked while my daughter was in school, so the hours were perfect. But there were times when I actually resented having to stop work to go pick her up or having to stay home with her when she was sick."

As time went by and her daughter grew into young adulthood, "the ministry became my life," she wrote. "I stayed longer and longer hours, even came in on my days off. I gave no real thought to spending time with my husband, to helping out with meal preparation or laundry. He did all of that himself. And I thought I was doing exactly what I needed to be doing . . . what I *loved* doing."

Do you sense the seduction here? Have you felt it yourself? Can you see the justifications that led Ellen to overlook the needs of her husband and child, to ignore the warning signs that these relationships were deteriorating, while focusing the bulk of her attention onto other tasks and relationships she enjoyed more—and wrapping it all in the guise of Christian service?

The day would come when my friend's mild-mannered, go-with-the-flow husband would say he'd had enough. She wrote:

> Joe got tired of being used, abused, and neglected,
> and found someone who—at the time anyway—
> seemed to enjoy pleasing him and wanted to be with
> him, and he liked it.

And just like that, Joe was gone—into the arms of another woman. Of course, Ellen was devastated. She had thought she was doing what God wanted. And in the eyes of most outsiders, she was the "innocent party" in this broken marriage. But over the next several months, her eyes began to be opened to ways she had torn down her home, rather than building it up (Prov. 14:1). Without excusing her husband's sinful choices, she began to accept responsibility for how she had devalued and neglected her husband, daughter, and home.

Through a miraculous work of the Spirit in both their hearts, Joe and Ellen ultimately reconciled. God gave them both the gift of repentance and a whole new set of priorities. They began in their forties to rebuild the relationship and home God had intended for them to establish and enjoy years earlier.

But just think what they missed during all those years when both their hearts were far from home.

Don't miss the message here. The point of Ellen's story isn't the importance of cooking and washing clothes for the family. It's not a warning against ever being involved in work or ministry outside the home. It's just a reminder that in God's economy, something vital is lost when we neglect our calling at home.

At the heart of the cross is the Lord Jesus opening His arms wide and saying, "I want you to come Home with me." When we cultivate homes where others can grow and be nurtured, we put the heart and character of God on display.

Ellen's disdain for the practical aspects of homemaking was symptomatic of deeper heart issues. She needed to come home to God's heart and to let Him give her a vision for how she could serve Him and others through being a keeper at home.

As, in the end, do we all.

A Grand and Glorious Goal

Have you ever thought about the fact that God Himself is a homemaker? Psalm 68:5–6 calls Him the "Father of the fatherless and protector of widows," the One who "settles the solitary in a home." Psalm 113:9 expands on that theme, reminding us that God

> gives the barren woman a home,
>> making her the joyous mother of children.

Jesus, too, is a homemaker. "I go to prepare a place for you," He said to His disciples on the eve of His betrayal. "I will come again and receive you to Myself, that where I am, there you may be also" (John 14:2–3 NASB).

At the heart of the gospel, at the heart of the cross, is the Lord Jesus opening His arms wide and saying, "I want you to come Home with me."

And when we cultivate homes where others can grow and be nurtured, where they feel welcomed, loved, and cared for, we put the heart and character of God on display.

When we bring order from the chaos of scattered toys and pantry shelves, or when we brighten a drab corner of the room with a spray of flowers or a new color accent, we reflect the One who fashioned the world out of a formless void. We point others to the Creator, giving those who live with or visit us a tangible glimpse of His beauty.

When we prepare tasty, nutritious meals for our families, we point them to the One who feeds those who are hungry and satisfies weary and thirsty souls. We stimulate their appetite not only for their favorite dishes and desserts, but also for the One who provides all things for them to enjoy.

When we make sure that children's closets and dressers contain clothing that fits them well and accommodates their needs, we cast a vision of God's faithfulness—how He not only meets our physical needs, but also clothes us in His righteousness.

This connection may not be immediately obvious to our families. We might not be consciously aware of it either. But what God can do in the hearts of our husbands and children and even housemates, working through the orderly, graceful, creative, muscular labors of our homemaking, is far more significant than what appears on the surface.

The welcoming atmosphere we provide for our family and friends, the errands we run, the outings we plan, the care we provide in times of illness, and the efforts we take to promote wellness—each of these daily actions and a thousand others, reveals in miniature an aspect of God's nature. The often tedious and mundane tasks of homemaking become acts of worship, our ordinary movements works of art.

This is the goal of all our "working" and "keeping" at home—the previews of heaven we're able to provide to our husbands, our children, our neighbors and roommates and guests. With every act of planning and nurturing, we demonstrate realities that are supreme and ultimate. We create a taste for things above. Just as Jesus prefaced His promise of a heavenly home by advertising it as a way for our "hearts" not to "be troubled" (John 14:1), so our efforts in creating a pleasant home environment can bring peace to those who live or visit there, even as they anticipate their eternal home in heaven.

My friend Jani Ortlund captures this vision:

> Our homes, imperfect as they are, should be a
> reflection of our eternal home, where troubled souls
> find peace, weary hearts find rest, hungry bodies find
> refreshment, lonely pilgrims find communion, and
> wounded spirits find compassion.[5]

It's no insignificant calling, this ministry of homemaking.

And no, I'm not trying to glamorize the job of scrubbing tile grout with a toothbrush or wresting a twelve-pound roast from its bloody packaging or trying to select one of the half-dozen varieties of Drano in the plumbing aisle. I'm not sure *anything* could glamorize tasks like that! In my experience, just about any job, no matter how impressive its title, requires a measure of grunt work, and housework is no exception. Nevertheless, the tasks involved in being a "keeper at home" (grunt work included!) provide important opportunities to invite heaven's realities into the lives of those you care about most.

The "excellent wife" described in Proverbs 31 is perhaps the best known biblical example of a woman creating such a taste of heaven in her home. And she's pretty impressive—rising before dawn to provide food for her household, equipping her husband and children with what they need, modeling diligence and good planning, preparing her family for the inevitabilities of winter. In summary, "she looks well to the ways of her household and does not eat the bread of idleness" (v. 27).

This woman is servant-hearted and conscientiously cares for the practical needs of her family and home. It doesn't hurt—it *helps*—that she is also financially savvy and has a good business head on her shoulders. And when all is said and done, her life shines a spotlight on the God she fears and loves.

My own mother embodied this ideal in many ways. She and my dad were not only new parents when I arrived as their first child (nine months and four days after their wedding!); they were also relatively new believers. They had a lot of learning to do. But the Lord gave them wisdom and grace as they sought Him.

There would be seven of us children altogether—the first six born within their first five years of marriage. So the task of planning and managing and corralling the hubbub of life and ministry in the DeMoss house was not for the fainthearted. And yet my mother oversaw all this and more with remarkable grace. She served her family and her Savior through her devotion to our home. And countless people found Jesus in that home, having been extended the gracious hospitality and gospel witness my parents offered.

My mother worked hard to create an atmosphere in our home that reflected God's beauty, His order, and His merciful, welcoming heart. In so doing, she gave our hearts a taste for heaven.

That's what can happen when women devote themselves to their marriages and families and homes. That's the kind of impact we can generate when our lives reflect the importance and value of home.

Bring It Home

"But my mother didn't teach me these things," I've heard young women lament. "I don't know how to do a lot of that stuff." Yes, and much to our bewildered surprise, no training manual arrives in the mail as a twenty-first birthday present, suddenly granting us the domestic knowledge that women of this age group are somehow supposed to possess.

That's precisely why Paul wisely delegated this "working at home" instruction to older women with years of home experience. Such mentors can come alongside younger women and offer practical lessons for running a household and, more important, transforming a house into a haven of peace, contentment, and joy, and a base of operations for spiritual growth and fruitfulness.

In the hands of such a mentor, a young wife may learn that by working to keep her house orderly, she introduces an ease into the atmosphere of her home that blesses her and others who live there.

Through the gentle input of a veteran mom, a young mother who finds herself slipping downward from overwhelmed to discouraged to depressed to nearly nonfunctional can rebuild her shaky confidence. She discovers how to serve family without being swallowed up by chaos and unrealistic expectations.

Under the tutelage of an encouraging mentor, a college girl can begin seeing her apartment or dorm room as a place of potential beauty and Christian hospitality rather than simply a crash site or a glorified laundry hamper.

Surely this is what Paul was imagining when he instructed older women to take a personal interest in their younger sisters and daughters in the faith. He wanted to see the transfer of both life skills and spiritual perspective across the generations. He wanted to open new gateways of opportunity where the gospel could enter in and take hold. He wanted to see the church thrive and bear witness to the strength and unity that exist when God's people are running together in the challenging race of life. And in few (if any) places does this Titus 2 dynamic produce a more lasting impact than when applied to homes and family relationships.

Having been single for so many years, I want to add that within the context of the family of God, the borders of "home" include more (though not less) than biological family members. This means any and all of us can share in the responsibilities and rewards of making and keeping a home.

More times than I can count, I have experienced the joy of being invited into others' homes and finding there the gifts of friendship, grace, peace, encouragement, nourishment for my body and soul, and loads of laughter. I have found sweet consolation and prayer in the living room of a friend when I was disheartened or carrying a burden too great to bear alone. I have received wise counsel from godly mentors. I have found family.

I have also had the great joy of opening my heart and home to others—for most of my life, as a single woman:

- making pumpkin pies or decorating gingerbread houses in my kitchen with children whose parents were out on a date
- ordering pizza for a spontaneous gathering of a few close families
- sitting on a sofa listening to a woman pour out her heart about a secret sin she'd never shared with anyone else
- weeping and kneeling together with a couple whose marriage had been ravaged by infidelity
- hosting weekly Bible studies with coffee and dessert
- hosting wedding receptions in the backyard

- having a houseful (and I mean *full*) to ring in the New Year with fellowship, sharing, praise, and prayer
- opening my home for a season to a newlywed couple or a missionary family on furlough or an older couple whose A/C had gone out in the middle of July

Just thinking about what has amounted to hundreds of such occasions over the years brings a smile to my face.

Has it sometimes meant extra stress, weariness, and expense?

For sure.

Does all the activity and interaction sometimes feel overwhelming for this introvert?

No question.

Have I at times resented the messes made by others and the wear and tear on my "stuff"?

Truth be told, yes.

But has it been worth it?

A thousand times, yes!

This is where deep, rich friendships have been forged. This is where lives—both mine and my guests'—have been molded. This is where I have acquired "adopted" parents, siblings, children, and grandchildren. This is where we have grown, shared, wept, repented, given and received grace, and rejoiced as we celebrated Christ together.

At home.

Something sanctifying occurs when we're fulfilling the tasks God has given us for whatever season of life we're living. Our minds are protected from deception, our hearts from distraction, and our feet from wandering when we are focusing on the places and roles He has assigned to us.

When disorganized chaos is the norm, when too many irons are in too many fires, when we're constantly running on fumes, chronically frustrated and short-tempered, something's out of whack with our priorities. We've all been there. But we can't continue that way indefinitely and expect to stay sane and spiritually strong.

The apostle Paul could've told us that years ago.

In fact, he *did* tell us that!

So *older woman*, it's time to put to good use all that hard-earned wisdom and experience you've gained by walking through those challenging seasons. Take a younger woman by the hand; gently help her sort through the many competing demands she faces; help her see the value of cultivating a heart for home. And when she feels overwhelmed or like a failure, help her fix her eyes on Christ and encourage her to listen for His voice through the din. Be willing to roll up your sleeves and provide hands-on coaching for the practical skills she needs to build a home that honors the Lord. Remind her that her endless, tiresome labors in her home really do matter. And give her a vision for how what she is doing can give others a taste of heaven.

> *Rather than looking wistfully at how your life may look different in a different season, embrace your current season and calling as a gift from God.*

And *younger woman*, thank God for that woman who has been further down the road than you have. Let God use her to encourage and support and train you—and learn well, because sooner than you think, it'll be your turn to take a younger woman under your wing and help her cultivate a heart for home. In the meantime, rather than looking wistfully at how your life may look different in a different season, embrace your current season and calling as a gift from God.

That's how we *all* come home to what matters.

Making It Personal

Older women

1. Being a keeper/worker at home looks different in different seasons of life. What does it look like for you in this season? What was it like for you in earlier years?

2. What insights and practical skills have you learned in managing your home that you could share with a younger woman to encourage her in making her home a place of fruitful labor and ministry?

3. Ask the Lord to put a younger woman on your heart who needs and desires encouragement, training, or practical help on the home front. Ask Him to make you alert and responsive to opportunities to serve in this way.

Younger women

1. What are some ways the gospel and the heart of Christ could be put on display through your heart for home?

2. Godly homemaking isn't about glamorizing mundane tasks, but rather taking advantage of every opportunity to "invite heaven's realities" into the lives of your loved ones. What do you see in Proverbs 31:10–31 that might help you carry out your own daily tasks to the glory of God?

3. In what area could you use some encouragement, training, or practical help from an older woman to be a more effective keeper/worker at home? Ask the Lord to direct you to an older woman who is willing and able to invest in this way.

Teach what accords with sound doctrine.

Older men are to be sober-minded, dignified, self-controlled,
sound in faith, in love, and in steadfastness.

Older women likewise are to be reverent in behavior,
not slanderers or slaves to much wine.

They are to teach what is good,
and so train the young women
to love their husbands and children,
to be self-controlled,
pure,
working at home,
kind,
and submissive to their own husbands,
that the word of God may not be reviled.

. . . so that in everything they may adorn
the doctrine of God our Savior.

TITUS 2:1–5, 10

CHAPTER 11

Need Help Lovin' That Man

Training Our Hearts for Relationship

Love through me, Love of God,
There is no love in me;
O Fire of love, light Thou the love
That burns perpetually.
AMY CARMICHAEL

WHAT IN THE WORLD HAVE I DONE?

Robert and I had been married for less than a month when that thought flooded forcefully into my mind. A series of circumstances and mishaps shortly following our wedding had taken their toll. I'll spare you a lot of the details. But to give you an idea . . . a water disaster in our home required replacing the wood floors on the first story and left us living and working virtually knee to knee in a tiny study for three weeks. (Did I mention I caused the flood?) That drama was compounded by misfiring relationally with some family members. And then there was the matter of serious sleep deprivation. (Let's just say sharing a bed after all those years of sleeping alone was a major adjustment for me.)

Anyway, in a panic-inducing moment, this man sleeping next to me in the bed—this amazing man who adored me and whom I adored—suddenly seemed like a total stranger. I found myself struggling to rein in my rogue emotions and wondering how we would ever build a loving, intimate marriage.

When I first led women through a study of Titus 2 many years ago, I was a single woman. Such thoughts and feelings—which I'm pretty sure most women who have ever been married have experienced at some point—were as yet unfamiliar to me.

Today, as I write this chapter, Robert and I have been married for just about ten months. We weathered that rough patch early on (thanks in large measure to my tender, humble, grace-filled husband) and came out the better for it. So I find myself looking at the subject of marriage with fresh eyes. For sure, I'm eager to learn more about what it means to love my husband well. (Robert says he loves living with a woman who is writing a chapter on how to love one's husband!)

And yes, loving husbands is right at the top of the list of what Titus 2 instructs older women to teach young women (v. 4). This is a vital way that married women and mothers live out their commitment to sound doctrine. This is how they adorn the gospel.

You and I may have vast knowledge of the Bible. We may have great gifts in teaching, leading, organizing, or serving. We may be star performers in our workplace and active in all kinds of church work and social concerns. But none of those things is worth much if we fail to love those in our own homes.

Radiant brides on their way to the altar can't imagine that the love they feel at that moment could ever fizzle out. So how is it that so many women who once gazed at their Prince Charming with stars in their eyes now look at him with eyes of hurt, hardness, and even hatred? What happens? Well, *life* happens. Problems and pressures and disappointments happen. Sin happens. No marriage is exempt.

And that's why young women need to be trained to "love their husbands."

But shouldn't love be a natural response? It should. But it isn't always—for a number of reasons. Sin kills love in marriages. Selfishness and pride kill love. And persisting in love beyond those other natural but deadly tendencies does *not* come naturally. By God's grace, however, and with the help and wisdom of spiritual mothers in the faith, it *can* be learned.

And keep in mind that this specific kind of training isn't just for married women. As one who was single for many years, I can testify to its value for *single women*. What a gift for those who contemplate future marriage to glean insight from women who've steered successfully through the marital rapids. And even those who never marry or don't expect to can learn how to develop appropriate relationships with men and how to bless and support the marriages of their friends and family.

Divorcees also need this kind of loving friendship as they seek to recover from the pain of dashed dreams and to be restored to a place of health and wholeness. Then, having been recipients of God's grace, they can become instruments of grace in others' lives. The presence of divorce in a woman's story need not disqualify her from training other women in loving their husbands. In fact, what the Lord has taught her as she hiked some of life's most treacherous paths can be invaluable in the lives of younger women who want a marriage that goes the distance and reflects the covenant-keeping love of Christ.

So though I speak directly in this chapter to married women, I hope those who don't have husbands will stay with me too. Because love is important to all of us—and all of us can use training in the dynamics of healing, encouraging, redemptive love.

Love That Feels Like Love

Markers on the graves of women from the New Testament era were occasionally known to bear the simple inscription *philandros* (husband lover) or *philoteknos* (child lover)—the same words Paul uses in Titus 2:4. The chief characteristic that marked these women's lives became the primary way of remembering them in death.[1]

They loved their husbands.

They loved their children.

And whether we're talking about then or now, it takes more than the heart palpitations of young love to enable a wife to love her husband for a lifetime. That kind of love requires intentional, woman-to-woman discipleship and mentoring.

"Train" them, Paul said, "to love."

This word—*philandros*—doesn't carry with it the physical, romantic, sexual aspect of love that is often so front and center in today's marital expectations. Romantic love is certainly an important aspect of the marriage bond, and the Bible does speak quite clearly, even quite graphically in spots (Song of Solomon, most notably), about the joys of sexual union. But that's not the emphasis Paul intended when he delivered his Titus 2 directive on love and marriage. His language instead conveys the idea of being a friend to our husbands, being fond of them, acting affectionately toward them, treating them with our utmost devotion.

Men long for respect and affection from their wives at least as much as they crave sexual expressions of love.

Enjoying them.

Finding pleasure in their company.

Liking them.

Loving them.

In many ways, this kind of love requires more effort and energy than other kinds of love. And it's important for wives to learn to love their husbands this way because of how men's hearts are fashioned by God. Here's something I've heard for years and am now learning first-hand to be true: Men long for respect and affection from their wives at least as much as they crave sexual expressions of love.

Wanting to test this premise, I once sent out an email to a few dozen male friends and coworkers, asking for their thoughts about how wives could bless and encourage their husbands. Some of these guys I knew to be soft-spoken individuals, men of few words. But not this time. This particular subject was one that drew each of them out.

Here are some of the common themes I heard from these men:

- They wanted their wives to express encouragement and belief in them and to compliment them for doing a good job, not just to consider it something that good husbands are supposed to do anyway.
- They wanted to be listened to long enough to get their full opinions out there before being critiqued.
- They wanted to be asked what they thought and to be noticed and thanked.
- When they messed something up or missed a relational cue, they wanted to know they would be met with grace instead of a lecture.

This last item seemed to be especially important to the men I surveyed. It wasn't that they wished to avoid responsibility for their actions or inactions. But a wife's forgiveness and mercy acted like rocket fuel, driving them to do differently the next time. Negative approaches like whining, rejecting, and pushing away just made it that much harder for husbands to keep trying to be the man they needed to be. The man they *wanted* to be.

The results of this informal poll reminded me that men flourish in an atmosphere of affirmation, encouragement, and respect. That's what motivates them to bless and serve their families. That's what feels like love to them.

Love for a Purpose

I've met many wives who are extremely responsible women. They serve their husbands faithfully and dutifully. But I wonder sometimes if these women really *like* the men they married. They don't seem to enjoy them. Their attitudes and their words don't indicate affection or fondness for them.

And I wonder what the church is missing by having so many marriages where this is the case. Because the most important objective behind befriending and thinking highly of one's husband is not simply to improve his self-esteem or free him from the fear of another rebuke. Rather, it's to move the marriage in the direction of its grander purpose. For loving our husbands well does more to honor Christ and make the gospel attractive than all our other words and actions combined, without that love.

Charles Spurgeon, the great British preacher of the nineteenth century, enjoyed a legendary love relationship with his wife, Susannah, or Susie, as he fondly called her. Both had major health issues—Charles suffering from chronic gout and seasons of deep depression, and Susannah unable to leave the house for fifteen years due to physical illness. Yet their love grew and remained strong even through intense trials and the challenges of a very public ministry. Their tender expressions of love and dedication, written to and about each other, are a joy to read. Spurgeon once wrote to Susie, for example:

> My Own Dear one—None know how grateful I am to
> God for you. In all I have ever done for Him, you have
> a large share. For in making me so happy you have

236

fitted me for service. . . . I have served the Lord far more, and never less, for your sweet companionship. The Lord God Almighty bless you now and forever![2]

Susannah, in turn, wrote of her deep love for her husband when she compiled his diary and letters (published as *C. H. Spurgeon's Autobiography* after his death):

> I deemed it my joy and privilege to be ever at his side, accompanying him on many of his preaching journeys, nursing him in his occasional illnesses,—his delighted companion during his holiday trips, always watching over and tending him with the enthusiasm and sympathy which my great love for him inspired.[3]

Such beautiful, affectionate marriages—at least in real life—don't just *happen*. They grow as two people purpose, as Charles and Susannah Spurgeon did, to live for each other and to dedicate themselves together to a cause greater than themselves.

The greatest blessings of marriage, in other words, come as a by-product of seeking something else.

A Goal for Marriage

I've often found myself in a store searching in vain for a wedding or anniversary card that expresses what I really want to say. At times, I've been tempted to start a whole new line of cards for such occasions. It's not that the sentiments expressed are *wrong*. It's more a matter of what they leave out.

Almost invariably, you see, the focus seems to be on happiness, romance, and blessings for the couple. But when's the last time you saw a wedding or anniversary card that said anything about a mission or purpose in marriage bigger than the couple themselves?

A lifetime of happiness and smiles and holding hands and romantic moments is far too small a goal. Marriage is designed to display to the world in Technicolor the covenant-keeping character and faithfulness of God.

Now, don't get me wrong. I want to experience happiness, romance, and blessings in my marriage, and I desire the same for all my married friends. But a lifetime of happiness and smiles and holding hands and romantic moments is far too small a goal. What I most want for my married friends—and for Robert and me—is a life defined by God's vastly superior blessings and grand redemptive purposes.

Marriage, at its heart, is a sacred covenant between a man and a woman, designed to display to the world in Technicolor the covenant-keeping character and faithfulness of God Himself. Just as the Bible is the story of the heavenly Bridegroom faithfully seeking out and staying true to His chosen Bride, human marriage is a story intended to draw people toward the gospel, showing them the love of God through two imperfect individuals whose lives become one in Him and who are devoted to one another for better or for worse . . . for life.

What Your Marriage Can Be

Does that sound like too lofty a goal—if not for marriage in general, at least for your marriage in particular? As you look at the two people whose faces appear in your wedding photos—especially the way you look today, having dealt with your share of differences and difficulties—you may calculate your chances of approaching this marriage ideal as somewhere between slim and none.

And yet that's not the way Bible math operates—because things are different when God is part of the equation.

Regardless of its weaknesses and challenges, your marriage can be a beacon of gospel truth and hope to your children, your grandchildren, your neighbors, your extended family, and to all who know you.

And here's the most surprising part: *this noble outcome does not depend on your husband's getting his act together.*

You might want to pause and read that sentence one more time.

It's hard to believe, I know, but it's true.

As a wife, you have the ability to demonstrate covenant love in your daily interactions with your mate—regardless of what he does or doesn't do to meet your needs.

You can learn to love your husband no matter how he acts, what he says, what he does.

"But that's not fair!" you may respond. "Doesn't he need to do anything? Who could live with such a one-sided relationship?"

Sure, I understand that marriage requires cooperation and effort from both mates. I realize that one partner's failure or indifference leaves an inevitable residue on the other. In fact, we could spend a lot of time addressing the unloving ways some men treat their wives, how they fail in their commitment to their marriage, and how that can affect whole generations coming behind them. If you identify with that storyline, it may feel unfair and insensitive not to address men as well as women in a chapter on loving your spouse.

But it's just us women having this conversation. And the truth is, regardless of what our men *should* do, we cannot *make* them do it. It simply isn't helpful—and can actually be harmful to our own hearts—to focus on what we cannot control.

That doesn't mean there's not a respectful, loving, even direct way of stating our opinions and injecting our perspective into matters of disagreement, disappointment, or disobedience on our husband's part. In fact, we can often help our husbands by speaking the truth in a timely way with carefully chosen words. But helping our mate is not the same as trying to change him. That's God's job.

God is powerful enough to speak to your husband's heart, getting through to him in ways you can't, no matter how logical your arguments or how earnest your appeals.

What's your job, then? From a biblical standpoint, your job is to be the person who uniquely completes your husband. To support him. To encourage him. To be a friend to him. To like him.

To love him.

Loving your husband does not mean brushing sinful behavior under the carpet. In fact, that would be unloving.

To love him even when he's hard to love.

Because the truth is, *no man is always easy to be married to.* (No woman is, either!) Your husband is not all *he* wants to be, much less everything *you* may want him to be.

Ruth Bell Graham, the late wife of Billy Graham, understood this. After experiencing the up-close frailties and failings of her husband, Ruth concluded that "it was my job to love Billy, and God's job to change him." Every wife could say the same about her own marriage.

"But what if there's nothing about him to love?" I can hear someone protesting, and I hear the frustration and pain behind the protest. My prayer is that this chapter will encourage you to believe that even in such a case, God can put true love in your heart, enabling you to love as He loved you.

Let me make clear, however, that loving your husband does not mean brushing sinful behavior under the carpet or just holding everything inside when there are issues you and your husband are unable to resolve. In fact, that would be *unloving*. It is appropriate and at times vital for you to confide in a wise, godly older woman or a pastor or counselor who can give you biblical perspective, provide emotional and spiritual support, and help you determine the best course of action. The purpose is not to find someone to take your side against your husband, but to help you discern how to deal with his actions and evaluate your own heart and responses. And if your husband is breaking the law or you or your children are being physically threatened or harmed—hard as it may be, you should contact local civil authorities and ask for their help. According to Scripture, they are "God's servant[s] for your good" (Rom. 13:4).

Even such difficult cases are not beyond God's grace and redemption. They can become opportunities to learn to love the unlovable, as God has loved us. But the truth is, the majority of marriages don't fall into these categories. For most of us, learning to love our husbands is more a matter of addressing petty, everyday sin and selfishness that can drain the love and intimacy from a relationship. And amazing things can happen when we let God's love flow through us.

Your marriage really can be more than it is today. It can be far stronger and more vibrant than the sentimental poetry and soft pastels found on the stock wedding or anniversary card. It can be a living testimony of God's power and grace. That can happen. It can *still* happen. And your part in building what God desires your union to be is to love your man.

To love—and to help others love that way too.

Older woman, here's your chance to do something transformational with those hard-fought lessons you've learned as a wife of many years, to turn them into something other than longstanding grudges to pull out in case you're ever losing an argument. By passing along your firsthand observations and experience to a younger woman (married, soon to be married, or one day hoping to be married), God can use both your good days and your bad days to help create better days ahead for yourself and for someone you care about.

Younger woman, you should crave this kind of input, objectivity, and time-tested wisdom. You will be a better wife to your husband—and understand him better than you ever thought possible—by making use of another woman's experience. Just think of the roadblocks and hurdles you may be able to get past with the coaching and assistance of someone who has walked this path before you.

Practical Training

I enjoyed a memorable visit over lunch one day with three adult sisters and their mother. A number of times during our meal, one or the other's cellphone would buzz. Friends were calling, work was calling, kids were calling. With each call they'd glance down at the phone, note the name on the display, then turn off the sound without interrupting our conversation.

"You know, there's something Mom's always told us," one of the women said as we shared a laugh over how intrusive our phones can sometimes be. "If it's your husband calling, you always take the call."

Others can wait, but he's always first in line.

Now there's a good piece of practical advice from an older woman, a nugget that's easy to grasp and to begin putting into practice. One that's sure to send a message to any husband about his wife's love and respect for him.

And these are the kinds of pearls of wisdom that can be transferred and received as women sit down together, younger and older, asking questions and offering counsel, intent on training and being trained in the fine art of loving a husband.

Just imagine if women were to have these kinds of conversations rather than ones in which they tore their husbands down and commiserated with each others' marital woes. Think how many conflicts could be defused or avoided altogether and how much room women would find for love in their minds and hearts if gripe sessions were replaced with true support and woman-to-woman wisdom.

Such wisdom has been invaluable to me in my somewhat unusual position of being both an older woman and a fairly new wife. For years, I've been encouraging other women to love their husbands well.

Now I'm learning how to love *my* husband well. And I'm being encouraged in that journey by the example of many women I've watched and learned from over the years.

I'd like to pass on a sampling of practical insights I've gleaned from these women, much of which I'm finding to be applicable in my own marriage. If you're an older woman, there probably isn't anything here you haven't heard before. But these are things it's easy for all of us—even those of us who know better—to neglect as life gets busy.

1. Put your relationship with your husband ahead of your relationship with your children.

It's not coincidental that "loving husbands" precedes "loving children" in Titus 2:4. I've seen women get that reversed and end up with a lifeless marriage or no marriage at all.

Of course, children demand a lot of time, attention, and effort. If you're not careful, tending to them can commandeer the bulk of your focus and energy, allowing walls and distance to grow between you and your husband. So in the midst of those exhausting child-rearing seasons—and even as your children become adults—it's important to be intentional about prioritizing your marriage. That means things like

- initiating conversations with your husband about topics other than the kids
- springing for a sitter or trading child care so you and your man can have focused "you and me" time together. (Trust me, this is important to your husband, even if you don't think it's feasible.)
- letting your husband know you're on his side when the kids challenge his instructions or attempt to divide the two of you. (They probably will!)
- honoring your husband when there's a difference of opinion by talking privately with him and keeping a united front before the children.

- setting aside time to pray together and make sure you're on the same page about family issues.

Keeping your marriage strong and thriving is actually one of the best possible gifts you can give your kids—providing them with a secure, stable environment and a model of what healthy love looks like. And if you and your husband keep your hearts connected in those busy seasons, you'll be far more likely to have a solid, enjoyable relationship with him once the kids are out of the nest.

 *Look for ways to keep your relationship fresh and growing.*

Daily life can be tedious and mundane. But you will do your marriage a big favor if you look for fresh, creative ways to love your husband, to enjoy him, to be his friend and his lover.

Remember the early days of your relationship?

- You were always looking for opportunities to bless or surprise him with simple acts of kindness.
- If he called at the last minute and said, "Can we go out for dinner tonight?" you probably didn't say, "Do we have to? I'm really tired." More likely you said, "I'd love to!" Then you dropped everything and got freshened up in record time.
- If he bought you something, you probably didn't protest, "We can't afford that!" or "I've already got two of those." Chances are you were delighted and thanked him for his thoughtfulness.
- If he threw his coat on a chair when he came in the house, you didn't huff and puff about his needing to grow up and be more responsible with his belongings. You were glad to hang it up for him without saying a word. So why do you make a big deal about it now?

That's not to say these kinds of issues should never be addressed. But rekindling some of the attitudes and practices you had when your relationship was young can help keep your marriage fresh. So can seeking out ways to enjoy being together, creating memories and staying connected. (Even after many years together, you might be surprised at what else there is to learn about each other.)

So in the midst of the routine and the endless tasks on each of your plates, take time to have fun together. To serve others together. To court one another and be romantic. To be spontaneous and also enjoy making plans for a special occasion. To develop new interests and shared experiences. Here are just a few ideas:

- Ask questions about your husband's day—and listen to the answers.
- Read a book together and share your thoughts.
- Drop your to-do list (and your honey-do list) long enough to snuggle up and watch some football or a movie with him.
- Invest in a pretty new nightie or evening outfit—something you know will please him.
- Text him a love note—or even a joke—in the middle of the day.
- Learn a new skill together (golf? a new language? guitar?).
- Stop what you are doing to wave good-bye or greet him at the door.
- Surprise him with tickets to a concert or event you'll both enjoy.

5. Be a student of your husband. Show interest in the things that interest him.

Robert is a lifelong Chicago Cubs fan. Becoming a Cubs fan myself (which first meant learning the basics of baseball!) has proven to be one practical way for me to love my husband. My interest in the "home team" has given us a new common interest.

Showing interest in Robert's DIY home-construction projects is another way I express my love for him. In fact, Robert is building a deck on our home this week, and I'm taking periodic time-outs from working on this book to ooh and aah over the progress, cheer him on, and replenish cold drinks and snacks. This says to him, *We're in this together. I'm thinking of you. I care about the things you enjoy.*

An important heart principle is at play here. Jesus taught that "where your treasure is, there your heart will be also" (Matt. 6:21). If you invest time, effort, and attention in your job or a hobby, your heart will be drawn in that direction. And when you invest "treasure" in your husband, your heart will be drawn to him. But if you choose to invest in someone else—a guy at work or an old boyfriend on Facebook, for instance—you may soon begin to feel things toward him that you've not felt for your husband in a long time.

> *It helps to remember that your husband's strengths and his weaknesses are exactly what you need to become the woman God wants you to be. And vice versa.*

This is how an affair can begin or you and your husband can simply "drift apart"—because you've been investing your energy outside your marriage. But if you make the deliberate choice to focus your time, attention, and interest in your husband, you'll eventually find your love for him growing.

Choose loving actions toward him, and your heart will follow.

4. Remember that you are both sinners.

It may be tempting sometimes to mentally compare your husband to some other man who seems to be further along in his maturity or faith—or to some imagined, "ideal" husband. You convince yourself that your life would be so much easier if you were married to someone like that. But you're not. He's not married to a perfect woman either.

Both of you are flesh-and-blood humans with the capacity for love, hate, support, and betrayal. Both of you make mistakes, sometimes big ones. Both of you need daily doses of grace just to get through the day. And the more you can keep that in mind, the freer you will both be to grow in love for one another. The truth is, even the best marriage involves two sinners perpetually humbling themselves, getting to Christ, and receiving and dispensing grace.

Charles Spurgeon's words can be aptly applied to marriage:

> He who grows in grace remembers that he is but
> dust, and he therefore does not expect his fellow
> Christians to be anything more; he overlooks ten
> thousand of their faults, because he knows his God
> overlooks twenty thousand in his own case. He does
> not expect perfection in the creature, and, therefore,
> he is not disappointed when he does not find it.[4]

Growing in grace as husband and wife involves a lot of acceptance and a lot of "I'm sorry; I was wrong." It means assuming the best of each other and not judging motives, trying to understand, not insisting on perfection. It also means extending mercy and forgiveness when you let each other down or hurt each other in small ways or big ones. (I promise it will happen—then happen again.) But it helps to remember that your husband's strengths *and* his weaknesses are exactly what you need to become the woman God wants you to be. And vice versa.

And once again, maintaining this awareness is not dependent on how well your husband accepts and extends grace to you. It's a matter of relying on God to give grace to both of you as you persevere in learning more and more about love.

When you and I stand before the Lord in eternity, He will not ask us: What were your husband's failures and flaws? Did he love you well?

But in light of Titus 2, He may well ask: How well did you love your husband?

"Root, Root, Root for the Home Team!"

I don't want to leave the impression that I do any of this perfectly. Not by a long shot. In the short time Robert and I have been married, I have learned that my attitudes, words, and behavior have a profound effect on this man's heart. I have the ability to make him feel encouraged and cherished. But I also have the ability—more than any other person in his life—to deflate and discourage his spirit.

I am an editor by trade and by natural bent. That means I have spent most of my adult life noticing and trying to correct mistakes. Robert says I can spot an error on a billboard while speeding by at eighty-five miles per hour. My ability to open a three-hundred-page book and spot the solitary typo is legendary. But while that skill is useful when it comes to proofreading, it's not particularly helpful in relationships, least of all in marriage. If I'm not careful, I am prone to notice and point out the one thing that's wrong (in my view) and much slower to identify the ninety-nine things that are right.

On occasion, Robert has said, "I feel like you're editing me." Ouch. I know that in those moments he feels I'm not pulling for him. What he needs in those moments is an encourager, not an editor. So I've made it my prayer and aim to build Robert up and to be a means of grace in his life.

From what I hear from other women, I know I'm not alone in my "editing" tendencies. And I know that focusing on our husband's faults and failures can be highly toxic in a marriage relationship.

Does that mean you should never point out needs in each other's lives? By no means. We all need honest input from those who know us best and can help us see blind spots we may be oblivious to. But our ability to give humble, helpful critique and have it be well-received is in direct proportion to the effort we make to give the gift of encouragement.

Knowing how important (and neglected) this gift is in a marriage, I have often urged wives to take what I call the "30-Day Husband Encouragement Challenge."[5] The challenge has two parts.

First, *for the next thirty days, don't say anything negative about your husband—to him or to anyone else about him.* That doesn't mean he won't *do* anything negative. It doesn't mean there won't be anything you *could* say. It just means you're just not going to say it. You're going to choose not to think about or focus on those things.

Then comes the second part, the positive one, which is equally important:

Every day for the next thirty days, encourage your husband by expressing something you admire or appreciate about him. Say it to him and say it to someone else about him. Tell your children. Tell your mother. Tell *his* mother. Each day think of something good about your husband and tell him about it, then tell someone else.

Now you may be thinking, *I can't think of thirty things I appreciate about my husband!* Well, then, just think of *one* thing and repeat it every day for thirty days!

In the years that I've been offering this challenge, I've seen marriages change in a way that has been nothing short of amazing. Here's just one of thousands of responses I've received from women who have taken this challenge:

> I was at my wits' end with my husband. We have only been married a little over a year and have had some awful knock-down, drag-out verbal fights. It has been a serious struggle to keep from walking out the door and writing off this marriage.
>
> Begrudgingly, I began my campaign of encouragement toward my husband. I started leaving him notes in his truck, in his wallet, on his computer,

taped to the mirror, but I did it with bitterness, anger, and hate in my heart. Right off the bat, my hard-hearted husband tried squashing my efforts, pouring out anger and frustration with me. I was hurt and about to quit what I'd started, but something made me keep going.

Throughout the day, every time a thought would come to my mind about something we had been fighting about, I began to look for the positive things instead of the negative things and would send him a text or email or leave a note for him.

This has been going on for over a week now. When I come home, the first thing I do is grab him and kiss him rather than just mumbling hello and going and changing my clothes.

Last night my hard-hearted, closed-off, non-communicative husband broke down, opened up, listened instead of barking orders, and sat on the couch with me. He said, "This is the best week I've ever had! To just be here holding my wife in my arms is the best way to end a day!" In just one week, my marriage is on the path to being mended! My husband and I had an absolutely romantic evening together this week that we haven't had since our wedding!

On a scale of one to ten, your relationship with your husband may be at a negative two right now. And this little challenge is probably not going to give your marriage an overhaul overnight. But if you persist for the full thirty days, I believe it will change you. It will give you a different perspective. And in time, as you water the soil of your husband's heart with affirmation, appreciation, and admiration, you may see him change as well. Either way, you can't go wrong.

You and I know women who would give anything just to have a husband to encourage. My mother, widowed at the age of forty, is one of those women. Throughout her married life, she was a wonderful example of what it looks like to love your husband. She was just nineteen when she married my dad (he was thirty-two). And almost from that moment, their lives, hands, and days were filled to the brim—raising a large family, launching a successful business, and being actively involved in many different kinds of ministry. Mother could easily have resented the busyness and the intrusion on their relationship. But she and my dad were in this together. They were friends. They enjoyed each other's company and loved doing life as a team. And the difficult times (devastating business losses, a brain tumor that could have taken her life, a fire that destroyed our home) only drew them closer.

As does every human being, my dad had his share of preferences and habits some women might have allowed to become a source of irritation. But my mother adored him. She admired and affirmed him. She didn't make issues out of things that didn't matter in the big picture. Amazingly, to this day, I don't recall ever hearing my mom say a negative, critical word about my dad.

It's not that she mindlessly agreed with everything he said or did. She is a smart, capable woman with strong views, and my dad solicited and valued her input even when she disagreed with him. But in the course of giving that input, she still showed him honor and respect. And whenever she talked about him to outsiders, she could be counted on to uphold and enhance his reputation.

Just two weeks before my dad died unexpectedly of a heart attack at the age of fifty-three, my mother wrote in a letter to an assistant he had just hired: "After twenty-one years of living with this man, I truly believe I am the most uniquely blessed woman in the world." Her husband knew she felt that way.

I want my husband to know I feel that way about him too.

Building and Rebuilding Love

I'm convinced that a majority of marriages today have settled for far less than what God intends for their relationship. Some women—including those who've been married a long time—have forgotten how to love and respect their husbands. Some never knew how in the first place. Some have become discouraged and just quit trying.

If one of those is you, start by being honest. Don't make excuses, and don't give in to the temptation to deposit all the blame onto your husband. The truth is, even if your husband was wonderful in every respect, you still wouldn't be able to love him the way he needs to be loved apart from God's love flowing through you to him.

Only the grace of God can enable anyone to love another unselfishly over the long haul. We humans just don't have it in us. But the good news is, we *do* have God, and His very essence is love. In fact, as 1 John 4:8 reminds us, "God *is* love." And He is able to infuse His supernatural love into the most love-depleted heart.

A colleague confided in me about a time when her marriage was in crisis:

> I so clearly remember lying in bed next to my
> husband and praying desperately, "Lord, I've tried,
> but I just can't love him, at least not right now. I don't
> even *want* to love him. So you're going to have to do
> it for me and through me." He did. He gave me the
> strength and the resolve to act in love even when I
> didn't feel the least bit loving. And it took a while,
> but I gradually reached the point where I could back
> up those actions with loving intentions and, eventually,
> feelings. In the process, my ability to trust God took
> a huge jump.

That can be true for you as well—I'm sure of it. Even if the love in your marriage has dwindled into grudging obligation or deteriorated into full-scale resentment and contempt, it can be rekindled. You can *learn* to love again—at the cross. On your knees. With older women coming alongside you to encourage and show you how it's done, and with younger women reminding you of a time when your love for your husband was fresh and pure.

In talking with women who are struggling to persevere in loveless marriages, I have often shared this little-known stanza of a hymn written by Fanny Crosby:

> Down in the human heart, crushed by the tempter,
> Feelings lie buried that grace can restore;
> Touched by a loving heart, wakened by kindness,
> Chords that were broken will vibrate once more.[6]

You may have long ago given up hope of ever experiencing genuine love and affection in your marriage. But the Holy Spirit who lives in you can restore and waken feelings that have been crushed by the tempter. And as you persist in grace, love, and kindness, He can quicken feelings that have long been buried—or perhaps never existed—in your spouse's heart.

That's not to say that if you love your husband well, he will automatically or quickly (or ever) reciprocate. God does not guarantee that your commitment to love your husband will solve all the issues in your marriage. You may have to continue living with unfulfilled longings. (Remember that we will all have unfulfilled longings this side of heaven.) You may need to seek godly counsel from a third party. And in some cases, loving your husband will mean appealing for intervention from the spiritual leaders of your church and/or legal authorities. But regardless of how your husband does or doesn't respond, God will bless your obedience and your faith. By His grace, He can give you

Part of the mystery of marriage is that we and our husbands are one — not only in joys and victories, but also in loss and brokenness.

strength and comfort and even unexplainable joy in the midst of your circumstances.

Every woman possesses the power to tear down her house "with her own hands" (Prov. 14:1), especially if she persists in focusing only on what *her husband* needs to do instead of what *she* needs to do. Whatever your husband's sins or failures may be, your responding to him in harsh, critical, and unloving ways is no less a sin. And even if you don't routinely treat him to a running commentary of his shortcomings—making him feel as though he could never earn your acceptance and approval—your sighs of resigned indifference can be more than enough to erode your relationship.

But the "wisest of women," that same proverb states, "builds her house." And that wise woman can be you. You can learn to love your husband by overlooking minor faults and flaws or matters of personal preference. By refusing to keep score. By relinquishing the right to exact payment for wrongs. By giving him grace instead of giving him grief. By seeking God instead of seeking your own way.

By building—or rebuilding—your house on a foundation of God's unfailing love.

A Lifetime of Love

Part of the mystery of marriage is that we and our husbands are one—one flesh—not only in joys and victories, but also in loss and brokenness.

Even in *his* losses and brokenness.

By being willing to love our husbands within full view of his imperfections, we can become living demonstrations to them of the heart and spirit of Jesus. We can become conduits of grace to someone who can experience it from us as from no other.

This mission of loving our husbands is truly a high and holy calling. As we embrace and fulfill that calling, we not only extend blessing to the men to whom we've joined ourselves by covenant, but we also enter into greater intimacy and oneness with our Savior. By choosing the way of love, we invite the love of Christ to rule in our hearts as well as in our marriage. And in the process, our default responses can be transformed until we actually start enjoying our husbands again.

No one, including God Himself, expects us to be able to love our husbands in the way we've described without help or effort. But He has promised to provide the help we need. And the effort is so worth it. It can make the difference between a satisfying, thriving marriage and one that just barely hangs on.

Ultimately, marriage is about so much more than romance and passion and the discovery of a soul mate. It's about making a covenant commitment to love and then, with God's help and the help of mature women He has placed in our lives for this purpose, getting trained in how to do it. It's about representing the grace of God to our husbands as well as to others who watch our devotion in action.

It's about adorning the doctrine of Christ by giving the world a picture of love that never fails.

Making it Personal

Older women

1. As we get older, it's easy to lose track of why we married our husbands in the first place. If that is true of you, what are some specific things you could do to rekindle and deepen your friendship with the man you married and to enjoy him more?

2. What insights and resources could you offer to a younger woman when she begins to discover her marriage can't survive on just romantic love?

3. What younger woman has God placed in your life who could use some encouragement in loving her husband? Pray about how to reach out to her.

Younger women

1. Can you think of an older Christian couple who models strong loyalty, friendship, and love? As you observe them, what can you learn about how that kind of love is cultivated?

2. Would your husband say you are his encourager or his editor? What are some practical ways you could encourage and affirm him?

3. Is there an older woman who is encouraging and coaching you in your relationship with your husband? If not, ask the Lord to lead you to someone who could offer insight and prayer.

Teach what accords with sound doctrine.

Older men are to be sober-minded, dignified, self-controlled,
sound in faith, in love, and in steadfastness.

Older women likewise are to be reverent in behavior,
not slanderers or slaves to much wine.

They are to teach what is good,
and so train the young women
to love their husbands and children,
to be self-controlled,
pure,
working at home,
kind,
and **submissive to their own husbands,**
that the word of God may not be reviled.

**. . . so that in everything they may adorn
the doctrine of God our Savior.**

TITUS 2:1–5, 10

CHAPTER 12

An Unexpected Blessing

Discovering the Strength and Beauty of Submission

Both women and men get to "play the Jesus role" in marriage—
Jesus in his sacrificial authority,
Jesus in his sacrificial submission.
KATHY KELLER

"I *HATE* THIS BOOK!"

Next in line at the book table, she darted at me waving her copy of my book *Lies Women Believe.* I wasn't sure if she wanted me to sign it or if she wanted to throw it at me.

"Uh . . . okay, well," I stammered. "Tell me what you don't like about it."

"It's that thing about *submission,*" she said, going on to declare that she'd never even *heard* of this notion before and that she certainly couldn't buy in to it. *Submission* . . . what in the world?

Our conversation didn't last long. Others were waiting. And believe it or not, standing in the same line was another woman who said essentially the same thing. Of course, they weren't the first (or last) readers to feel this way. But what surprised me about these exchanges was that they took place at an event for women's ministry leaders and Bible study teachers, hosted by a respected evangelical seminary.

Not long after I got back home, I was sitting at dinner with a handful of friends. I wanted to hear their thoughts on the subject, so I motioned to everyone around the table and said, "When you were a young wife, what was your concept of submission? Did you get it?"

These, too, were women I would have expected to be well acquainted with the idea, even as younger women. But they all responded in so many words, "No, I was clueless about submission—what it was, what it meant." One woman said, "My idea of submission was doing what my husband wanted as long as I agreed with it. [Ha-ha!] Otherwise . . ."

Such reactions—from basic misconceptions about what biblical submission means and what it should look like in a marriage, to vehement rejection of the whole concept—are not uncommon today.

And that's yet another reason why Titus 2 training is so needed today.

We focused in the last chapter on the first direct marriage exhortation in Paul's list: "Train the young women to love their husbands" (v. 4). And now we turn to the second: "Train the young women to . . . [be] submissive to their own husbands" (vv. 4–5).

At this point Paul could hardly be more out of sync with our fiercely independent, egalitarian Western world. Bring the subject up in most settings—even among some in the church—and you can expect to have people look at you as if you were an alien from another planet.

The tragic reality of domestic abuse makes the whole idea even more objectionable to many. In fact, it is often asserted that the church's teaching of submission in marriage actually promotes and fosters abuse of women. Those who take this biblical concept seriously are often ridiculed as unenlightened at best or misogynists (woman haters) at worst.

One column I read contends that "the sacred belief of male

headship, held by anyone in a position of authority or influence, poses a danger to human rights."[1] And a chapter I wrote on this subject some years ago elicited this strong reaction from a reader:

> How can you actually believe and print these things?
> Do you know that men, here in the US and in other
> nations, use things like this to dominate, beat, and
> kill their wives?

The whole idea of submission makes some women feel weak, worthless, and vulnerable to controlling or angry men. This is not surprising, when we consider how many women have experienced mistreatment at the hands of male authority figures.

From a human perspective, I get this reaction. To our finite, fallen minds, the whole idea sounds unfair, even preposterous.

The wisdom of God, however, is infinitely higher than human wisdom. He values and esteems many of the things we despise and reject. If we only could grasp His eternal purposes, we would be enthralled with the perfection and splendor of His ways. So when it comes to this (or any other) topic, we need to earnestly seek His wisdom rather than relying on our own limited, flawed perspectives.

And that's my goal in this chapter: to explore God's wisdom in relation to this question of submission in marriage. What does it mean? Why does it matter? How are our lives adorned as we submit to our husbands? How does our submission adorn the doctrine of God?

And by the way, if you're unmarried and perhaps starting to feel left out of these proceedings, please don't check out. As a relatively new wife, I'm so grateful for the opportunities I had as a single woman to cultivate a submissive heart. The principle of submission applies to all of us in one way or another, and understanding it will help you in many different relationships—with parents, children, employees and employers, and church leaders, not to mention a future spouse. It will also help equip you to the train younger women in your life in what it means to submit to their husbands.

Foundational Assumptions

So what are we to make of this *S*-word?

Let's start with two foundational assumptions:

1. Submission was God's idea.

It's not an idea some chauvinistic guys cooked up to suppress women. No, it's built into the original plan of our sovereign Creator, who wove relationships of authority and submission into the very fabric of the universe.

This is how He created everything to operate.

With structure. With order.

In the church. In the workplace. In the courtroom. In the White House.

And yes, in your house.

Not only are God's ways true and right; they are also beautiful and good.

There are those who do theological gymnastics to conclude that the Scripture doesn't actually call wives to submit to their husbands. But a plain reading of the text, both here in Titus 2 and elsewhere in the Scripture (see, for instance, 1 Cor. 11:3, Eph. 5:22–33, Col. 3:18, and 1 Pet. 3:1–6), clearly sets forth the principle of headship and submission in the marriage relationship.

The Bible is the pure, authoritative revelation of God and His will. It is the operator's manual for our lives. We don't get to pick and choose which parts we like. And this is *good news*. For who better knows how life should function than the Creator and Designer of life Himself?

2. God's ways are good.

Not only are God's ways true and right; they are also beautiful and good. He delights in the creatures whom He fashioned with His own hand, into whom He breathed the breath of life. And He wants them to delight in Him and to experience every blessing possible.

Our good, wise, loving God would never ask of us something that is not for our ultimate benefit. If we abandon or reject His good plan, we do so to our own harm, as well as to the harm of others and the gospel itself.

I'm not saying submission is easy. It can be excruciatingly hard.

I'm not saying it comes naturally. It doesn't.

We are all born with a rebel spirit (or, as I sometimes say, in a kickative mood). Apart from having a new spirit imparted by Christ, we all naturally resist yielding to the authority of another—whether divine or human.

But regardless of how we may feel about it at times, biblical submission is a gracious gift from the Lord. A good thing. A beautiful thing. It's a heart attitude and a way of life to be embraced not only for the glory of God, but also for our own blessing and the blessing of others.

In the Beginning

To find the roots of biblical submission, we need to travel back to the garden of Eden, where God first revealed His transcendent principles for the human experience. One of these is the relationship between husband and wife, which like the rest of creation was intended to exhibit God's glory and bring Him the worship and praise He deserves.

Genesis 1 describes the moment when God completed the pinnacle of His creation:

> God created man in His own image . . . *male and female* He created them. . . . And behold, it was very good. (Gen. 1:27, 31 NASB)

Genesis 2 unpacks this further, filling in details of how the woman was made from the man and for the man, then given to the man to complete him and to partner with him in fulfilling God's holy, eternal purposes.

That brings us to Genesis 3, where everything goes awry—including our understanding of submission.

Some theologians believe that submission in marriage is a direct outcome of the Fall, a consequence of the curse of sin that is reversed by the gospel. They base this view on God's prediction to Eve in Genesis 3:16 (NASB), following the forbidden-fruit episode:

> Your desire will be for your husband,
> and he will rule over you.

But by the time these prophetic words were spoken, the divine plan for ordering the universe and human interactions was already in place. God had established the divine arrangement of headship and submission as part of the original created order, *before* the Fall. In God's good, wise plan, the man and the woman were designed for different roles. And through their union they would depict distinct and complementary aspects of the redemption story that unfold throughout history.

Many centuries later, the apostle Paul and other New Testament authors would explicitly confirm this meaning. Some dismiss the New Testament teaching on submission in marriage in Titus 2 and elsewhere as being culturally bound and irrelevant for today's readers, simply an acknowledgment of the cultural norm of the day. These writers, they say, were simply giving women advice on how to live a righteous, holy life within that now-outdated cultural system.

But Paul himself, writing under the inspiration of the Spirit, specifically sets forth the divine order of headship and submission as being timeless and transcultural—the husband-wife relationship patterned after the God-Son relationship and the Christ-man relationship.

> I want you to understand that the head of every man
> is Christ, the head of a wife is her husband,[2] and the
> head of Christ is God. (1 Cor. 11:3)

For a wife, submission means accepting God's good order for her life, just as a husband submits himself to God in accepting God's order for his life. And it gives her the privilege of representing the mystery and the beauty of the Son's submission to the Father. For even within the Trinity, we see this paradoxical arrangement—seamless unity with separate roles and different identities, perfect equality with pure submission.

The Father and the Son, we know, are both equally God. And yet the Son chooses to submit Himself to the will of the Father:

> For I have come down from heaven, not to do my own
> will but the will of him who sent me. (John 6:38)

The submission of Christian wives to their husbands is a powerful and beautiful picture of the Son's submission to His Father and of the church's submission to Christ. These wives, together with husbands who love them selflessly and sacrificially, put the gospel story on vivid and compelling display.

What Submission Is Not

But let's get practical here. What does biblical submission mean in the context of our daily lives, as we wrestle with the inevitable rub of relationships?

I am convinced that much of the resistance to this idea comes from a faulty understanding of its meaning. It's especially important for those of us who are older women to be prepared to deal with the misconceptions that exist around this subject if we want to carry out our mandate to train younger women to be "submissive to their own husbands."

Here are some basics we all need to understand:

1. A wife's submission is not to men in general.

Every person—man or woman, young or old—has relationships that require submission, whether to parents, a boss, civil authorities, or spiritual leaders in the church. And all of us as believers are to have a humble, submissive attitude toward one another in the body of Christ (Eph. 5:21). However, when Scripture instructs wives to submit, it is specifically to "their own husbands," who have been established by God to serve as the head of their wives and to love them and lay down their lives for them.

2. Submission does not mean a wife is inferior to her husband.

Scripture affirms unequivocally that men and women are both created in the image of God and therefore have equal worth. They have equal access to the Father and are equally coheirs with Christ, sharing equally in the Holy Spirit, equally redeemed and baptized into Christ, equally partakers of His spiritual gifts, and equally loved and valued by God.

3. Submission doesn't subject a wife to a life of forced compliance.

The word used in the New Testament for "submission"—referring to the orderly fashion of following a leader—speaks of an act that is voluntary. In a proper understanding of marriage, no husband should ever force his wife to submit to him through coercion or manipulation. Submission is her willing decision not only to follow *him*, but ultimately and supremely to follow in obedience to her Lord.

4. Submission doesn't amount to slavish, groveling subservience.

A wife is not a hired maid. Not an employee. Not a child. Not a second-class citizen who bows at the feet of her superior. Submission is rather a joyful, glad-hearted, intelligent, loving responsiveness to your husband's God-ordained position as your spiritual head (see Eph. 5:22–23). And that headship doesn't mean your husband has absolute authority over you. Husbands are not the supreme authority over their wives. God is. Husbands have been *delegated* authority by God, and they will answer to God for exercising it in a humble, sacrificial, loving way.

5. Submission doesn't minimize a wife into mindlessness.

Being submitted to your husband doesn't doom you to a fate of blind, unquestioning obedience. You still possess valid opinions and the right to express them in a humble, godly way. As your husband's helper, in fact, you would be derelict in your duty not to bring things to his attention that he either doesn't see or doesn't seem to understand.

6. Submission doesn't mean husbands are always right.

Your husband is not God. (You already know that.) He is every inch the sinner you are. (You know that too.) So biblical submission cannot possibly be based on how wise or godly or capable your husband is, nor on whether his style or manner or personality is to your liking. Bottom line—he is not the one who makes this pattern work in marriage. God is. And God is the One to whom you and I are ultimately submitted in our marriages.

7. Submission never requires a wife to follow her husband into sin.

Your ultimate allegiance and loyalty are to Christ. If your husband abuses his God-given authority and requires of you something that is contrary to the Word and will of God, you must obey God rather than your husband.

> *Whenever women are instructed in Scripture to submit to their husbands, there is a corresponding command for husbands to love and cherish their wives.*

However, my observation from listening to many wives in difficult marriages is that often their struggle is with being led in a way they don't prefer to go or just don't think is best, rather than in a way the Bible and conscience forbid. It's important to distinguish between the two in responding to a husband's direction.

8. Finally, a wife's submission never gives license to her husband to abuse her.

Never. Whenever women are instructed in Scripture to submit to their husbands, there is a corresponding command for husbands to love and cherish their wives. There is no possible justification for a husband to abuse his wife, whether in overtly physical or verbal ways or in more "respectable" types of manipulation and intimidation—what one pastor calls "polite abuses."[3]

If you are being abused (or suspect you are being abused), you must get help. There is nothing in the biblical teaching on submission that permits such treatment. If you (or your children) are being physically harmed or threatened, you should get to a safe place and contact both civil and spiritual authorities for protection.

Wherever people abuse the order God has established for any sphere, the problem does not stem from flaws in God's plan, but from humanity's sinful distortions of it. Therefore, the solution to problems that arise when this principle is applied in marriage is not to throw submission out with the bathwater, but rather to align our understanding and practice with what Scripture really says. Because when the system is working according to God's design, blessings flow to us from heaven, revealing to us, in us, and through us the beauty of His character and ways.

The Cost of Submission

That's not to say, however, that biblical submission—properly understood, faithfully followed, not twisted by abuse—comes easy. As we have already seen, it doesn't. Even those who agree with the principle of submission find its practice to be difficult at times.

For proof of its difficulty—if you need any proof—I take you to the epistle of 1 Peter. The prevailing theme of this New Testament letter is how to maintain hope and joyful endurance through suffering. The apostle Peter wrote it to the persecuted early church, urging them to remember Christ's example, to keep their eyes on their coming heavenly reward, and not to be ashamed of their faith even when it seemed they were standing alone amid fiery trials.

This theme of suffering runs through chapters 1 and 2 of 1 Peter. It is also prominent throughout chapter 4 and again in chapter 5. And I don't believe it's an accident that Peter brings up the subject of marriage (in chapter 3) right smack in the middle of these chapters.

Setting up the teaching on marriage, the last paragraph of chapter 2 (vv. 21–25) is a powerful testimony of how Christ submitted Himself to the will of His Father, even when it required suffering. All the while, rather than threatening or retaliating against sinners, Jesus "continued entrusting himself" to God, knowing His wise, loving Father would vindicate Him in the end. He did this all *for us*, leaving us an example, "so that you might follow in his steps." As a result of His obedience and His trust in God, He brought us spiritual healing and restored our wandering hearts to the Shepherd of our souls.

The very next paragraph, starting in chapter 3, verse 1, begins this way: "*Likewise* [in the same way], *wives*, be subject to your own husbands" and goes on to give some examples and reasons (vv. 2–6). Verse 7 continues, "*Likewise, husbands,* live with your wives in an understanding way, showing honor." And then the rest of the chapter centers on the theme of suffering for righteousness' sake, as Jesus did for our sake.

In tying the redemptive suffering of Christ to marriage, Peter wanted us to understand that both husbands and wives sometimes have to suffer in order to fulfill their God-given role and responsibility toward their mates. He reminds us that we can trust our situation and the outcome of our obedience to God, and that our willingness to follow in Jesus' steps (2:21), even when it is hard, can bring healing and restoration in the lives of others.

In his words to wives, Peter specifically addresses women whose husbands are not believers—a situation that was common in the early church. For a Christian wife whose husband does not share her faith—who perhaps resists her or ridicules the things that matter most to her—submission and showing respect can be a struggle. And yet for these women, as for those who persevere through *any* affliction with dignity and faith in God, the experience only serves to make their faith and character shine more brilliantly.

According to Peter, "respectful and pure conduct" and a "gentle and quiet spirit" are what give wives "imperishable beauty" (1 Peter 3:2, 4). This is how they adorn the doctrine they claim to believe. Far more effective than any tactics of manipulation, nagging, or angry tirades, a wife's submission to Christ—expressed in respectful submission to her husband—is the means most likely to reach her husband's heart and win him to become an obedient follower of Christ.

And this principle can be applied to any woman whose husband is not being obedient to the Word of God. When a woman denies the natural urge to resent her husband or retaliate against him, when she runs to the cross instead of running her mouth, when she maintains a gentle and quiet spirit and steadfastly hopes in God, regardless of her husband's behavior—that is no spineless, mousy, whimpering puddle of dominated femininity. *That is a woman of power.*

The hard-fought, God-honoring response of a submitted wife can be a means of drawing the most resistant husband to submit to God. This kind of submission is a mark not of groveling, but of greatness.

"But What if I Believe He's Wrong?"

"But," many women beg to know, "what do I do when I disagree with my husband's decisions or direction?"

Actually, this is the only time submission really becomes an issue in marriage—when the husband and wife don't agree on something. As long as everyone is on the same page, no one really needs to submit to anyone about anything. It's only when you look up and realize the two of you aren't on the same page—or even in the same chapter, book, or library—that submission is put to the test.

Such testing can involve minor disagreements that surface in the course of daily life. Or it can encompass bigger issues related to (for example) parenting decisions, financial matters, or sexual expectations and desires. Then there are the really thorny matters—such as the ones our ministry team sometimes hears about from women whose husbands are asking them to do something they believe is contrary to God's will:

- "My husband is not saved. I am supposed to be submissive to him. He does not want me to tithe. This is a big issue for him. What am I to do?"
- "What if he is an unbeliever and takes your young children to see R-rated movies when you plead with him to consider an alternative? Or what if he tells you to go to work and put your kids in daycare?"
- "My friend's husband has a large collection of evil music— sex, drugs, etc. He says he is a Christian, but he refuses to dispose of it. My friend does not like having it in her home (they have six children), but feels that to be submissive she cannot tell him to get rid of it."

The women asking these and other tough questions need more than a stock response from a remote counselor, author, or teacher who doesn't know them or their situation. They need someone who will walk with them, pray with them, weep with them, challenge them or advocate for them when needed, stick with them over the long haul, and help them discern step-by-step the best course of action.

That, of course, is exactly what Titus 2 provides for these women. And it is why ongoing, life-on-life relationships between younger women and seasoned, older women—in the context of the local church, where pastoral leaders can be brought in if necessary—are so important, and can be a great source of practical wisdom and encouragement.

That said, there are some general principles I have found useful when walking women through situations where they are being asked to submit to direction they believe is unwise or unbiblical.

1. Ask yourself: Am I generally submissive?

Biblical submission is first a heart attitude—an inclination or bent toward being leadable. The submitted wife has a general pattern of yielding to her husband's leadership rather than resisting his ideas and leadership. To be sure, a wife's submission involves actions and behavior. But what she *does* (submits) flows out of who she *is* (a gentle-spirited, responsive, amenable woman).

When biblical headship and submission work the way God ordained, the husband and wife are able to work together to accomplish a common goal rather than being pitted against each other. They are playing on the same team. And as with sports teams, when each position plays their part, the team wins games.

To change the metaphor, it's kind of like ballroom dancing. For the dance to work, someone has to lead and someone has to follow—but both partners can and should inspire the other to do better. When wives submit to their husband's leadership, it is easier for husbands to love and lead. And when men love and lead, it is easier for their wives to submit.

That's something to think about when you find yourself in a marital tug-of-war. Step back and evaluate the normal pattern in your responses to your husband. Is your response to your husband generally receptive and responsive? Or do you tend to reflexively push back and resist, making it tough for your husband to make suggestions or decisions without bracing for your inevitable objections?

Late one night, as I was writing this chapter, Robert shared with me a concern about my need to be a better steward of my time while under my looming book deadline. He gently challenged me to make some practical changes that he felt would make me more effective.

My knee-jerk reaction was to defend my way of getting things done, explaining that we are just wired differently (which is true). But the Spirit reminded me that this was an opportunity to humble myself and yield to my husband's counsel, realizing he has been given the responsibility to provide leadership in our marriage and trusting that God is using him to help make me more like Jesus.

So I swallowed my pride, thanked Robert for his input, and purposed to take it to heart. And over the next couple of days, I saw more clearly the wisdom of what he had said. I also began to experience a sweet infusion of God's grace in my life as I responded to his leadership.

This example may seem trivial compared to far bigger issues you are facing in your marriage at the moment. But our responses to these everyday exchanges really do impact our husband's responses to us. I've observed that men tend to choose one of two faulty alternatives when faced with their wife's resistance. They'll either become *overbearing*—just taking the ball and running with it—or they'll acquiesce into *passivity*. Neither one, of course, makes for good decision making or a healthy relationship. But the second—passivity—can actually be the most vexing for a wife. In fact, one of the most common frustrations I've heard expressed by Christian women is regarding their husband's slowness to step up to the plate and lead.

One friend said to me, "My husband doesn't like conflict or

confrontation, so he doesn't tend to give direction that he doesn't think I will want to comply with." Sometime later, when I asked this man for his perspective, he explained: "If a husband feels like his leadership is going to threaten the relationship, he will protect the relationship and not lead."

Another husband told me, "If everything is challenged and questioned, it's more difficult to lead than do nothing. So men may choose to do nothing instead of risking failure."

The point is, when a husband develops ingrained patterns of conflict avoidance, he'd rather just let his wife make the calls instead of risking damage to his pride or inviting further strife into the relationship.

And as a wife, that's not a good place for you to be. It leaves you exposed and unprotected, overloading your already full plate of responsibilities. It also makes you feel lonely and unsupported—because your partner has essentially opted out of engaging with important issues.

So it's helpful to consider . . . what's your bent?

To submit or to resist?

That's a good place to start.

2. Make sure you want God's will and glory more than you want your own way.

I realize that the command to submit to our husbands may feel like the height of unfairness. At times, the sense of vulnerability and loss of control can provoke fear. But it helps to remember that the ultimate issue is not our surrender to human leadership—to our husband—but rather to God. When you think about it, being asked to align ourselves under a God-ordained authority is really just asking us to be like Jesus.

"My food is to do the will of him who sent me," Jesus said (John 4:34), indicating that His greatest satisfaction came from doing what His Father asked Him to do. This decision was obviously costly to Him: "Being found in human form, he humbled himself by becoming obedient to the point of death, even death on a cross" (Phil. 2:8). But as a result of Jesus' chosen submission, the Father "highly exalted him" (v. 9), favoring Him with blessing that far outweighed the high price of His surrender.

The battles you face at home can sometimes put you in what feels like an impossible position. But if you could drill down to the heart of your struggle, you might be surprised by what you'd find. Could it be that you're simply afraid that what will honor God in this situation might be different from what you want?

I've discovered that once we've truly submitted ourselves to the will of God, it often becomes easier to submit to human authorities.

3. Share your concerns, but watch your attitude.

There's a way to say no, and there's a way to say no. You know what I mean? One of those ways can be accusatory and threatening, whiny and wearisome, demeaning and demanding. But the other way comes from a heart that is humble, loving, respectful, and aware that you likely hold in your hand the difference between a clash of wills or a calm, adult discussion.

Attitude is so important.

And attitude, obviously, begins in your heart. You may be able to control your tongue and facial expressions by force of will alone—sometimes. But you can only do it consistently when submission comes from within, not merely from outward compliance.

This is another reason why God's call to submission is a blessing—because it trains our hearts to resist what our runaway emotions would demand. And so the more deeply a wife yields—to God first, and therefore to her husband—the more likely it is that gentleness and well-spoken truth will bubble up from inside her instead of harshness and poorly worded arguments.

By making a difference in *you*, submission can make a difference in how issues in your marriage (or elsewhere—in the workplace or at church) work themselves out.

4. If you're still in disagreement, make your appeal—gently.

Share your heart—prayerfully, kindly, with carefully chosen words, and at an appropriate time. Sometimes this means waiting until your emotions have calmed down and your husband is in a better frame of mind to really hear your heart.

One helpful example of appealing to authority can be seen in Queen Esther, an orphaned Jewish girl who ended up married to the King of Persia. King Ahasuerus was an impatient, angry, volatile man, known in history for cruelty and horrible fits of rage. If you're familiar with this Old Testament account (in the book of Esther), you know that the king's chief official, Haman, manipulated Ahasuerus into declaring extermination on her people.

Esther's guardian, Mordecai, pleaded with Esther to ask her husband to halt these evil plans. And not surprisingly, Esther hesitated, fearing for her own safety. Finally she marshaled the courage to risk the king's possible rejection—or worse. But she prudently resisted the temptation just to blurt out her case all at once. To do so could have made Ahasuerus feel accosted or blindsided. Instead she invited both him and Haman—twice—to a sumptuous feast she had prepared. Only then, when the king was relaxed and in a favorable mood, did she make her request of him. And her approach proved to be a wise one. Haman's treachery was exposed, and Esther's people were saved.

I've often thought of this account when I have been tempted to dump my concern onto my husband or another person in authority rather than exercising restraint and considering the most judicious timing and approach. You might compare her tactics to a wife's saying, "Honey, there's something I really need to talk with you about. When would be a good time for us to sit down and let me share with you what's on my heart?"

Now, Esther had no guarantee the king would change his orders and call off the death squads, any more than a wife's gentle approach guarantees that her husband will come around to her way of thinking.

But the example of Esther's appeal to her evil husband illustrates that the timing and tact of a woman's appeal can make a man more open and inclined to listen and to consider her perspective.

This is not a matter of being coy or manipulative to get your way. We're talking about using gentleness and tact in making your case.

Granted, the line between the two can be a thin one. And Esther and Ahasuerus' marriage certainly cannot be held up as a model worthy of emulation. Nevertheless, I believe her example can be instructive when it comes to approaching a husband (or any other authority figure) with a difficult matter or a disagreement.

5. Once you've made your appeal, wait for God to intervene.

I had a boss once who wisely and kindly told me, "Nancy, it's fine to put your cards on the table, but once you put them there, take your hands off. Don't keep pushing."

My natural, firstborn temperament, I confess, is a lot more pit bull than golden lab. I can sink my teeth into something and not let go until whoever is on the other side of the issue finally says, "Okay, fine, you win."

Unfortunately, as I am learning, such pit-bull tendencies are seldom effective or productive in marriage—or in any other relationship. I've seen that when I approach Robert about a concern with a gentle spirit, *What a relief it is to know we are not responsible for wringing obedience out of our husbands. Only the Lord can do that.* then leave the matter with him, things go much better. When he knows I'm trusting God to work through his leadership, he's actually *more* inclined to listen to what I am saying. He feels a greater sense of responsibility and a heightened desire to seek the Lord and to love me well.

What a relief it is to know we are not responsible for wringing obedience out of our husbands. Only the Lord can do that. What you and I need to do is *pray* for the men we married—and pray about our issues of disagreement as well. If there's wisdom in what we're asking our husbands to consider and they don't seem inclined to listen to us, then the best way to get through to him is go "over his head" to the One who can move his heart to do what is right.

This process requires patience. But it will show how big we really believe God is and whether we trust that He is powerful, sovereign, and good. In these seasons, the words of the psalmist are just what we need:

> Wait for the Lord;
>> be strong, and let your heart take courage;
>> wait for the Lord! (Ps. 27:14)

As the days go by, of course, we may find it's *our* hearts that God turns, not our husband's. Or perhaps we will find some sweet combination of the two. But however the Lord chooses to act, we will have chosen to walk in the place where His peace dwells and where He can do a deep, sanctifying work in our life and marriage.

Someone once told me about a time when she and her husband had come to an impasse over a particularly contentious issue. She felt strongly about what needed to be done and kept badgering him with her opinions. His opinions were just as strong, and he dug in his heels. Tensions escalated. Walls were going up. Her husband wasn't bending, and she sure wasn't going to be the first one to crack.

But one day, following yet another heated exchange, the Lord convicted my friend's heart about some of the things she had said and the attitude she was displaying. She went to her husband with a humble apology, explaining that God had caused her to see the harm she was doing and that she was fully prepared—even though she still disagreed with him—to submit to him and to his decision. "I'm praying for you, honey," she said, "and I'll keep praying over this matter. But I will back you on whatever you decide."

When this wife took her place under her husband's authority, he didn't take it as a thumbs-up victory. Instead, he began to feel the sheer weight of what was at stake and the need to listen to the Lord and follow His direction. All this husband wanted to do now—with his wife's trusting support—was to make sure he got this right, even if the right way was the one that had been her way all along.

This woman could've said, "I lost. I gave in. He won. I let him get away with it."

But no, she didn't lose.

She won, just as he won.

They won—because her trust in the Lord motivated her husband to a new level of discernment and obedience and a desire to do what was truly best for his marriage and family.

The Promise of Grace

What we need to remember—and what is so easy to overlook or minimize—is that our husband's role is a difficult one. No, not all husbands take it as seriously as they should, and many contribute to making their wife's obligations harder to fulfill than necessary, just as many wives make things difficult for their husbands. But do you know what? Whether your husband realizes it or not, God has placed on him the responsibility for the condition of his marriage and family. And he will be required to stand before the Lord to give an account for how he managed this stewardship.

God doesn't hold us responsible for fulfilling our husband's role. But He does hold us responsible for filling *our* role—not simply submitting to our husband, but pulling with him and upholding him in prayer. And yes, things can still go awry, even on the other side of our obedience. But even then, God promises (and never fails to deliver) grace sufficient for every challenge.

As we hope in God, as Jesus Himself did when suffering unjustly (1 Peter 2:23), we can experience freedom from fear. And our submission and trust in the Lord will showcase the beauty of the gospel:

> For this is how the holy women who hoped in God
> used to adorn themselves, by submitting to their own
> husbands, as Sarah obeyed Abraham, calling him
> lord. And you are her children, if you do good and do
> not fear anything that is frightening. (1 Pet. 3:5–6)

In the opening chapter of this book, I shared about a few private moments I spent with my lifelong friend Vonette Bright just before I walked down the aisle to become Mrs. Robert Wolgemuth. In true motherlike fashion, she wanted to be sure I was adequately prepared for this new life I was stepping into. Toward the end of our brief conversation, Vonette said something I've not forgotten—a bit of wisdom that has proved to be one of the sweetest wedding gifts I received.

"Submit to whatever brings him pleasure—in everything," she said with a smile, "and you'll be just fine!"

I've hesitated to share this advice, knowing it could easily be misconstrued. By no means was she encouraging me to satisfy any sinful desires my husband might have. And she was not implying that I would be my husband's slave, existing merely to fulfill his every whim. But this precious widow, who had enjoyed a deeply loving fifty-four-year marriage, knew firsthand the joys of having a disposition—an inclination—to follow and yield to her husband's leadership.

Vonette's words have come to mind many times since my wedding day. My natural bent is to push for what I want—what brings *me* pleasure. But in those moments when I have felt reluctant to be inconvenienced or to make a sacrifice to serve and bless my husband, this timely counsel from an older woman has helped recalibrate my thinking. And as I have tried to choose the pathway of submission, I have watched my kind, tender husband bend over backward to serve and please me.

I understand that not every husband will respond this same way and that some wives will not see the fruit of their obedience to God's Word in the short term.

I also understand that too often the concept of submission has been used as an excuse and cover for bullying or for a kind of spineless acquiescence. We should not turn a blind eye to such situations. Depending on the nature and severity of the circumstances, perpetrators need to be confronted and held accountable for their behavior, and those on the receiving end need to receive compassionate counsel and practical relief. But we cannot afford to let those distortions and perversions of submission cause us to miss out on the real thing.

We eagerly await the day when our great God will right all wrongs and will reward the faithfulness of those who have endured patiently under ungodly authorities—whether tyrannical rulers or selfish, domineering husbands.

In the meantime, He calls us to follow in the steps of our Savior, to hope in God, and to train each other in this biblical truth, trusting in His wisdom, goodness, and love, and experiencing the surprising beauty and power of humble submission.

Making It Personal

Older women

1. What are some of the ways you have struggled (or still struggle) with biblical submission in your own life and marriage? What have you learned? How could your experiences be a source of encouragement for a younger woman in your life?

2. How can you model and teach submission to younger women in a way that helps them see it as a blessing and not a burden?

3. What can you do to walk alongside a woman who is struggling with her husband's decisions? How can you offer support and encouragement while challenging her to think biblically?

Younger women

1. Would you consider yourself a biblically submissive woman? What does that look like for you? Is your general inclination to be responsive or resistant toward authority?

2. Do you often find yourself wanting your own way rather than seeking to honor the Lord and follow His direction through your husband or other authorities? How might a proper understanding of submission to the will of God help you? How does Christ's example inspire you?

3. Who is an older, mature woman or mentor you could ask for encouragement and counsel when you struggle to respond to authority in a biblical manner?

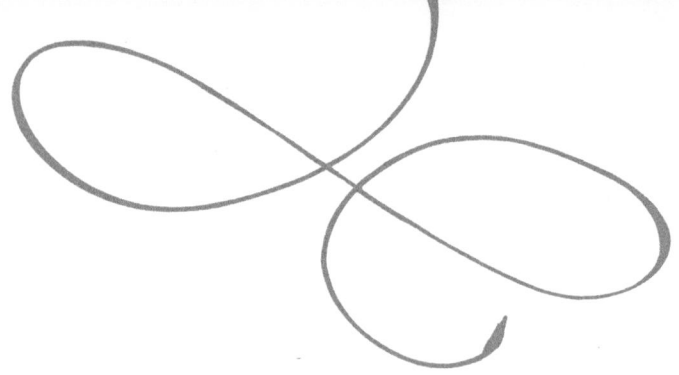

Teach what accords with sound doctrine.

Older men are to be sober-minded, dignified, self-controlled,
sound in faith, in love, and in steadfastness.

Older women likewise are to be reverent in behavior,
not slanderers or slaves to much wine.

They are to teach what is good,
and so train the young women
to love their husbands and children,
to be self-controlled,
pure,
working at home,
kind,
and submissive to their own husbands,
that the word of God may not be reviled.

. . . so that in everything they may adorn
the doctrine of God our Savior.

TITUS 2:1–5, 10

CHAPTER 13

Life-Givers in Training

Embracing the Gift of Motherhood

Mothering is at the essence of womanhood.
To live out a life as a nurturer in this self-centered,
godless culture will cost you. But the rewards ... are rich indeed.
BARBARA HUGHES

YOU MAY HAVE SEEN A HUMOROUS PIECE ON THE INTERNET that proposes a series of "tests" for people who are thinking of having children. The activities the author describes are attempts to simulate what life with kids is like, giving people a taste of the real thing before they actually make the commitment. The tests include things like going to bed (again) at 2:45 a.m. and getting up when the alarm goes off at 3:00 a.m., spooning soggy cornflakes into a swinging melon suspended from the ceiling, inserting a coin into your car's CD player, and attempting to stuff a live octopus into a string bag so no arms hang out.[1]

We can all get a laugh (or more likely a knowing sigh) from these makeshift simulations of the high-wire acts and pyrotechnics that make up a typical day for a mother with little ones. But the jest is only effective up to a point. Taken too seriously, it can reveal a mindset I fear many young women bring with them into marriage—the idea that parenthood, for all its fanciful ideals and Facebook photo ops, is mostly just a hard grind of self-depletion.

As we seek to gain God's perspective on the calling and gift of motherhood, we need to ask what influences may have shaped our underlying beliefs on this topic (and others addressed in Titus 2):

- Are we just mimicking what we experienced growing up without stopping to evaluate whether those ways are true and good and wise?
- Do we mindlessly accept the philosophies promoted through popular culture—magazines, media outlets, or mom blogs?
- Or . . . are we looking to God's Word to determine His purposes for us in our various roles and callings as women, wives, friends, church members, workers, sisters, and, yes, mothers?

Kari was a mom in her midthirties when she attended one of the first True Woman conferences hosted by Revive Our Hearts. We had a booth set up where people could record a video testimony of how the Lord had met with them at the event. In her video, Kari told how she had received Christ shortly after the birth of her first child and how she and her husband had welcomed seven children into their home over the course of the next twelve years. She was a devoted mom who obviously valued children. And yet during that weekend, the Lord had exposed anger and frustration that had been building up in her heart for a long time. Without even realizing it, she had harbored a lingering sense that her husband, her children, life, God—all of them, really—had taken advantage of her, had stolen from her, had drained away opportunities and freedoms from her.

Kari's voice broke and tears started to flow as she haltingly testified to what had happened to her at the weekend event. Through the teaching of His Word, God had renewed her passion for motherhood.

Now the joy of what He had given her to do filled her heart. She was eager to get home to her little ones, to enjoy the privilege of being their mother and leading them to know and walk with Christ.

We posted Kari's video on our *True Woman* blog the following week, and the site was immediately flooded with responses from moms who related to her story. Many of them shared that they'd also come to resent God and their husbands for the burden of responsibility placed on them, that they'd often mourned the loss of desires and plans that had been laid aside to care for their families, that they'd chafed at not being able to go to Walmart when they wished or even to the bathroom by themselves. They bore witness to ways that unbiblical philosophies that circulate so freely in our culture had subtly (and sometimes *not* so subtly) invaded their thinking and left them feeling perpetually deprived and depleted. But they, too, revealed that God was recapturing their hearts and minds, rekindling their zeal for the high and holy calling of motherhood.

He can do the same for you.

No, the fresh winds of truth won't stop your toddler from throwing up on the morning you're leaving for vacation. They won't prevent your middle schooler from informing you in the car on the way to school that forty dollars and a signed permission slip for next month's band trip are due *today*. They're not likely to win over an angry stepchild or bring a prodigal son or daughter immediately to his or her senses after years of wandering.

Life goes on. Costs go up. Parenting is demanding, complex, and short on immediate rewards, no matter how passionate you are about motherhood.

But if you're a mother—a birth mom, a stepmom, an adoptive or foster mom, or anyone else actively involved in nurturing children—Titus 2 can help you remember that you've got a vital calling and ministry right there in the house with you, a ministry that isn't necessarily a drive to church or a Kenyan mission trip away. And it will assure you that your efforts in raising those little ones for His glory are not—and *will* not be—in vain.

I want to acknowledge at the outset that I'm not a mom—at least, not in the traditional sense. I now have the privilege of embracing Robert's two daughters and their husbands, and five teen and young adult grandchildren as "family"—an unexpected gift in this season of my life.

However, God, in His providence, has not chosen to give me children of my own. So what you will hear in this chapter is not so much the voice of my personal experience as it is the voice of my many mom friends. I have walked with these women and cheered for them through various seasons of motherhood. These moms have helped me better understand what it means to love children—little ones, adolescents, and adult kids; those who love and follow Christ and those who have walked away from Him; sons and daughters who embrace the values of their parents and others whose choices have broken their parents' hearts.

One thing I know for sure: God cares about children. Which is why He wants us to. All of us.

Delightfully Yours

But here's a news flash you don't have to be a mom to get: motherhood can be hard.

It's always been difficult, and today's supermom expectations—driven by media and the competitive spirit of today's culture—can make it even harder. No wonder so many young women today are postponing children or even deciding against having them at all. No wonder, if they do have children, they feel pressured to turn family into a contest, outdoing friends and neighbors, an extension of their own personal brand.

And all too often, they're feeling the strain. Mothers caught inside this constant buzz of activity may actually spend less time *with* their children than *around* their children. Even when they manage to keep the trains running on time (on most days, in most ways), they often forget which light they're supposed to be chasing at the end of the tunnel.

Looking back at Titus 2, we're reminded that Paul instructed the older women to "train the young women to love their husbands *and children.*" And the kind of love he was talking about, you'll recall, was fondness and affection, friendship and enjoyment, taking delight in the objects of our love and finding pleasure in their company.

Most people will never see the sacrifices you make to parent your children, nor will you likely get a bonus at the end of the year to recognize and reward you for your efforts.

If you're in the parenting season at the moment, then you know that *delighting* in your children often takes a back seat to meeting the *demands* of your children. And that can turn the joy of loving children into nothing more than a series of repetitive, thankless duties to be fulfilled day after endless day.

You wouldn't be human not to wear down at times under the strain. And most people will never see the sacrifices you make to parent your children, nor will you likely get a performance review or a bonus at the end of the year to recognize and reward you for your efforts.

But if you're not careful, if you're not prayerful, if you let the days just pass by without being determined to use them for God's highest and best purposes—to remember the real reason you're doing all this—then the blessings He intends for you in this season may slip through your fingers. And your children may miss out on the vision of God's love you were intended to give them.

So how do you hold this impossible task in balance?

With help! And not only God's help, though of course that is

The Bible invariably describes children as gifts from God.

available to you. But God has chosen to work in your life through other women—Titus 2 women. Women who've been down this road, sharing life lessons they've learned along the way, providing support and encouragement to help guide you through the twenty-five-hour days of parenthood. Helping you remember to . . .

Enjoy children.

If you're a mom, you know better than I that the sometimes uncomfortable months of pregnancy and the hours of labor and delivery are just the beginning of many challenges ahead: sleep deprivation, colicky crying marathons, headstrong temperaments, anxious moments. And those who are watching their older children—even grown children—struggle and backtrack, stumble and fall could tell you stories that make the shoe-tying trials of toddlerhood seem tame by comparison.

Yes, mothering is hard. Initial enthusiasm for this season is often eclipsed by exhaustion, delight by drudgery.

But these children—as you know, yet perhaps need to be reminded —are *blessings.* The Bible invariably describes children as gifts from God. As a heritage. As a reward. As hope for the future. As something to be thankful for and enjoy.

"I will bless her," God said to Abraham, promising a son to Sarah. "I will bless her, and she shall become nations; kings of peoples shall come from her" (Gen. 17:16).

Isaac's blessing for Jacob included the prayer that God would "bless you and make you fruitful and multiply you" (Gen. 28:3).

When Esau met up with his brother years later in open country, amazed by the size of the approaching entourage, he asked, "Who are these with you?" Jacob answered, "The children whom God has graciously given your servant" (Gen. 33:5).

And the psalmist exclaimed,

> Like arrows in the hand of a warrior
>> are the children of one's youth.
> Blessed is the man
>> who fills his quiver with them! (Ps. 127:4–5)

Jesus recognized children as blessings and rebuked those of His followers who tried to shush them and shuttle them away as a bother and inconvenience. "Let the little children come to me and do not hinder them," He said (Matt. 19:14).

Jesus was expressing what most parents know but can easily forget amid the pressures of daily life. That little ones are blessings.

I once asked a woman who has a large number of children if she and her husband had always wanted a big family. "No, not at first we didn't," she said. "But as God began to bring children into our lives, I started noticing what He says about children in Scripture. His perspective is that they are a blessing and reward. And I thought, *Well, if God wanted to give me some other kind of blessing, like, oh . . . thousand dollar checks, I wouldn't say to Him, 'No more blessings! We don't have room for all those blessings you're trying to give us.'"*

How true. And on days when you don't know if you

As we open our hearts to children, we reflect the heart of our heavenly Father, whose love for His children never fails.

can butter another piece of toast or settle another argument or read another story or sit through another soccer game in subfreezing temps, remember that these children are in your home for a relatively short period of time. And underneath all the dirt and diapers and doctor visits, even the hardships imply the presence of blessing that many would trade whole fortunes to possess.

So take a deep breath. In the midst of the hubbub, ask the Lord to slow your racing heart and to silence the voices of others' expectations that are ringing in your head. Look around to where life is happening for you right now.

And thank God for your children—whatever their age and size. Ask Him for a heart to enjoy them. Enjoy them when they're lovable and it comes naturally. And when they're difficult or demanding or disrespectful, don't lose sight of the fact that they are still a gift. A blessing. A sacred stewardship.

And if you don't have children of your own, enjoy others' children. Do it for Jesus' sake. Do it for the children's sake, and for the spread of God's kingdom to the next generation.

As we open our hearts to children, we reflect the heart of our heavenly Father, whose love for His children never fails.

Express affection.

A friend was cleaning out her purse one day and found a little piece of paper. (Who knows from how long ago; we women can sometimes span presidential terms between pocketbook purges.)

The note said simply, "Thanks, Mom, for coming to my game tonight."

Can you imagine the joy this mom felt when she read those words again? Amid a crinkly collection of store receipts, appointment reminders, and cough-drop wrappings, she had found treasure.

And if we adults are moved by such a tender expression of affection, imagine how your children need—and will one day remember—your verbal infusions of love and affection.

This brings to mind Jesus' baptism, when the Holy Spirit visibly descended in the form of a dove and the Father's voice echoed from heaven: "This is my beloved Son, with whom I am well pleased" (Matt. 3:17). It was an epic moment, with the three members of the Trinity all actively involved. But it was also an incredibly tender moment—

a Father declaring to a Son (and the world) that He loved Him and was pleased with Him.

Our heavenly Father set an example for all parents and for those who love and care for children of every age when He spoke those words of affection, affirmation, and approval.

I know it may sound elementary, but say the words often. Say them out loud. In writing. In texts. In private. In public.

- "I love you."
- "I thank God for giving you to our family."
- "I'm cheering for you!"
- "I'm so blessed to be your mom."
- "You're a blessing, a treasure!"

Whenever possible, underscore your words with loving physical touch. You can't do it enough. You can't do it too often. And though your kids may sometimes wipe off your kisses or wriggle to escape your hugs, those expressions of affection will not be lost on them. Each tender word, each kiss and hug, is an investment that will pay out across future years and generations as a rich inheritance of love.

When the apostle Paul wanted to express to his children in the faith how much he loved them, he likened his feelings to a mother's love for her children:

> We were gentle among you, like a nursing mother
> taking care of her own children. So, being affectionately
> desirous of you, we were ready to share with you not
> only the gospel of God but also our own selves, because
> you had become very dear to us. (1 Thess. 2:7–8)

Gentle. Nurturing. Caring. Affectionate. Desirous. Sharing. Self-sacrificing. Very dear. This is the kind of heart Paul calls for older women to help younger women cultivate toward their children. A heart that makes the gospel beautiful in the eyes of children and adults alike. A heart that needs to be expressed both in actions and in words.

What truly inspires us to love the children God has put in our lives is His calling, not the sweet expressions on their faces or the attention we gain from their adorable presence or their accomplishments.

We love them because *God* loves them, and we love them because He's *called* us to love them—even on those days when they are anything but sweet and adorable.

My dad died suddenly of a heart attack on the weekend of my twenty-first birthday. One of my brothers was killed in a car wreck at the age of twenty-two. In both cases, everything that was going to be said between us needed to be said before that day arrived so unexpectedly. So I'm acutely aware of how important it is to express our love now. Because even if everyone in a whole family lives to be a hundred, our opportunities for expressing love to one another are still limited.

So if you can, if there's a way—even with children who live far away or who are estranged—do it before it's too late.

Say it today: "I love you . . ."

Make children a priority.

You hear a lot today about "hover mothers" and "drama mamas," who wrap their own needs too tightly around their children, often failing to let them establish their personal identities and learn to take responsibility for their lives. But in my observation, another concern is that for some moms, their children's needs rank fifth or sixth on the priority list—behind work, friends, personal time, buying new stuff for the house, sometimes even church and ministry.

Your children need a mom who is attentive to the condition of their souls.

My husband and I sat in a restaurant recently and watched as two women friends at the next table enjoyed a long, leisurely lunch and conversation. That whole time, the preschool son of one of them sat affixed to an iPad, isolated beneath a set of headphones, with absolutely no interaction with either of the grown-ups.

I'm not saying there is never a time for adults to converse and let children entertain themselves, and I don't believe children should always be the center of attention (an opposite and equally unwise extreme). But your children *need* you. They need a mom who is tuned, alert, attentive to their needs and the condition of their souls, who is intentional about engaging their little hearts now and for eternity.

Children live with their parents such a short time before they are grown and gone. So if your little ones are still at home, please make this time count. There will be time later for those other activities that you choose to put on hold until they are safely out of the nest.

And I would repeat this encouragement to women like me who do not have children of our own. We are part of the body of Christ, and we are all in this Titus 2 sisterhood together. That means children should be a priority for us too—as they were for Jesus when He was here on earth.

You may or may not particularly like kids. They may strike you as messy, disruptive, and unnecessary. But to love and welcome children is to be like Jesus (see Matt. 19:13–14). So let's be alert to ways we can reach out to them and bless them, as big sisters and spiritual mothers and grandmothers.

Seek them out and speak to them at church. Compliment them when you see evidences of grace in their attitude or behavior. Let them know you notice them and that you care about them. Come alongside their parents to support the raising of these children, whether by offering to babysit occasionally so Mom and Dad can go out by themselves or by engaging more directly in their lives.

One of the great joys of my life has been cultivating relationships with others' children:

- attending their sports events
- taking them out on lunch dates
- celebrating their special occasions
- staying connected through notes and texts and calls
- asking them questions and listening to their answers
- rooting for them through different seasons and transitions
- extending grace and staying engaged when they struggled in their faith journey

And some of the closest relationships I enjoy today are with the now-adult children I reached out to when I was in my twenties and thirties.

I have been blessed to participate in many of their weddings. And now they have children of their own, some of whom call me Yaya (Greek for grandmother). So my life as an older woman continues to be enriched and multiplied by nurturing relationships with children, teens, and young adults. Never anticipating that I would one day marry, I've said for years that I didn't fear growing old alone because all these kids who have been such a precious part of my life would care for me when I couldn't care for myself! Truly the Lord "gives the barren woman a home, making her the joyous mother of children" (Ps. 113:9).

Everyone benefits when we all join together to make "loving our children" a priority and to pass the baton of faith on to the next generation.

But don't put children first . . .

Now, this may sound contradictory to the whole idea of making children a priority. It is certainly a paradox. But embracing this paradox may be the key to loving your children well.

You've been uniquely tasked with transmitting the gospel—day by day, year by year, experience by experience—to the little ones you've been privileged to raise and nurture. It happens, Paul says, as you "love" your children—sharing with them the affection that God has for His children. So you must make the sharing of this love a priority—but *not* your first priority.

Here's what I mean.

Moms can be so overwhelmed by the mental, physical, and emotional outlay of parenting—in combination with other necessary responsibilities—that they forfeit time with the Lord in exchange for what feels like better ways of recharging. As a result, they simply don't have the capacity to give their children the love they need. Without meaning to, they have distanced themselves from the Source of true love for their children.

Certain seasons of parenting, of course, do make it difficult to consistently set aside chunks of time for prayer and Scripture reading. But even in such busy, stressful stretches, loving children well necessitates drinking from the fountain of God's grace and love.

I love the memory one of my friends shared of a morning when the phone started ringing. She was back in her bedroom trying to get some much-needed time alone with the Lord. One of her little ones, however, picked up the phone and, after a brief hello, told the caller, "I'm sorry, but my mommy is meeting with God right now. You'll have to call back later."

So sometimes, ironically, the best way to make your children a priority is to make time with God an even greater priority. That may mean weeding out other good but nonessential activities for a season. It may mean narrowing the number of activities your children are involved in. But at the end of the day, the time you carve out to spend in the Word and prayer—alone and with your children—will settle your heart, strengthen you, and enable you to love the little ones in your life better, and to see them for the blessings they are. In the process, you will be pointing them to Christ, training them to seek out His love as well.

The Privilege of Giving Life

So moms (and others), I hope you will delight in your children. Enjoy them. Let the priorities spelled out in Titus 2 shape your life so that the little ones as well as the bigger ones—all the ones who call you Mom (or Auntie or friend)—are able to legitimately describe you as "the joyous mother of children" (Ps. 113:9).

Motherhood is a privilege and responsibility like none other. What you're doing is vital, quite literally life-giving. I'd like to park on that term—life-giving—for a moment. It takes us back to the first mother. Have you ever realized it was only after their tragic fall into sin that the woman actually received a personal name like her husband, Adam?

It was Adam who named her: "The man called his wife's name Eve" (Gen. 3:20).

But . . . Eve. Why Eve?

Eve's very name is a statement of faith in the promises and redeeming love of God.

Adam didn't just take Eve's name at random from a book of names—eyes closed, finger circling in midair, then pressed down at random to the page, going with whatever it landed on.

No, the name *Eve* held (and continues to hold) enormous significance, not only in God's plan for women and motherhood, but also in His grand design of redemption. For when Adam named his wife, the two of them had just made a fatal choice. In violating God's command not to eat from the only forbidden tree in the garden, they had called down upon themselves and future generations the justified curse of death.

And yet it was in that moment, when death was looming, that Adam named his wife *Eve*, which sounds like the Hebrew for "life-giver."

Eve's very name, in other words, is actually a statement of faith in the promises and redeeming love of God. The woman whose actions had brought death to the human race would now become, by the restorative action of a gracious God, the one whose body would produce physical *life* for the human race.

This legacy can be seen in the hands and hearts and physical capabilities given by God to generations of women who have carried on—and still carry on—the giving of life by bearing children and nurturing them. And we should marvel at this.

No, not all of us are given the privilege of bearing physical children. Some of us never have the opportunity to nurture children of our own, and some are called to raise children that other women gave birth to. And we are worth no less to the Lord than those with two, four, six, eight, ten biological children featured in the picture frames that line their hallways at home. But the tremendous value and responsibility invested in us as women by God, as those uniquely given the capacity to be bearers of life, means that we all share in His purpose for the ages. We all participate in Eve's life-giving legacy. And when we love children as He has instructed us to do—*our* children, *their* children, *your* children, *all* children—the gospel grows and brings forth the fruit of eternal life.

> *Motherhood is a privilege. But inherent within this precious privilege is also the potential for pain.*

Privilege, Pain, Promise—and Perez

Motherhood is indeed a privilege. Having children in our lives is a privilege. It's all part of the life-giving blessing of being a woman. But inherent within this precious privilege—on this side of the Fall—is also the potential for pain, because anyone who accepts the call of motherhood risks having her heart broken as a result.

Mary of Nazareth experienced this pain more deeply than any mother who has ever lived. When she and Joseph took her infant Son to the temple forty days after His birth, the aged Simeon spoke divinely inspired words to prepare the young mother for what she would face:

> And Simeon blessed them and said to Mary . . . "Behold, this child is appointed for the fall and rising of many in Israel, and for a sign that is opposed (and *a sword will pierce through your own soul also*), so that thoughts from many hearts may be revealed." (Luke 2:34–35)

Yes, Mary was uniquely blessed to be the mother of the Son of God. And yes, this calling would bring exquisite joys. But with the privilege would come excruciating pain. Not the pain caused by her child's sin—something every other mother experiences—but the painful price her Child would pay for the sin of the world.

You are not Mary, of course. Her role in history—and in motherhood—is unique. But no mother escapes the pain of motherhood entirely—and neither will you.

Your children will disappoint you at times, just as you will disappoint yourself as a parent—something that happens most every day in small or large ways. You'll give in to their pleas and feed them junk food. You'll overreact. You'll lose your temper. Or you'll let yourself get distracted on a day when one of the kids wanders from your sight and inadvertently puts himself or herself in danger—a terrifying experience, even when everything turns out all right.

Even on the best days, a mother's job can be fraught with worry, fear, and guilt—which means moms must recognize their utter dependence on the grace of God, both for themselves and for their children. When mistakes and shortcomings rear their ugly heads, when yesterday's meltdown is seen more clearly in the light of a new morning, they can experience afresh the truth of the gospel that invites them to turn to Christ, receiving His mercy and forgiveness, and walking in renewed hope.

Motherhood is indeed a means of sanctification, meant to deepen your confidence in the One who can supply every grace to you through the indwelling Spirit of Jesus. That's true when the troubles you encounter are "ordinary" and relatively minor. But what about when your troubles with your children are major?

- When your marriage has failed or your husband has died and you're struggling as a single mom to reach past your pain to parent your children.
- When you suspect—or know—that a child is drinking or doing drugs.
- When your six-year-old is kicked out of school for fighting—again!— or your sixteen-year-old is failing classes left and right.
- When a child's special needs threaten to sabotage your marriage.
- When a son or daughter has embraced an immoral lifestyle.
- When a child rejects the truth of God's Word you've tried so hard to implant.
- Or when the phone rings with the news that there's been a terrible accident . . .

I can't tell you how many stories I've heard from mothers who have earnestly sought to love their children well and to lead them into a real relationship with Christ, and who still experience heartache over their troubled kids—sometimes for years. For so many, motherhood is a roller-coaster ride, with periods of crisis followed by brief glimpses of calm. No sooner do they dare to hope again than they are plunged back into a familiar place of anxiety, regret, guilt, heaviness, and too many fractured emotions to count.

If that's what loving your children has been requiring of you lately, I want to point you to a passage of Scripture that may give you fresh hope and courage.

The occasion was the improbable wedding of Ruth and Boaz, and the setting was the outpouring of blessing given to them by the people and elders gathered at the city gates.

> May the LORD make the woman, who is coming into your house, like Rachel and Leah, who together built up the house of Israel. May you act worthily in Ephrathah and be renowned in Bethlehem, and may your house be like the house of Perez, whom Tamar bore to Judah, because of the offspring that the LORD will give you by this young woman. (Ruth 4:11–12)

Perez. "Like the house of Perez."

Who's he?

Here's the story, which happened long before the days of Ruth and Boaz. Judah, one of Jacob's twelve sons, who would eventually be father to one of the twelve tribes of Israel—married a Canaanite woman (which was never a good thing) and had three sons. The older two were wicked and were put to death at the hand of the Lord. At some point thereafter, Judah's wife passed away as well. And some time after *that*, Judah took what amounted to a business trip, traveling to a certain city to shear his sheep. While there, he was intimate with a woman masquerading as a prostitute, who became pregnant from their casual union and gave birth to twin boys.

The woman in question, Tamar, was actually the widow of Judah's older deceased son. And the elder of the twin boys who were born to Judah and Tamar was . . .

Perez.

If you've gotten lost in this soap opera, don't feel the need to go back and unravel it. Suffice it to say the whole story was a convoluted, dysfunctional mess. Bad things happened and then got worse. But God's heart is always beating in the rhythm of redemption. And through this illegitimate, nearly incestuous birth, the line of Perez would extend to Boaz, the husband of Ruth . . . to David, the great-grandson of Boaz . . . and ultimately to Joseph, the husband of Mary, the mother of Jesus (see Matthew 1).

And that's the promise of the house of Perez.

We have a redeeming God who is continually in the process of making all things new and who is always working—even through our messy lives and stories—to write His story and to display His glory.

There is no situation, no matter how broken or bleak, into which our redeeming God cannot step, bringing supernatural help, healing, and hope.

Giving Life to One Another

Perhaps you identify with some of the details in Perez's family line. One or more of your children may have been born as the result of foolish or sinful choices, whether yours or others. One of your grown or teenage children may have brought an "out of wedlock" child into the world and into your family circle. Perhaps you're dealing with some other painful circumstance in the life of your child, and heartbreak is squeezing you like a vise, causing you to wonder whatever is to become of this one you love so deeply and intensely. Or perhaps the worst has happened, and you're wrestling with a grief that seems insurmountable.

But there is no situation, no matter how broken or bleak, into which our redeeming God cannot step, bringing supernatural help, healing, and hope. It might take time, and it might take you places you never expected to go. It probably won't look the way you would have scripted the story. But God is faithful, and He loves your kids more than you ever could. He *will* show up. When He does, I suspect, He will be fragrant with the incense of your prayers (Rev. 5:8) and carrying the container where He's captured every tear you've shed

(Ps. 56:8)—along with the prayers and tears of all the Titus 2 women you have turned to in your pain. And in time, no doubt, He'll have someone in mind who needs a mentor she can relate to, a woman who will need the encouragement of your testimony about God's faithfulness and grace even when your eyes were filled with tears.

Motherhood, like marriage and other callings in a woman's life, was never intended to be attempted alone, without counsel and comfort, without teaching and training.

Older woman, your hardest mothering days may be behind you. Your children may be launched, your direct influence on their lives diminished significantly. But your job is not done yet. Following in your steps are some tired young moms who need you. They need your voice of encouragement, calling them to press on in the race. They need your wisdom, gained in the trenches. They need your helping hands, reaching out to hold a crying baby. They need your time, perhaps to offer them an afternoon break or even an overnight getaway. They need your love for Jesus and your love for them, inspiring them to love Him and to love their husbands and children.

And *younger woman*, when you want to shriek, "My name's not *Mommy* any more—go call someone else!" and when you feel like a motherless child needing to be held yourself, remember that God has made provision for this very time. He has placed older women in the Body for just such moments, to be a means of grace in your life. Don't be afraid to let them know you need them. Don't be too proud to ask for practical help, insight, and prayer. You'll be giving them an opportunity to do what God has called them to do. These older women need you as much as you need them!

And, by the way, don't miss an older single woman who might be standing in the wings wondering if there is a place for her in this Titus 2, life-to-life arrangement. The opportunity to encourage young moms in a variety of ways during my years of singleness was a huge blessing to me, allowing me the joy of being a life-giver and forging many, lasting sweet friendships with families.

The writer to the Hebrews—seeking to bolster the faith of believers living in difficult days—emphasized the importance of avoiding isolation and maintaining such vital relationships:

> And let us consider how to stir up one another to love
> and good works, not neglecting to meet together, as is
> the habit of some, but encouraging one another, and
> all the more as you see the Day drawing near. (Heb.
> 10:24–25)

We women, we givers of life, are called to give life to one another as well as to the children He entrusts to our care. When the days are difficult, as they often will be—or even when they're just ordinary and entire days seem to be lived on autopilot—moms can find strength, courage, and wisdom by walking together with other like-hearted women.

As older women train and encourage younger women to love their children, the next generation will experience the beauty of Christ's love and their hearts be captivated by it—the Titus 2 way.

Making It Personal

Older women

1. Do you know a young mom in your church or community who is angry or frustrated about mothering? What can you do to encourage her and gain her ear so you can begin to gently pour God's wisdom about motherhood into her life?

2. Do you have a heart for nurturing children? How is that expressed? How can your life model biblical motherhood in positive, nurturing ways to the young women in your world?

3. Whether you're called "Mom," "Auntie," "Grandma," or "friend," your life can make a difference in younger women's lives. Examine your relationships today. How can you step up your teaching or mentoring influence in their lives? How can you love and encourage them or offer some practical relief?

Younger women

1. How has the way you were mothered shaped your perspective and feelings about motherhood? To what extent do those feelings and thoughts line up with God's perspective on motherhood?

2. God uses other women—Titus 2 women—in our lives to help equip us for our calling. Who are the women in your life you can call on for counsel and encouragement? How might one or more of them be able to help you deal with the "impossible task" of motherhood?

3. How might an older woman's insight, prayer, or practical help encourage you right now? How might your requests for help bless *them*?

Teach what accords with sound doctrine.

Older men are to be sober-minded, dignified, self-controlled,
sound in faith, in love, and in steadfastness.

Older women likewise are to be reverent in behavior,
not slanderers or slaves to much wine.

They are to teach what is good,
and so train the young women
to love their husbands and children,
to be self-controlled,
pure,
working at home,
kind,
and submissive to their own husbands,
that the word of God may not be reviled.

. . . so that in everything they may adorn
the doctrine of God our Savior.

TITUS 2:1–5, 10

CHAPTER 14

Instruments of Grace

Showing a Deeper Kind of Kindness

*Pure kindness flows from God's saving grace and colors
our lives with a joy that is winsomely contagious.*
MARY BEEKE

FROM THE LOOK ON WOMEN'S FACES whenever the subject of Titus 2 womanhood comes up, it seems many of them are drawn to this ideal. They respect and desire the kind of character this passage calls them to, and they are intrigued by the possibilities of what God could accomplish *in* them and *through* them if they were to engage in the intergenerational friendships Paul describes in this passage.

I think that's why you and I are still here, digging into the Word to find out what the Titus 2 woman looks like, what sort of principles she embodies, and what she does to adorn the gospel—to see if she could actually look like us.

But God is not only interested in *what* we do. He is equally concerned with *how* we do what we do—with the heart behind our actions.

That's why I believe Paul included an admonition about being kind right in the middle of his core curriculum for women in the church (Titus 2:5). In fact, "kind" falls right on the heels of "working at home"—it's included in the context of our most intimate family relationships. I believe Paul is saying it's not enough to tend to the tasks and people assigned to us. God also cares about our motives and our disposition—how that service is carried out, how we treat and respond to our family, friends, and others.

Paul is the one, remember, who famously wrote, "If I speak in the tongues of men and of angels . . . if I have prophetic powers, and understand all mysteries and all knowledge . . . if I give away all I have, and if I deliver up my body to be burned, but have not love, I gain nothing" (1 Cor. 13:1–3).

Nothing.

He might similarly say, of women who serve their families and care for their homes, "If I have a house so spotless that people could eat off the kitchen floor . . . and if I can whip up incredibly scrumptious meals on a tight budget . . . and if I've transformed our home into a magazine-quality showcase . . . but I don't do it all with kindness, it's nothing."

Because, yes, Jesus can be seen and worshiped through such ordinary things as a crisply ironed dress shirt, a made bed, a ride to soccer practice, even a fresh batch of chocolate-chip cookies.

But not when they're performed without kindness.

Without that quality, those "good" things we do for others amount to noisy gongs and clanging cymbals. (Paul's words again.) And nobody can hear or feel our love for them over the tired, exasperated, frustrated racket we're making.

Like Jesus' friend Martha, we are sometimes "distracted with much serving" (Luke 10:40), "worried and bothered about so many things" (v. 41 NASB). We become stretched thin and stirred up, bothered and brittle.

And, all too often, unkind.

But I think there's often something more than just stress behind the sharp tone or impatient attitude that sometimes bubbles up and spills over as unkindness in our relationships. It's something we've already discussed in this book—the lack of a "sound mind."

A self-controlled—*sophron*—mind.

Because when we're not *sophron*, we're apt to see only what frustrates us, so we begin to resent the very people God has called us to serve.

When we're not *sophron*, we let ourselves get overwhelmed by our schedules and agendas rather than concentrating on the "one thing" Jesus said was "necessary" (Luke 10:42)— experiencing life in His presence.

When we're not *sophron*, we don't have any margin or heart for kindness.

So why don't we just pull over here for a while and drop in on Martha at her home in Bethany. And see what the lack of *sophron* did to one woman's mind in particular.

A Tale of Two Sisters

The occasion, you may recall, was a visit by Jesus and a band of His followers. (You can read the whole story in Luke 10.) We don't know for sure how many people were with Him, but it was probably a good-sized traveling party, perhaps two or three dozen people. And Martha, with her take-charge, firstborn temperament, was the de facto hostess for this impromptu gathering.[1]

At first, we assume, Martha was excited to see Jesus and the others in the doorway, thankful for the privilege of hosting her friend in the home she shared with her sister (Mary) and brother (Lazarus). But as Martha scrambled to clean and cook and make sure everyone was properly served and comfortably settled (while Mary chose to sit at Jesus' feet and listen to Him teach), a host of turbulent thoughts and attitudes began swirling in her head and heart.

I'm sure, like me, you'll recognize some of them:

- *Self-centeredness.* "Lord, do you not care that my sister has left me to serve alone? Tell her then to help me" (v. 40). Notice all the first-person language in these biting words, all the concern about "me"—what this responsibility is costing me, what people should be doing for me.
- *Insensitivity.* People had gathered around to listen to Jesus teach. But that didn't keep Martha from barging in, interrupting Him, disturbing everyone. She was more concerned about how she was being inconvenienced than about what others were needing or experiencing.
- *Accusation.* Asking if someone could give her a hand would have been an understandable request. But her words were accusatory—both toward Jesus ("do you not care?") and toward her sister ("my sister has left me to serve alone").
- *Resentment.* We can guess that Martha may have already been clattering the dishes in the kitchen a little more loudly than necessary. Her inner martyr had likely been muttering under her breath for quite a while. And when no one picked up on her "hint, hint" clues, she stopped even trying to squelch her rising anger. Out it came—loud and whiny and, yes, unkind.

Martha had grown irritated, impatient, demanding. There was an edge in her spirit, harshness in her voice. Serving was no longer a privilege—lovingly, gladly, graciously given—but a burden. The friends she had set out to serve had become to her a bother, a nuisance.

And beyond just being selfishly upset, Martha was willing to risk building a wall between herself and her sister. If not for Jesus' wise, gentle, corrective rebuke, we could easily imagine a few subsequent days of . . .

"Is something wrong, Martha?"

"Nothing's wrong."

"Well, *something's* wrong. I can tell."

"No, Mary. It's *not!*"

"Well, it sure seems like it."

"Would you please just stop?"

"Oh, Martha, don't tell me you're still—"

"I don't want to talk about it anymore, okay?"

"It was just that Jesus was here, and—"

"Exactly! And I would have been fine if you'd . . ."

The Scripture doesn't tell us what took place between the sisters after Jesus' visit. But when *sophron*—a sound mind, self-controlled thinking—goes missing, unkindness all-too-often shows up in its place, and relationships take a hit.

Older woman, many younger women in our lives are tired, frustrated, and feel alone in their efforts, as if no one cares about the sacrifices they are making. Their relationships at home and elsewhere are frayed. We are called to model kindness for them and to train these young women to develop a kind heart and walk.

Younger woman, this quality is essential to learn if you want to honor the Lord. It flows out of a *sophron* mind and a heart that is fixed on Christ, and it makes all the difference in the world—both in your personal well-being and in the atmosphere you create around you.

If we wish to progress together toward the Titus 2 model for women, if we want to adorn the doctrine and gospel of Christ and His beauty to the world, we need a different kind of heart.

A *kind* kind of heart.

Gifts in Kind

On the surface, a study on kindness could seem insignificant compared to the weightier subjects we've been addressing. It's easy to underestimate and overlook the importance of this quality. But I assure you that kindness is no trifling notion in the Christian vocabulary. I believe

Paul intended it to matter as much to us as all the other essentials of the Titus 2 curriculum for women.

That's because a woman's spirit and tone has the ability to determine the climate around her, whether at home, at work, at the gym, or at church. And this makes kindness indispensable—in our relationships with others and for our gospel witness in the world. When we submit to Christ's lordship and serve others with humility and kindness, our words and actions can have a greater impact on those around us than a hundred sermons and orchestrated church outreaches. But when we don't, when we give in to unsound thinking and unkind attitudes, everyone suffers.

Let's be intentional about pursuing kindness.

So with the same concern we feel for being pure and self-controlled, for avoiding slander and sins of the tongue, let's also be intentional about pursuing kindness—because it is every bit as important as the others.

Good and Kind

The Greek word translated "kind" in Titus 2:5—*agathos*—is rendered as "good" almost every other time it appears in the New Testament. Sometimes it is used as an adjective to describe another word, as in "good works" or "good deeds." Various Bible scholars and commentators define this word as meaning "good and benevolent, profitable, useful,"[2] "beneficial in its effect,"[3] and "kind, helpful, and charitable."[4]

What Paul is exhorting here, in other words, is more than simply a nice, friendly feeling. *Agathos* is kindness that goes somewhere. It's a benevolent disposition coming to life, turning into active goodness.

The kindness inside us, in other words, becomes the goodness that others receive from us. It's a process that starts inside and inevitably moves outward. It's not just *wanting* to be kind or having kind thoughts and feelings, but *being* kind.

Author Jerry Bridges reminds us that this kind of kindness and goodness is rooted in humility and others-centeredness—no small challenge, as our natural bent is just the opposite:

> Apart from God's grace, most of us naturally tend to be concerned about *our* responsibilities, *our* problems, *our* plans. But the person who has grown in the grace of kindness has expanded his thinking outside of himself and his interests and has developed a genuine interest in the happiness and well-being of those around him.[5]

Am I a kind woman? In heart attitudes as well as outward actions? This is a question that pierces us when God's Word holds up a mirror in our family rooms and kitchens and hallways, our cars and minivans and workplaces. At times, instead of kindness and goodness, what we see reflected back is harshness and criticism. Barking and berating. Touchiness and irritability.

We may try to justify ourselves. After all, aren't we the ones who make sure everybody gets their meals and has their clothes washed?

Yes.

Will we leave the office early tonight and leave everyone to do our work for us?

No.

Will we fail to show up when we're scheduled to help out at church?

Of course not.

Will we come around later, if necessary, to apologize if we reacted sharply toward someone earlier in the day?

Maybe—although we may be tempted to point out the circumstances that provoked us.

The people in our lives know they can count on us to be there when they need us. And if our spirit isn't always kind while we do our serving, is that really such a big deal? Shouldn't they just be thankful for all we do for them?

So we go through our days, checking off items from our to-do lists. We perform the duties others demand or expect of us. But are we doing it with a kind heart?

And if not, then what good are we really doing, and how are our relationships being affected?

Channels of Blessing

I love the New Testament account of a follower of Christ most commonly known as Dorcas (the Greek equivalent of her Hebrew name Tabitha). The book of Acts tells us that she "was full of good [*agathos*] works and acts of charity" (9:36).

Here was a woman whose relationship with Christ moved her to pour out her life in practical acts of kindness toward those in need. Her life was a picture of true kindness in action. And the phrase "full of" ["abounding with"—NASB] implies that her charitable acts were not performed as begrudging service or out of a mere sense of duty. That became even more clear when tragedy struck, and the life of this generous-hearted woman was snuffed out:

> In those days she became ill and died, and when they
> had washed her, they laid her in an upper room. Since
> Lydda was near Joppa, the disciples, hearing that Peter
> was there, sent two men to him, urging him, "Please
> come to us without delay." So Peter rose and went with
> them. And when he arrived, they took him to the upper
> room. All the widows stood beside him weeping and
> showing tunics and other garments that Dorcas made
> while she was with them. (vv. 37–39)

This poignant description of the widows she had blessed, grieving next to her lifeless body, suggests that Dorcas genuinely cared for the people she served with her acts of kindness. They didn't just miss what she had done for them. They missed *her*.

Who will weep at your funeral as they think about your kind heart and the ways you have served and blessed them and demonstrated the kindness of Christ to them?

And how will you be remembered by your family, your closest friends, and others who knew you? Will they remember only what you did for them, or will there be a lingering fragrance because of how you did it?

Will they remember both the sacrifices you made *and* the smile they could always count on to warm their day?

Will they remember the extra time you took *and* the way you put your arms around them at the end of the day and told them how much you loved them?

Will they just remember the chugging sound of the washing machine running while they were drifting off to sleep, or will they also recall the soft sound of your voice humming a tune while waiting for the last load to dry?

Will they remember you as both a hard worker *and* an instrument of grace and goodness?

It's not clear what Dorcas' friends expected Peter to do when they called for him to come after the beloved benefactress died. But what happened next quickly got the attention of the whole town:

> Peter put them all outside, and knelt down and prayed; and turning to the body he said, "Tabitha, arise." And she opened her eyes, and when she saw Peter she sat up. And he gave her his hand and raised her up. Then calling the saints and widows, he presented her alive. And it became known throughout all Joppa, and many believed in the Lord. (vv. 40–42)

All that time and effort spent making clothing for widows who had no other means of support had spelled L-O-V-E. And such kindness stood in stark contrast to the unbelieving world, where widows were often left to fend for themselves and faced probable destitution. Dorcas' life shone a spotlight on the love of Christ. It endeared her to those who had witnessed and been touched by her kindness. The power and beauty of her life moved them to call for the apostle when she died. And as a result of her being raised back to life, "many" put their faith in Him.

And that's the ripple effect of Christian kindness and the impact it can have on our witness in the world.

Kindness—true goodness—sometimes shows itself in tireless effort and sleepless nights. It can translate into grocery shopping for the family instead of shoe shopping for ourselves. It can mean relinquishing our plans for the afternoon when a daughter really needs to talk or hosting neighbors on a Friday night instead of enjoying a quiet evening to ourselves.

When we serve people, we serve Christ.

But the goal of it all is to show others the goodness of Christ—on a practical, personal, you-matter-to-me basis. And to do that consistently and well, we all need the training, accountability, and support Titus 2 relationships can provide. Older women need to model *agathos* for younger women and teach them the value of kindness. And younger women need to learn from older women that *people* matter more than any other *tasks* you might accomplish.

And, yes, people can be perturbing. Marriage and family life would be a lot less stressful if husbands and children didn't sometimes act irresponsibly or disregard our feelings or instructions. Ministry would go more smoothly and be less demanding if people weren't so needy or would just get their act together. Many of the issues we face in our jobs would go away if it weren't for inexperienced coworkers, demanding clients, or impatient customers.

Yes, people may cause the lion's share of our headaches. But when we serve people, we serve Christ. And when we treat people with kindness rather than indifference or impatience, we become channels of blessing, dispensing gracious words and actions that can't help but adorn the gospel of Christ.

Kindness Begins at Home

The woman whose description we know so well from Proverbs 31 is another lovely, biblical model of kindness in action. Wherever this strong, gifted, diligent woman goes, she leaves a trail of goodness, and she ministers grace to everyone around her:

> She opens her mouth with wisdom,
>> and the teaching of kindness is on her tongue. (v. 26)

But note who benefits first from this woman's industry and goodwill. For her, kindness begins at home. With her family. With her inner circle. With those who share her daily life. Her kindness toward her husband, for example, is displayed in a daily commitment that remains undiminished with the passing of time or when their relationship may be in a hard place:

Nowhere am I more tempted to be selfish and lazy than in my home and my closest relationships. Too often, we show more concern and kindness for complete strangers than for those who live under the same roof with us.

> She does him good, and not harm,
>> *all the days of her life.* (v. 12)

Not a day is wasted by lashing out in frustration and anger or being passive-aggressive. Every day is seen as an opportunity to do her husband good with her attitude, words, and actions. This is a huge gift she gives to him—and to herself, as her husband responds with the highest of praise for his wife.

The Proverbs 31 woman's selfless, thoughtful deeds also bless her entire family as she labors tirelessly and faithfully to ensure their needs are met.

> She is not afraid of snow for her household,
> for all her household are clothed in scarlet. . . .
> She looks well to the ways of her household
> and does not eat the bread of idleness.
> Her children rise up and call her blessed . . . (vv. 21, 27–28)

The fact is, nowhere am I more tempted to be selfish and lazy than in my home and my closest relationships. And I fear this is true for most of us—wives and moms, as well as those who live with other family members or friends. Too often, I'm afraid, we show more concern and kindness for neighbors, colleagues, store clerks, or complete strangers than for those who live under the same roof with us or who are related to us by blood or marriage.

If a couple were staying at our house for the weekend, we'd be sure clean towels were in the bathroom, their linens were freshly washed, dinner was flexible to their schedule, and a fresh pot of coffee was brewing in the morning. But when our own kids and husband need something—well, they know where the refrigerator is and how to turn on the oven.

Right?

Managing a busy household, dealing with the daily tasks related to serving husbands and kids—or whatever other responsibilities you may have—requires diligence and discipline day in and day out. It requires hard work, sometimes exhausting work. But it also requires kindness—or as one commentator put it: "a lack of irritability in light of the nagging demands of mundane and routine household duties."[6]

And that's where things can get challenging. It's so easy for us to be like the woman who once lamented to me with refreshing candor, "I'm only good enough to look good to the world." At home, it's often another story.

When I'm out speaking at a conference, I can be exceedingly gracious, kind, and patient with long lines of women who want to share their burdens and their (at times long, detailed) stories, looking them in the eyes, never complaining about my tired, aching back and feet. But when those closest to me—in my home, my family, or our ministry—need a listening ear, an attentive heart, or a thoughtful act, I can be preoccupied, unfeeling, or just too busy.

Who among us hasn't had the experience of being in the middle of a tense, unkind exchange at home, only to instantly change our tone and talk warmly with an outsider who calls or stops by? What does that say to our loved ones about how we value them and about the authenticity of our "kindness" to others?

Yes, kindness at home takes extra effort. Home is where we experience most acutely those daily annoyances and disappointments that tempt us to develop an attitude. So kindness at home also requires extra helpings of grace, which in turn requires daily dependence on God and the support of our Titus 2 sisters.

Already, in the short time I've been a wife, I've witnessed at moments the distance-creating, intimacy-killing impact of a lack of kindness on my part toward my husband. Unkind words spoken thoughtlessly, kind words left unspoken, inconsiderate actions; being too self-absorbed to notice and celebrate an accomplishment in my husband's business; wounding him in sensitive areas with insensitive teasing; being too busy with my own stuff to carry out small acts of kindness that would serve and bless him.

But I've also experienced the incredible importance and power of kindness in a marriage. I have seen it modeled in the marriages of some of my closest friends and of my Titus 2 mentors. And Robert's tender heart and his consistent kindness—always looking for ways to serve and bless me—have inspired me to be more tuned in to how I can do good to him. Being the recipient of his kindness has increased my desire to outdo him in this area.

Often, I've found, it's the little things—the simple expressions of gratitude and kindness—that express love to my husband and set the tone in our relationship. Leaving encouraging sticky notes in his *One-Year Bible* when he is headed out on a trip. Turning down the sheet on his side of the bed at night. Delivering a sandwich and cold root beer on a hot day when he's outside working on a project. Stopping in the middle of a busy work day to head downstairs to his study and find out how his day is going. Honoring his preferences over mine. Assuming the best when he forgets to tell me a piece of news. Choosing to overlook some perceived (or real) slight rather than grinding his nose in it. A kind heart expressed in kind words and kind deeds oils our relationship and softens and draws our hearts toward each other.

Your call to kindness at home will probably take different forms from mine. It may involve curbing a sharp reaction to a childish accident, replenishing the fridge with snacks for a teen, helping a roommate with a project, repeating yourself gently to an elderly parent. But if we were all to demonstrate true kindness toward the people who know us best and see us at our worst, our more public displays of affection would likely ring more true. And I suspect that if we showed more kindness at home, we'd also find ourselves growing genuinely kinder toward everyone else.

From Home and Beyond

Kindness needs to start at home and in our closest relationships. But it doesn't need to *stay* there. As we train each other and let ourselves be trained in kindness, here are some of the other places where our goodness could—and should—be evident.

The family of God

"As we have opportunity," the Bible says, "let us do good to everyone, and especially to those who are of the household of faith" (Gal. 6:10).

Especially to those.

Many people view "church" as primarily a place to show up once a week and invest an hour of time into their spiritual savings account. But that's not what church is supposed to be! Jesus intended His church to be a family—a "household." Not a place, but a people who live out the gospel daily; redeemed men and women who gather together regularly for worship, encouragement, instruction, and service. And the many opportunities for kindness that exist within these relationships—woman to woman, friend to friend, older to younger, younger to older, family to family—can provide a rich source of blessing that builds each other up and keeps each other going.

The roots of this kind of mutual care and consideration among God's people can be traced back to the Old Testament, where the law prescribed, for example, that if you saw an ox or a sheep wandering astray, you weren't allowed to just ignore it. If you knew the person it belonged to, you were to walk it back to its owner. If you weren't sure whose it was or if the journey was more than you could manage, you were to take the animal home with you and keep it safe until the owner came looking for it (see Deut. 22:1–4).

That's the kind of loyalty and kindness that is meant to mark our relationships with fellow members of Christ's body. For as 1 John 4:20 tells us, "he who does not love his brother whom he has seen cannot love God whom he has not seen." And when we open our hearts in generous love and a spirit of kindness toward our fellow believers, we testify to the kindness we've received from God.

So as you encounter fellow believers at church, at Bible study, as they come to mind through the week, or even as you interact online, consider how you might be able to extend kindness that goes deeper than shallow "Hi, how's it going?" hallway conversations. Because most people *aren't* doing "fine, thanks." And your gift of timely kindness—asking sincere questions, expressing interest in the happenings in their life, offering practical assistance for a need they're facing, or stopping to pray together—may be the means by which God ministers grace to them that day.

The poor and needy

Throughout the Scripture we see God's heart for the underserved and the overlooked, the weak and the disenfranchised. The noble woman of Proverbs 31 expresses that heart as she

> opens her hand to the poor
> and reaches out her hands to the needy. (v. 20)

No, it's not our responsibility to solve everyone's problems, to feel as if the weight of people's suffering is ours alone to bear. But God does call each of us to be sensitive toward the plight of those He brings to our attention. And He calls us to demonstrate His kindness to them in practical, need-meeting ways.

And who better than those who have been on the receiving end of God's amazing kindness to be on the lookout for people who are in need of His grace—especially those who may not be expecting anyone's help.

Reaching out in kindness can be as simple as choosing to "see" a person panhandling on the street instead of looking the other way—looking that person in the eye and offering a little something without judging how they will spend it. It can involve asking a widow to sit with us at church, helping out at a food pantry, offering to take a senior in the neighborhood to doctor appointments. But as God leads and as we follow, the borders of our kindness may eventually reach far beyond our natural comfort zone or our normal circle of relationships.

I've watched in awe, for instance, as many of my friends have opened their hearts and homes to care for "the least of these"— orphans, abused or neglected children, special needs children— through foster care, providing "safe homes," and adoption. What a beautiful way to put on display the heart of our heavenly Father who opened His heart and home to bring us into His family when we had nothing to offer Him except our poverty, dysfunction, sin, and need.

If it weren't for Christ showing kindness to us, not one of us would have a single blessing to our name.

In recent years, I have received much joy through occasional involvement at a women's prison where God is at work in an unusual way. The opportunity to offer the kindness of Christ to damaged, broken women who are incarcerated on drug charges or as sex offenders, even some who are serving life sentences for first-degree murder, has reminded me that grace grows best in hard places. It has opened my heart to experience deeper streams of His kindness and blessing, often through the very women I am reaching out to.

Our enemies

And now for the most radical sphere of all—showing kindness to enemies. Responding with gentleness and goodness to those who dislike or even hate us. Doing good for those who would do us harm. Actively seeking the good of those we have reason to fear. That's a prospect that can tie our stomach in knots.

But if it weren't for Christ Himself showing kindness to *us*, not one of us would have a single blessing to our name. We would simply be God's sworn, forever enemies, with no hope on our part of anything except His righteous wrath and just judgment.

Paul says as much in the third chapter of Titus:

> For we ourselves were once foolish, disobedient, led
> astray, slaves to various passions and pleasures, passing
> our days in malice and envy, hated by others and
> hating one another. (v. 3)

That's a description of *you and me* before Jesus saved us. Even for those of us who came to know Him as young children, at our core, we were disobedient, malicious, and hateful. So how did God treat us? Here's how:

> But when the goodness and loving kindness of God
> our Savior appeared, he saved us, not because of
> works done by us in righteousness, but according to
> his own mercy . . . (vv. 4–5)

His goodness and kindness toward us were not based on how we treated Him or on any worthiness in us. Likewise, the kindness we are to show to others is not conditional on their behavior or acceptability. Rather, it's an expression of the kindness we have received from Christ, flowing through us to others.

Even to our enemies.

"I don't have any enemies," you may say. But think again. We're not necessarily talking about supervillains here. Your enemies could simply be people with whom you seem to be at odds. Think about who annoys you or resents you, who often hurts or angers you, who you tend to approach warily if at all. They may be among your family or within your church or from your past. They may live near you, necessitating all-too-frequent contact. Or you may be distanced from them, preferring never to see them again if you can help it.

But consider: what might the kindness of God be leading you to do if your heart was like His heart? And what might it look like if your response toward these people reflected the blessing Christ poured out on you when you were still His enemy?

To be kind is to be like God. And when we are kind to those who are undeserving and unkind to us, we show them the amazing, undeserved kindness of God.

Christ-Centered Kindness

"Be kind to one another," writes Paul in Ephesians 4:32.

"Teach what is good, and so train the young women . . . to be . . . kind," he adds in Titus 2:3.

Agathos—kindness of heart, kindness in action—is an indispensable part of the Titus 2 curriculum for both older and younger women.

Such kindness can be costly—costly to our time, our plans, our comfort, our privacy. But when we exercise it in Jesus' name, kindness can provide us with some of our best opportunities to do what we've been put on this earth to do—to bring glory to God and make known the life-giving, transforming gospel of Christ.

Our kindness may be the window through which those around us are enabled to see His beauty.

Our kindness may be the window through which those around us are enabled to see His beauty. Because kind women—younger and older together—paint an exquisite picture of the gospel. Our lives put on display "the riches of [God's] kindness"—the kindness that "is meant to lead [us] to repentance" (Rom. 2:4). The kindness that can bring about true transformation in those who experience it through us.

The kindness that adorns both us and the gospel we proclaim.

Making It Personal

Older women

1. Dorcas showed the kindness of Christ by helping the poor and needy around her. How might you use your skills to show kindness? How might you mentor or encourage a younger woman in the process?

2. Many younger women feel tired and overwhelmed and can become frustrated when their service and sacrifices appear to go unnoticed. What did you learn in that season that could be helpful to share with a younger woman who is struggling?

3. How could you reach out in kindness to a younger woman in a way that would encourage her and help lift her load?

Younger women

1. Who comes to mind when you think of a Dorcas—a woman who loves Jesus and is a model of kindness and ministering to people's practical needs? What can you learn from her example?

2. Would the people who live in your home and work with you consider you a kind woman? Why or why not?

3. When we get stretched and overly busy with tasks, it's easier to be cranky than kind (think of Martha). How could meditating on the kindness of Christ be an encouragement and motivation to show kindness when you're in that place?

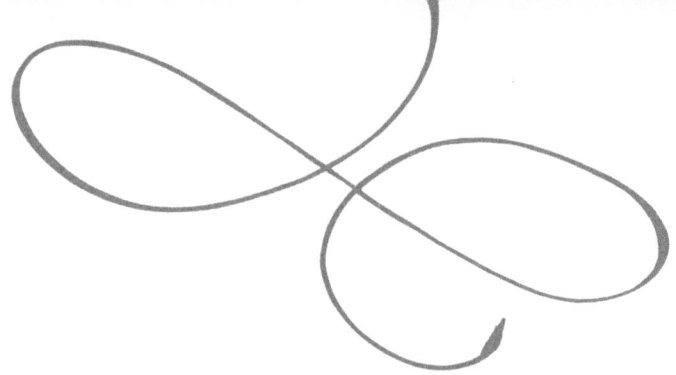

Teach what accords with sound doctrine. . . .

Older women likewise are to be reverent in behavior,
not slanderers or slaves to much wine.

They are to teach what is good,
and so train the young women
to love their husbands and children,
to be self-controlled, pure, working at home,
kind, and submissive to their own husbands,
that the word of God may not be reviled.

Show yourself in all respects to be a model of good works,
and in your teaching show integrity, dignity,
and sound speech that cannot be condemned,
**so that an opponent may be put to shame,
having nothing evil to say about us.**

**. . . so that in everything they may adorn
the doctrine of God our Savior.**

TITUS 2:1–10

A Woman Overjoyed

Tying It All Together . . . Beautifully

This city shall be to me a name of joy,
a praise and a glory before all the nations of the earth
who shall hear of all the good that I do for them.
JEREMIAH 33:9

WE BEGAN THIS BOOK WITH A WEDDING. MY WEDDING. God's wonderful surprise gift to me long after I assumed it would never happen.

Now, as I sit here putting the final touches on this book, Robert and I are approaching our first anniversary. And a lot has changed since that never-to-be-forgotten wedding scene. My lovely white wedding dress is packed up in a box, sitting in storage. There's no make-up artist or hair stylist anywhere in sight. In fact, I haven't done a thing to my hair since yesterday and don't have a drop of make-up on. Robert is out of town, and I'm dressed in work-at-home-no-plans-to-see-anyone attire. (I do plan to change before he gets home later this evening!)

Our home is generally quiet these days, and our lives have settled into a "normal" routine that includes conversation (lots of it), simple meals, church, friends, relaxation, sleep, prayer, and meaningful but

We are not the picture-perfect couple that smiles back at us from the wedding photos displayed in various places around our home. We believe it's worth the price for our marriage to be able to point others to the loveliness of Christ.

strenuous and time-consuming work. Like most people we know, we live a pretty unremarkable, unglamorous life—quite unlike the glorious three-day celebration we experienced on our wedding weekend and the sweet days that followed at a friend's home in the Caribbean.

Robert and I love each other even more than we did the day we said "I do," and we've experienced many happy times in our first year of marriage. But as I've already mentioned, we've also had our share of misunderstandings, missteps, mistakes, and stressful moments—figuring out how to blend our different lifestyles and patterns into our new life as one. Some tears have been shed along the way. The days always seem too short to do everything we had hoped to get done. And at times we fight the temptation to become isolated from one another and independent in spirit—to forget that we need each other.

For sure, we are not the picture-perfect couple that smiles back at us from the wedding photos displayed in various places around our home. We know better than anyone else how weak and frail and sinful we are.

Yet even in our more difficult moments we press on—together—because we believe we are called to this. We remember that we can't do this alone. We realize that the dailyness and even the struggles we face are forging for us a deeper oneness and joy than would otherwise be possible. We believe it's worth the price for our marriage to be able to point others to the loveliness of Christ. And we know that unfettered, unsullied joy will ultimately be ours at the end of the journey.

It seems to me that Robert's and my experience of the last year has some similarities to your experience and mine as we seek to live out the calling of Titus 2.

You and I know that Christ and His gospel are exceedingly lovely. We know it is an extraordinary privilege to belong to Him. We aspire to be the women He made us to be and to fulfill His calling for our lives. And we are exceedingly grateful for those moments when we sense His nearness and revel in His presence, when we are enthralled with His beauty, when we know the joy of being and doing what He has put us here on this earth to be and to do.

But then there are the days—perhaps most days—when we feel more like earthbound plodders than heaven-bound pilgrims. When we lament our selfishness, sinfulness, stubbornness, and slowness to grow in these qualities we know to be pleasing to Him.

Yet we press on in our mission. We keep pursuing our calling to magnify Christ, and we persevere by faith, with the grace we receive from Him each day. We know the challenges and hardships are deepening our oneness with the Savior and conforming us to His likeness. We believe it's worth any price to put His beauty on display during our sojourn in this world. And we trust we will experience unending, unclouded joy when we see His face at the end of the race.

Growing Pains

As we've traveled through these verses from Titus 2, at times you may have felt—as have I—woefully inadequate, convicted by how far short you fall. I would remind you that the point of exposing our sin and insufficiency is not to burden us down with our failure. Rather, the goal is to get us to Christ, whose mercy and grace are our only hope, and to make us realize our utter dependence on Him for anything resembling Christian character in our lives.

If you're a believer in Christ, He has already imputed to you His righteousness. You couldn't possibly be any more pleasing to the Lord,

There are days when we feel more like earthbound plodders than heaven-bound pilgrims. Yet we press on in our mission.

even if you tried—because not an iota of your personal standing with Him is based on your personal effort. His covenant love is based on *His* performance, not yours. And it is His love and faithfulness that motivate and enable you to walk in a way that honors Him.

The conviction you feel, therefore, is not meant to induce you to try harder, as if you could somehow work yourself into better favor with God. No, it's intended to let true repentance lead you back to the true Source of all this love, kindness, and self-control—the only One who's able to make you a beautiful, adorned Titus 2 woman.

Yet even if you've taken God's grace to heart, I suspect that some of what we've talked about in this book still feels a little—or a lot—overwhelming. No book can change our lives into totally manageable, easily handled, pieces. As long as we live here as fallen people on a fallen planet, the puzzle pieces will never quite look like the picture on the box. There will be days—many days—when everything seems like an incomplete jumble, and only the Spirit of Christ, at work in us and empowering our obedience, can keep moving us in the right direction.

But that's part of the beauty of Titus 2! It brings to these messy realities the promise of reinforcements for the struggle, and recovery of our divine calling and purpose.

Younger woman, it comes in the form of practical and spiritual mothering that meets you at your points of inexperience and your need for training. This gift of intergenerational connection and community helps to settle your heart and to set you on a sound path for the future—not to mention providing another set of hands to help you get there. And even when your questions seem to have no answers, at least now you have a caring prayer partner and confidante to walk with you and encourage you during the waiting times.

And *older woman,* you have the opportunity to see fruit growing again on seasoned, perhaps long-dormant limbs—not just by writing another check or promising to pray (important and valuable as those are), but also by investing one-on-one, face-to-face in the lives of younger women who, perhaps to your surprise, are eager for what you have to offer. The vacuum of an empty nest or semiretirement is filled by a sense of mission that makes you eager to get out of bed in the morning.

And so, even with life a complicated maze of obligations, disappointments, longings, and uncertainties—new health scares, financial strain, painful losses, and bone-tired weariness—God settles and stabilizes our hearts, even as He broadens us beyond ourselves and our own personal concerns. He places us in close-knit, Christ-centered relationships, through which we can experience and express more of His love. He makes us at home in others' homes—and others at home in ours—to unite us across generations and protect us against our tendencies toward insecurity and isolation.

To give us friendship.

To give us growth.

To give us hope.

To give us . . .

Joy.

Yes, we will feel overwhelmed at times. Choosing to invest in other women or to receive another's counsel and care involves cost and sacrifice. But none of that can compare with the refreshment, connectedness, and joy we receive from these relationships, not to mention the greater joy of glorifying God through fruitful lives.

What's at Stake

Throughout his short letter to Titus, Paul gives instructions to believers in various seasons and stations in life. He shows us what it looks like when all believers live in a way that "accords with sound doctrine" (2:1).

In this book we've focused intently on three verses in chapter 2 that address specifically how the beauty of the gospel is put on display as women—older and younger—live it out together.

We've grappled with what it means when Paul says we should be reverent in behavior, not slanderers or slaves to much wine. We've examined his curriculum for what older women are meant to model and convey to their younger daughters and sisters in the faith—to love their husbands and children, to be pure and self-controlled, to be working at home, kind, and submissive in their marriages.

And we've seen that what Paul has drawn for us in this description is really a portrait of the heart of Christ—His love, His purity, His self-control, His kindness, His submission to the will of His Father. We are to make it our aim to look and act and talk and think like Jesus!

In the rest of Titus 2, Paul goes on to remind us (vv. 11–12) that it is the grace of God (undeserved as it is) that not only saves us, but enables us to live that kind of life "in the present age."

He also encourages us (v. 13) with the promise and blessed hope of seeing Jesus when He returns—a joyous prospect that helps us stay the course and press on when we are tempted to give up or when our efforts seem fruitless.

But there's one more thing I want you to see in Titus 2, something that helps us understand *why* it matters so much that we learn and practice these qualities. This understanding puts a frame around the picture we've been admiring and reminds us what is at stake here.

Paul didn't just toss around these concepts as being good ideas, you see, nor did he intend that these truths were solely for the purpose of our personal spiritual growth, or even for the benefit of other believers with whom we learn and live them out. In Titus 2, he lays out three "purpose clauses" that give us an even grander, greater motivation for taking this message seriously. These three clauses, which are three different ways of making essentially the same point, remind us that our lives as believers have a major impact on how those around us view and respond to our message.

In other words, the *reason* we are called to live as Titus 2 women (and men) is so . . .

1. *"That the word of God may not be reviled" (Titus 2:5)*

A comparison of other translations gives us a fuller sense of Paul wants us to understand:

- "that the word of God will not be dishonored" (NASB)
- "that God's message will not be slandered" (HCSB)
- "that no one will malign the word of God" (NIV)
- "that the word of God may not be blasphemed" (NKJV)

This last rendering is actually a transliteration of the Greek word used in this verse. It's the word *blasphemeo*. It means just that: "to blaspheme, revile . . . to hurt the reputation of."[1] One commentator offers this paraphrase: "so that God's Word may suffer no scandal."[2]

Paul's point is simple and sobering. When we call ourselves Christians and claim to believe God's Word but do not live according to it, the Scriptures will be dishonored in the eyes of those who are watching us. Any disconnect between what His Word says and the way we live will give them ammunition to speak evil of God and His ways.

Instead, the example of our lives should earn the respect of onlookers, making the Word of God more attractive and compelling to them, not more repulsive.

2. *"That an opponent may be put to shame, having nothing evil to say about us" (Titus 2:8)*

Paul was not afraid to speak out against the hypocrisy of those who taught one thing to others but whose lives contradicted their message. To such people he would say, horrified, "The name of God is blasphemed among the Gentiles because of you" (Rom. 2:24).

In Titus 2:8, he warns against that same hypocrisy, cautioning us not to give others reasons for rejecting Christ by allowing there to be a gap between what we profess and what we practice. The consistency of our Christian character should keep people from being able to accuse us of pretending to be something we're not.

3. "That in everything [we] may adorn the doctrine of God our Savior" (Titus 2:10)

Or as the NIV puts it, "so that in every way they will make the teaching about God our Savior attractive." Just as our lives can cause people to revile the truth, they can also cause people to admire it.

Just think. We have been given the opportunity—and the responsibility—to live in such a way that people who have no respect or love for the gospel will be compelled to ooh and aah over its beauty.

These three purpose clauses all address the quality of our witness. They call us to conduct ourselves in such a way that our lives reveal the inherent beauty of the message of the gospel. Although only one uses the actual word, they are all about *adorning* the doctrine of God.

Life to Life

History has preserved for us a letter written by Clement of Rome, one of the early church fathers, to the believers in Corinth, just across the Mediterranean waters from the island of Crete. This epistle, dated around AD 96, was written to express concern over the backslidden, divided condition of the church—a situation he reminded them was "highly incompatible with God's chosen people" and had brought their good name "into serious disrepute." But Clement also reminded these believers of an earlier season, when their behavior had beautifully adorned the gospel they professed. He observed the profound impact the gospel had made on people's lives, making specific mention of the women:

Nobody could spend even a short while among you without noticing the excellence and constancy of your faith. . . . Your womenfolk were bidden to go about their duties in irreproachable devotion and purity of conscience, showing all proper affection to their husbands; they were taught to make obedience the rule of their lives, to manage their households decorously, and to be patterns of discretion in every way.[3]

Clement clearly recalled seeing the gospel on visible, enthralling display in the lifestyles of everyday Christian women in Corinth, and he was eager for this to be the case once again. As I read this description of the gospel at work in and through women's lives, I can't help but believe that if it could happen in a profane, debauched culture such as that of the first-century Roman Empire, then surely it could happen today.

And I think it does happen. In fact, I've witnessed and participated in this dynamic—women living out the beauty of the gospel together—over and over again.

I've watched it transform resistant, reclusive teenage girls into shining models of Christian faith and beauty.

I've seen it redirect young wives and mothers from giving up on their marriages and walking away from the whole stressful mess.

I've observed older women dare to return from the sidelines and get back into the race, discovering that what young women really want and need from them is not an impressive personality and résumé, but simply a heart that truly desires Christ and is seeking to obey Him.

My own life has been molded and changed in precious ways—both as a younger woman, and now as an older woman—by this gift of intentional, life-to-life friendship, community, and discipleship.

I'll admit I came to a point, somewhere around age fifty, where my heart and body just wanted to start coasting. I was tired. And I was tempted to believe I'd already done enough, that I could afford to take it easy from here.

But here's what my heart knows to be *really* true, even when my feet and back are screaming otherwise. I can't live for Christ and live for me at the same time. If I choose myself, I'm choosing to miss out on something a lot more valuable than my self-centered desires and comfort. And I can attest that as I have chosen Him, He has continually amazed me with His persistent faithfulness and joy.

He has let me stand close enough to the action when He captures a younger woman's heart that the abundance He pours out into her overflows to refresh my own spirit.

And whenever my heart has grown weary, He has kept me close to older women who continue to inspire me out of the overflow of their walk with God.

Throughout this book, I've told you about the influence of older women like Vonette Bright, Leta Fischer, and my own mother. I want you to meet one more Titus 2 woman—a dear friend who touched my life in a beautiful way.

Joyce Johnson—known to many of us whose lives were blessed by her influence simply as Mom J—exemplified the joy older women can experience as they pour themselves into younger women.

Joyce died less than three months after the passing of her husband, to whom she'd been married for almost sixty-five years. She had known significant loss along the way—including the tragic death of her seventeen-year-old daughter, the oldest of their five children, less than a month before high school graduation. Yet Mom J's resiliency and trust in God's sovereignty only deepened and grew through such experiences, guarding her heart from self-pity and resentment.

I first got to know Joyce when she and her husband, friends of my parents, invited me to live with them in Southern California while I finished my last two years of college. She was in her early sixties at the time, and the mark she left on my life was indelible. I wasn't the first young person she and Dad J had received into their home, nor would I be the last. Her ministry of mentoring would continue all the way to the finish line of her race.

One of the last times I spoke with her, in fact, she told me excitedly about the twenty-year-old single girl she was regularly discipling and meeting with. At age ninety-two! And loving every minute of it.

Mom J never stopped blessing me with her interest and love. As I said half-seriously when I spoke at her funeral, I didn't know if I'd be able to write any more books after she was gone—not without knowing that Mom J was out there marinating them in her faithful prayers. I recall the passion God gave her for holiness while she prayed me through the writing of a book on that topic.[4] She eagerly began marking in her Bible every reference to holiness she could find. For the better part of a year she wrote to me often, exuberant and convicted over what God was showing her along those lines.

She never stopped growing and learning. And whatever God taught *her*, she transferred to others—life to life.

I want to be a Mom J.

And I want to see a whole generation of Mom Js raised up.

Every glimpse I see of that taking place causes my heart to rejoice. As I was in the final stages of writing this book, a dear friend—an empty-nest mom and grandmom—wrote to me:

> When I was a young adult, I saw no one in my church or sphere of influence who taught or modeled these things. *Taking Titus 2 to heart changed the entire course of my life.* I take legacy and living a life of mentorship seriously. My heart's desire is to be one of those older women.

How might our homes and churches be different if they were filled with such women?

What kind of impact might these women make among unbelievers in our families and our communities?

And what might it look like to see a genuine, God-ignited revival, spreading like wildfire through the linked arms and hearts of women (and men) who are passionate about adorning the gospel of Christ? This is the vision Paul had for that band of believers on the isle of Crete in Titus' day. And this is the vision the Lord has put in my heart for our day.

The women around you, overwhelmed by the undertow of life, need more than a book to read or a class to attend. They need you.

Our *goal* for what we're talking about here is as grand as the glory and majesty of God. But the *method* He has prescribed for us is as simple as women sitting down together, opening up their lives and the Word, receiving and passing on to others the baton of faith and Christlike character.

The women around you, overwhelmed by the undertow of life but longing to be beautiful—adorned—need more than a book to read or a class to attend or more worship music to play.

They need you.

They need your presence, your concern, your prayers.

As we live out the beauty of the gospel—younger and older women together—we will be beautified and blessed and, yes, overjoyed. That beauty will spill over into our homes, our churches, our workplaces and communities, and ultimately into our world.

And in the end, Christ will be "glorified in his saints, and . . . marveled at among all who have believed" (2 Thess. 1:10).

Such pure beauty. Such eternal joy.

Let's pursue it—let's pursue Him—together.

Notes

Chapter 1: A Woman Adorned and Adorning

1. Nikolaus Ludwig von Zinzendorf, "Jesus, Thy Blood and Righteousness," 1739, tr. John Wesley, 1740.

Chapter 2: Doctrine, You, and Titus 2

Epigraph: John Piper, "The Ultimate Meaning of True Womanhood," message delivered at the 2008 True Woman Conference, Desiring God, http://www.desiringGod.org/resource-library/conference-messages/the-ultimate-meaning-of-true-womanhood.

1. Blue Letter Bible Lexicon, s.v. "anatrepō" (Strong's G396), Blue Letter Bible website, version 3, https://www.blueletterbible.org/lang/lexicon/lexicon.cfm?Strongs=G396&t=ESV.
2. Charles R. Swindoll, *Insights on 1 and 2 Timothy, Titus*: Swindoll's New Testament Insights (Grand Rapids: Zondervan, 2010), 256.
3. Paul uses this term not only for non-Christians, but also for those who claimed to be in the faith but whose doctrine and lifestyles gave no such evidence.
4. John MacArthur, Jr., The MacArthur New Testament Commentary: *Titus* (Chicago: Moody, 1996), 88.

Chapter 3: Don't Give Up on That Modeling Career

Epigraph: John MacArthur, "God's Plan for Older Men and Older Women," sermon delivered February 7, 1993, Grace to You, http://www.gty.org/resources/sermons/56-13/gods-plan-for-older-men-and-older-women.

1. Helen Roseveare, "A Call for the Perseverance of the Saints," address delivered at the Desiring God National Conference, September 29, 2007, http://www.desiringGod.org/messages/a-call-for-the-perseverance-of-the-saints.
2. Warren Doud, *The Epistle to Titus: A Grace Notes Bible Study,* online study downloaded as pdf from Grace Notes: Online Training in Bible Teaching, http://www.gracenotes.info/TITUS/Titus004.pdf, 30.

Chapter 4: Grow Up and Step Up

Epigraph: Cathe Laurie, "How to Bake a Pie," Cathe's Notes, Virtue, October 24, 2014, http://www.harvest.org/virtue/sections/cathes-notes.html/?p=11050.

1. Tom Nelson, "The Priesthood of the Believer," sermon preached at Denton Bible Church, Denton, TX, September 23, 2007, https://www.dbcmedia.org/?s_cs=1&s=1269.

2. Daniel C. Arichea and Howard A. Hatton, eds., *A Handbook on Paul's Letters to Timothy and Titus*, UBS Handbook Series (New York: United Bible Societies, 1995), 284.

Chapter 5: Revival of Reverence

Epigraph: Rochelle Fleming, "Titus 2 Women—Reverent Behavior," pdf downloaded from Light-Work blog, http://lightwork.typepad.com/lightwork/files/Reverent.pdf, 2.

1. William Barclay, *The New Daily Study Bible: The Letters to Timothy, Titus, and Philemon*, 3rd ed., rev. (Louisville: Westminister John Knox, 2003, orig. pub. 1956), 279.

2. "Titus 2:3-4 Commentary," s.v. "hieroprepes," Precept Austin, http://www.preceptaustin.org/titus_23-4.htm.

3. Thomas C. Oden, *First and Second Timothy and Titus*, Interpretation: A Bible Commentary for Teaching and Preaching (Louisville: John Knox Press, 1989), 115.

4. Frederic William Farrar, in *Streams in the Desert*, vol. 1, comp. Mrs. Charles E. Cowman (Cowman, 1925; Grand Rapids: Zondervan, 1965–66), September 13.

Chapter 6: You Don't Say

Epigraph: Jon Bloom, "Lay Aside the Weight of Slander," Desiring God, December 19, 2015, http://www.desiringGod.org/articles/lay-aside-the-weight-of-slander.

1. Martin Luther, *Luther's Works, Vol. 21: The Sermon on the Mount and the Magnificat*, 41, quoted in Jason Garoncy, "Luther and Calvin on Slander (and Women)," January 14, 2010, http://jasongoroncy.com/2010/01/14/luther-and-calvin-on-slander-and-women/.

2. Spiros Zodhiates, *The Complete Word Study New Testament*, reissue ed. (Chattanooga: AMG, 1991), 913.

3. William Barclay, *The New Daily Study Bible: The Letters to Timothy, Titus, and Philemon*, 3rd ed., rev. (Louisville: Westminster John Knox, 2003, orig. pub. 1956), 280.

4. Jonathan Edwards, *Memoirs of Jonathan Edwards*, vol. 1 in *The Works of Jonathan Edwards* (Carlisle, PA: Banner of Truth, 1976), xlvi.

Chapter 7: At Liberty

Epigraph: Renee Johnson, "I Found Life," quoted in "Finding Liberty from Addiction," Revive Our Hearts Radio, October 10, 2008, https://www.reviveourhearts.com/radio/revive-our-hearts/finding-liberty-from-addiction. Used by permission of the author.

1. John MacArthur, Jr., *The MacArthur New Testament Commentary: Titus* (Chicago: Moody Press, 1996), 78.

2. Elizabeth Cohen, "Line between Overeating and Binge Disorder Is a Thin One," CNN.com, February 24, 2007, http://www.cnn.com/2007/HEALTH/

conditions/02/22/VS.binge.eating/index.html.

3. Study published in *Alcohol Health and Research World*, quoted in Sharon Hersh, "Even Good Women Get Hooked," *Today's Christian Woman*, July 1988, http://www.todayschristianwoman.com/articles/1998/july/8w4082.html.

4. Joan Caplin, "Confessions of a Compulsive Shopper," CNN Money, November 4, 2005, http://money.cnn.com/2005/07/20/pf/shopper_0508/index.htm.

5. John McDuling, "This Chart Suggests America's Addiction to Television Is Not Normal," Quartz, http://qz.com/178161/this-chart-suggests-americas-addiction-to-television-is-not-normal/.

6. Shannon Ethridge, "What Women Must Know about Lust," *Charisma*, June 22, 2011, http://www.charismamag.com/site-archives/610-spiritled-woman/spiritled-woman/13881-what-women-must-know-about-lust.

7. Lindsay Roberts, "I Was Addicted to Romance," *Today's Christian Woman*, September 2008, http://www.christianitytoday.com/mp/2002/004/1.34.html.

8. Jon Bloom, "Lay Aside the Weight of Self-Indulgence," Desiring God, August 29, 2014, http://www.desiringgod.org/articles/lay-aside-the-weight-of-self-indulgence.

9. Gabrielle Glaser, *Her Best-Kept Secret: Why Women Drink—And How They Can Regain Control* (New York: Simon & Schuster, 2013), 17–18.

10. This is apart from what the law considers to be legal intoxication alcohol levels for operating motor vehicles.

11. National Institute on Alcohol Abuse and Alcoholism, "Alcohol's Effects on the Body," https://www.niaaa.nih.gov/alcohol-health/alcohols-effects-body, accessed June 29, 2016.

Chapter 8: A "Sophron" State of Mind

Epigraph: J. Hampton Keathley III, "Marks of Maturity: Biblical Characteristics of a Christian Leader," https://bible.org/seriespage/mark-10-self-control.

1. W. E. Vine, *The Expanded Vine's Expository Dictionary of New Testament Words: A Special Edition* (Minneapolis: Bethany, 1984), 1057.

2. Ibid.

3. Spiros Zodhiates, *The Complete Word Study New Testament* (Chattanooga: AMG Publishers, 1991), 947.

4. William Barclay, *The New Daily Study Bible: The Letters to Timothy, Titus, and Philemon* (Louisville: Westminster John Knox Press, 2003), 278.

5. A pdf of this chart is available at www.ReviveOurHearts.com/sophron. Permission is granted to reproduce the full pdf for yourself or others.

6. This is not to suggest that treatment for people with severe mental illness may not be necessary or helpful or that an encounter with Christ will automatically and immediately free them from their infirmity. However, no treatment will solve problems that originate in the heart, apart from cooperating with the Spirit of Christ in dealing with those issues.

Chapter 9: Passionate about Purity

Epigraph: Quoted in "25 Quotes about Purity," Christian Quotes, http://www.christianquotes.info/quotes-by-topic/quotes-about-purity/#ixzz42zs1XjC2.

1. W. E. Vine, *The Expanded Vine's Expository Dictionary of New Testament Words: A Special Edition* (Minneapolis: Bethany, 1984), 175, 903.

2. J. P. Louw and Eugene Albert Nida, eds., *Greek-English Dictionary of the New Testament: Based on Semantic Domains*, quoted in William E. Wenstrom, Jr., "1 Timothy 5:21–22," pdf downloaded from Wenstrom Bible Ministries website, www.wenstrom.org/downloads/written/exposition/1tim/1tim_5_21-22.pdf, 58.

3. Warren W. Wiersbe, *Be Faithful: It's Always Too Soon to Quit!*, New Testament Commentary, 1 & 2 Timothy, Titus, Philemon (Colorado Springs: David C. Cook, 2009), 124.

4. Patrick F. Fagan, "The Effects of Pornography on Individuals, Marriage, Family and Community," Research Synthesis, December 2009, pdf downloaded from MARRI (Marriage and Religion Research Institute) Research, http://downloads.frc.org/EF/EF12D43.pdf. Read a summary of the full report at http://marriagegems.com/2010/04/02/porn-use-increases-infidelity-divorce/.

5. Gerhard Kittel and Gerhard Friedrich, eds., *Theological Dictionary of the New Testament,* tr. Geoffrey W. Bromiley (Grand Rapids: Wm. B. Eerdmans, 1964), 1:122–24.

6. My booklet *The Look: Does God Really Care What I Wear?* (Niles, MI: Revive Our Hearts, 2003) offers a fuller treatment of this subject. Available at www.ReviveOurHearts.com/look.

Chapter 10: Taste of Heaven

Epigraph: Carolyn McCulley with Nora Shank, *The Measure of Success: Uncovering the Biblical Perspective on Women, Work, and the Home* (Nashville: B&H Books, 2014), 22.

1. "Titus 2:5 Commentary (Titus 2 Resources)," Precept Austin, updated February 21, 2015, http://www.preceptaustin.org/titus_25.htm.

2. "Criticism of Southwestern Homemaking Course Angers Professor, Radio Host," Baptist News Global, July 10, 2007, https://baptist news.com/2007/07/10/criticism-of-southwestern-homemaking-courses-angers-professor-radio-host/.

3. I am indebted to my friend Carolyn McCulley for helping me better understand the history of the home and for her input on this chapter. She expands on these ideas in her excellent book (with Nora Shank), *The Measure of Success: Uncovering the Biblical Perspective on Women, Work, and the Home* (Nashville: B&H Books, 2014).

4. McCulley with Shank, *The Measure of Success,* 57. Emphasis is the author's.

5. Jani Ortlund, *Fearlessly Feminine: Boldly Living God's Plan for Womanhood* (Colorado Springs: Multnomah Books, 2000), 147.

Chapter 11: Need Help Lovin' That Man

Epigraph: "Love Through Me," poem in *Edges of His Ways* by Amy Carmichael, ©1955 The Dohnavur Fellowship. Used by permission of CLC Publications. May not be further reproduced. All rights reserved.

1. J. H. Moulton and G. Milligan, *Vocabulary of the Greek Testament* (Peabody, MA: Hendrickson, 1997), 668.

2. "The Love of Charles and Susannah Spurgeon," Christianity.com, http://www .christianity.com/church/church-history-timeline/2001-now/the-love-of-charles-and-susannah-spurgeon-11633045.html.

3. Charles Haddon Spurgeon, *C. H. Spurgeon's Autobiography: Compiled from His Diary, Letters, and Records, by His Wife and His Private Secretary*, vol. 2, 1854–1860 (London: Passmore & Alabaster, 1899), 291–92.

4. Charles Haddon Spurgeon, "Ripe Fruit," sermon no. 945, delivered August 14, 1870, at The Metropolitan Tabernacle: Sermons Preached and Revised by C. H. Spurgeon During the Year 1870 (London: Passmore & Alabaster, 1871), 448.

5. For daily ideas and support in this exercise, visit the "30-Day Husband Encouragement Challenge" at www.ReviveOurHeart.com/challenge.

6. Fanny J. Crosby, "Rescue the Perishing," 1869.

Chapter 12: An Unexpected Blessing

Epigraph: Kathy Keller, "Embracing the Other," ch. 6 in Timothy Keller with Kathy Keller, *The Meaning of Marriage: Facing the Complexities of Commitment with the Wisdom of God* (New York: Riverhead Books, 2011), 201.

1. Jocelyn Anderson, "Submissive Question: We Have a Right to Know Sacred Beliefs," *Orlando Sentinel,* August 23, 2011, http://articles.orlandosentinel.com/2011-08-23/ news/os-ed-michele-bachmann-theology-0823120110822_1_michele-bachmann-male-headship-beliefs.

2. Some translations of this phrase use the words *woman* and *man* instead of *wife* and *husband.* The original Greek words can have both meanings, so the translation must be based on the context. The context of this verse is clarified in the ongoing discussion of 1 Corinthians 11:7–9, which refers to the original man as head of the original woman, the man being the husband and the woman being his wife. In this way, 1 Corinthians 11:3 parallels Paul's teaching in Ephesians 5:22–33, which sets forth the headship of a husband and the submission of a wife.

3. Dave Dunham, "A Word About Polite Abusers," Pastor Dave Online, June 30, 2016, https://pastordaveonline.org/2016/06/30/a-word-about-polite-abusers.

Chapter 13: Life-Givers in Training

Epigraph: Barbara Hughes, *Disciplines of a Godly Woman* (Wheaton, IL: Crossway Books, 2001), 167.

1. Colin Falconer, "Are You Ready to Have Babies? Take the Test," *The Huffington Post,* February 11, 2014, http://www.huffingtonpost.com/colin-falconer/are-you-ready-to-have-babies_b_4377307.html.

Chapter 14: Instruments of Grace

Epigraph: Mary Beeke, *The Law of Kindness: Serving with Heart and Hands* (Grand Rapids: Reformation Heritage, 2007), 31. Quote adapted with permission from the author.

1. Scripture does not explicitly state that Martha was the eldest sibling in her family. But many commentators believe the text suggests that this was the case—also that the home belonged to her and that she was responsible for managing the household.

2. Spiros Zodhiates, ed., *The Complete Word Study Dictionary: New Testament,* rev. reissue ed. (Chattanooga: AMG, 1993), 62.

3. W. E. Vine, *The Expanded Vine's Expository Dictionary of New Testament Words: A Special Edition* (Minneapolis: Bethany, 1984), 493.

4. Matthew Henry, *Commentary on the Whole Bible,* ed. Leslie F. Church (Grand Rapids: Zondervan, 1961), 1902.

5. Jerry Bridges, *The Practice of Godliness: Godliness Has Value for All Things,* rev. ed. (Colorado Springs: NavPress, 2008), 189.

6. Thomas D. Lea and Hayne P. Griffin, *1, 2 Timothy, Titus,* vol. 34 of *The New American Commentary* (Nashville: B&H, 1992), 301.

Epilogue: A Woman Overjoyed

1. Spiros Zodhiates, *The Complete Word Study New Testament,* reissue ed. (Chattanooga: AMG, 1991), 884.

2. William Kelly, cited in John MacArthur, Jr., *The MacArthur New Testament Commentary: Titus* (Chicago: Moody, 1996), 88.

3. Clement of Rome, "The First Epistle of Clement to the Corinthians," in Andrew Louth, ed., *Early Christian Writings: The Apostolic Fathers,* tr. Maxwell Staniforth, rev. ed. (London: Penguin Classics, 1987), 23.

4. Nancy Leigh DeMoss, *Holiness: The Heart God Purifies* (Chicago: Moody, 2005).

Heartfelt Thanks

I HAVE QUIPPED THAT THIS BOOK about younger and older women growing together has taken so long to write that in the process I have transitioned from the young woman category to the older woman one—not to mention transitioning from being a single woman to being a married one.

For sure, there have been lots of twists and turns along the way—a lot of life lived and lessons learned—and more sweet providences than I can count. Not the least of these are the many humble, gifted, servant-hearted friends who believe in this message and have partnered with me to see it take shape in the form of this book. Among them . . .

- *Greg Thornton, Paul Santhouse, Randall Payleitner, Judy Dunagan, Erik Peterson, Ashley Torres, Connor Sterchi, and the entire Moody Publishers team*—whose faithful, diligent efforts, along with their patience, prayers, and encouragement have been a great gift

- *Lawrence Kimbrough*—who took 144 pages of my notes and hours of my audio teaching on Titus 2 and organized, framed, and fashioned it all into an excellent working draft

- *Anne Christian Buchanan*—editor extraordinaire, who stuck with me through at least four complete, painstaking rounds of substantive edits on a 350-page manuscript

- *Mike Neises*—Director of Publishing and Events for Revive Our Hearts, who has played an invaluable, mostly unseen, role in the development of each book I've written

- *Erik Wolgemuth and the rest of the Wolgemuth & Associates team*—who dove in headfirst midway through this project and have been a great help in getting it to the finish line

- *Tim Challies*—for his thoughtful theological review and his help in sharpening specific points to make them more clear, helpful, and biblical

- *Tom and Roz Sullivan*—who lovingly assisted with grocery shopping and delicious meals, so my husband (who was also working on a book) and I could stay at it

- *Martin Jones, Sandy Bixel, Hannah Kurtz, and Leanna Shepard*—who graciously provided administrative support and kept countless plates spinning to enable me to write with a minimum of distraction

- *Dawn Wilson*—who tirelessly assisted with research, dug up quotes, and suggested Making It Personal questions

- *Paula Marsteller*—who kindly read through the manuscript twice with her great eye for details, made many helpful edits and suggestions, and collaborated on the Making It Personal questions

- *Jennifer Lyell, Carolyn McCulley, Mary Kassian, and Kimberly Wagner*—who gave feedback on certain chapters and helped me grapple with how to communicate effectively and biblically on specific issues

- *"The sisterhood"*—whose friendship, wisdom, prayers, encouragement, and love are one of the greatest blessings of my life

- *My dear "Praying Friends"*—who faithfully carry me through every significant undertaking with their earnest prayers on my behalf

- *Robert Wolgemuth*—my precious husband and cheerleader, whose prayers, encouragement, and input have been wind beneath my wings as I worked on this book over the past year

These women and men are "my fellow workers . . . beloved in the

Lord" (Rom. 16:3, 8). They each deserve far more credit than they will get this side of heaven, and they adorn the gospel with their lives, their love, and their labors. My life is more fruitful and this book is more effective as a result of their partnership. To them and to the Lord Jesus I offer my deepest gratitude.

Also by Nancy

A 30-Day Walk With God in the Psalms

A Place of Quiet Rest: Cultivating Intimacy with God through a Daily Devotional Life

Becoming God's True Woman, ed.

Brokenness: The Heart God Revives

Holiness: The Heart God Purifies

Surrender: The Heart God Controls

Brokenness, Surrender, Holiness: A Revive Our Hearts Trilogy

Choosing Forgiveness: Your Journey to Freedom

Choosing Gratitude: Your Journey to Joy

Lies Women Believe: And the Truth That Sets Them Free

The Companion Guide for Lies Women Believe

Lies Young Women Believe: And the Truth That Sets Them Free
(coauthored with Dannah Gresh)

Lies Young Women Believe Companion Guide

Seeking Him: Experiencing the Joy of Personal Revival
(coauthored with Tim Grissom)

The Quiet Place: Daily Devotional Readings

The Wonder of His Name: 32 Life-Changing Names of Jesus

True Woman 101: Divine Design: An Eight-Week Study on Biblical Womanhood
(coauthored with Mary A. Kassian)

True Woman 201: Interior Design: Ten Elements of Biblical Womanhood
(coauthored with Mary A. Kassian)

Voices of the True Woman Movement: A Call to the Counter-Revolution, ed.